Command and Control
on the Western Front

The British Army's Experience
1914–1918

COMMAND AND CONTROL ON THE WESTERN FRONT

THE BRITISH ARMY'S EXPERIENCE 1914–1918

edited by

Gary Sheffield and Dan Todman

SPELLMOUNT
Staplehurst

British Library Cataloguing in Publication Data:
A catalogue record for this book is available
from the British Library

Copyright © Spellmount Limited 2004

ISBN 1-86227-083-X

First published in the UK in 2004 by
Spellmount Limited
The Village Centre
Staplehurst
Kent TN12 0BJ

Tel: 01580 893730
Fax: 01580 893731
E-mail: enquiries@spellmount.com
Website: www.spellmount.com

1 3 5 7 9 8 6 4 2

The right of Gary Sheffield and Dan Todman
and the individual authors to be identified
as the authors of their work has been asserted by them
in accordance with the Copyright, Designs
and Patents Act 1988

Typeset in Palatino by MATS, Southend-on-Sea, Essex
Printed in Great Britain by
T.J. International Ltd
Padstow, Cornwall

Contents

List of Maps

For V and N

The views expressed in this book are those of the individual authors and do not represent those of the Joint Services Command and Staff College or any other organisation or body.

Acknowledgements

The editors owe a huge debt of gratitude to our publisher, Jamie Wilson, for his exemplary support and patience in the writing of this book. We acknowledge the contribution of Dr Stephen Badsey, who was originally going to be a co-editor, but who sadly had to drop out of the project because of unforeseen circumstances. Gary Sheffield would like to thank his family for putting up with yet another book, and his colleagues, past and present, academic and military, for providing intellectual stimulation over the last nineteen years. The Australian Army gave him a grant which enabled him to undertake archival research in Australia. Daniel Todman would like to acknowledge the support of Pembroke College, Cambridge and the Department of War Studies, Royal Military Academy Sandhurst.

The editors and authors are grateful to a number of people and institutions for permission to quote from material to which they own the copyright.

Extracts from the Bean papers are reproduced with the permission of the Australian War Memorial.

Extracts from the Burnett-Stuart papers by permission of G S Burnett-Stuart and the Trustees of the Liddell Hart Centre for Military Archives.

Extracts from the Cox papers are reproduced with the permission of Dr Jo Cox.

Extracts from the French papers are reproduced by permission of the Trustees of the Imperial War Museum.

Extracts from the Haig papers are reproduced by permission of the Earl Haig and the Trustees of the National Library of Scotland.

Extracts from the Howell papers are reproduced by permission of the Trustees of the Liddell Hart Centre for Military Archives.

Extracts from the Liddell Hart papers are reproduced by permission of the Trustees of the Liddell Hart Centre for Military Archives.

Extracts from the Maxse papers are reproduced by permission of A J Maxse.

Extracts from the Uniacke papers are reproduced by permission of the Royal Artillery Institution.

The British Library is thanked for permission to reproduce extracts from documents in its care in the Hunter-Weston collection.

Crown copyright material appears by kind permission of the Public Record Office (now the National Archives) and the Australian War Memorial.

The editors have made every effort to locate copyright holders, and wish to apologise to anyone whose copyright we may have unwittingly infringed.

All photographs are reproduced by kind permission of the Trustees of the Imperial War Museum, London, except No. 9, which is reproduced by kind permission of the State Library of New South Wales, Sydney, Australia.

The Contributors

Dr Gary Sheffield is Senior Lecturer in Defence Studies at King's College London, based at the Joint Services Command and Staff College. He has published many books on military history, his most recent being *Somme* (2003). He contributed to the Templer Medal-winning *The British General Staff: Reform and Innovation, 1890–1939* (edited by D French and B Holden Reid, 2002).

Dr Dan Todman is Lecturer in Modern British History at Queen Mary College, University of London. He was co-editor, with Alex Danchev, of the best-selling *War Diaries 1939–45: Field Marshal Lord Alanbrooke* (2001). His book *The Great War, Myth and Memory* will be published in 2005.

Dr Niall Barr is Senior Lecturer in Defence Studies at King's College London, based at the Joint Services Command and Staff College. His major study *Pendulum of War: The Three Battles of El Alamein* appeared in 2004.

John Lee is Treasurer of the British Commission for Military History. He is the author of *A Soldier's Life: General Sir Ian Hamilton 1853–1947* (2000).

Chris McCarthy is Head of Conservation at the Imperial War Museum. He is the author of *The Somme: the Day-by-Day Account* (1993) and *The Third Ypres Passchendaele: the Day-by-Day Account* (1995).

Dr Sanders Marble is an historian at the Office of Medical History, Office of the Army Surgeon General. Formerly Project Historian in the National Museum of American History at The Smithsonian Institution, Washington DC, he was awarded a doctorate in 2001 for a study of British artillery in the First World War, which was published in the Gutenberg-e programme by Columbia University Press in 2003.

Professor Peter Simkins is Honorary Professor in Modern History at the University of Birmingham. Formerly Senior Historian at the Imperial War

xv

Museum, he has published widely on the Great War, including the Templer Medal-winning *Kitchener's Army* (1988).

Dr Andy Simpson is the author of *Hot Blood and Cold Steel* (1993) and *The Evolution of Victory* (1995). In 2001 he was awarded a doctorate by the University of London for a study of the Corps level of command in the First World War.

CHAPTER I

Command and Control
in the British Army on the Western Front

Dan Todman and Gary Sheffield

'First, we have naming of parts': our title begs definitions of command and control. In his useful study, Martin van Creveld discusses the concept of 'command'. He divides the responsibilities of 'command' into 'function-related' – the fulfilment of the army's needs in terms of men, supplies and organisation – and 'output-related' – enabling the army to carry out its mission through the gathering of intelligence and the planning and monitoring of operations. Van Creveld defines 'command' as 'a function that has to be exercised, more or less continuously, if the army is to exist and to operate'. He points out that a massive quantity of effective command goes almost unnoticed when historians concentrate on individually important battlefield decisions.[1] Although van Creveld was keen to collapse the complexities of command and control into a single term, for the purposes of this study, we might accept his definition of *what* a commander does, and go on to define 'control' as *how* he does it: the structures and systems, formal and informal, defined and less tangible, through which command is exercised. The two are, of course, intimately related, and it is as well to accept that the boundary between the two is blurred so that they may become indistinguishable.

Command and control will clearly be exercised at different locations throughout an army from the lance corporal organising his half-section of men to the field marshal directing the movements of whole armies. The subject is obviously a vast one; military historians are only beginning to scrape at its surface. The purpose of this book is to bring together a number of 'snapshots' of command and control at different levels in the British Expeditionary Force (BEF) on the Western Front, from General Headquarters down to individual battalion level.

Issues of the BEF's command and control have been the subject of debate and controversy virtually from the time the first British soldier landed in France in August 1914. Soldiers had an understandable interest in the quality of the direction they received, although for most

1

infantrymen the competence of their platoon and company commanders was of more immediate concern than that of more senior, more distant figures. Civilians too discussed the conduct of the war, as the wartime poster warning against despondency – 'Don't think you know better than General Haig' – suggests. Journalists also debated command and generalship. Some, such as Charles Repington, were fairly outspoken. By contrast, Philip Gibbs was far more critical in his post-war writings than he was prepared to be while the fighting was still in progress.[2]

These debates continued after the war's end, although more extreme expressions may have been limited by the widely held belief in the need to spare the feelings of the bereaved. At the time of Sir Douglas Haig's death, in 1928, newspaper obituarists acknowledged that his wartime career was still the subject of controversy, even as they praised his post-war dedication to veterans' welfare.[3] Some books published in the interwar period took an unashamedly pro-High Command line, such as the two-volume work co-written by Haig's private secretary, Lieutenant Colonel J H Boraston. Moreover, a number of unit and formation histories examined the Western Front with an objectivity that has stood the test of time.[4] The series of official histories edited by Brigadier General Sir James Edmonds was, contrary to popular belief, by no means uncritical of British generals and generalship, although criticism was often oblique rather than overt.[5]

However, the influence of such books was relatively limited. Three other interwar books, Churchill's *The World Crisis*, Liddell Hart's *The Real War*, and Lloyd George's *War Memoirs*, adopted a distinctly more critical tone towards British generalship, and between them set the direction of study on the war for several decades to come. The authors portrayed the struggle on the Western Front in terms of the personalities of the senior commanders involved.[6] The first two books were more moderate in their criticism of British High Command than subsequent recycling of their work has made apparent. All three formed the basis for much subsequent writing, filling the vacuum left by the absence of documentary material.

The early 1960s saw renewed evidence of public interest in the war, with the publication of a large number of popular histories, as well as representations of the war on stage and screen. Again, these popular histories tended to focus on war from the top down, examining the actions of generals. However, the period saw little original research using previously unpublished materials; instead, there was heavy reliance on published texts. The result was that the military history of the war seemed to descend into a series of semantic debates about casualty figures and passages from Haig's diary. Although some useful work was done – for example by John Terraine in pointing out that Haig's perception of the Western Front as the key arena for the struggle with Germany was essentially correct – this tended to be overwhelmed by squabbles based on a personality-driven approach to the war. This tendency was only heightened by the appearance of popular works, such as the musical drama (and subsequent film) *Oh! What a Lovely War.*

Although how they were perceived at the time is still a matter of study – and it is apparent that there was a heavier undercurrent of nostalgia than has generally been appreciated – representations of the First World War in the 1960s formed the basis for a set of myths which were to become dominant in the 1970s and 1980s and continue to inform popular opinions on the war.[7] These myths portrayed First World War officers as upper-class twits, and generals in particular as asinine incompetents, feasting in châteaux far behind the lines whilst their men were despatched in a series of muddy, bloody massacres: a view utilised to remarkable comic effect by the 1989 BBC television series *Blackadder Goes Forth.* Such myths caused some military historians – to whom it was apparent that this was far from an accurate picture of the war – considerable pain. However, whilst they argued against them in their own terms, they did little to dispel them, and might even have only served to strengthen the conviction of those who sought to convict British generals as 'butchers and bunglers'.[8]

Even as the view of the British army in the Great War as 'lions led by donkeys' established a seemingly unbreakable grip over modern popular representations of the war, two developments began that were to move forward the study of the military history of the Western Front. First, developments within the academic study of how the war was fought led to efforts to break away from the focus on individual senior personalities, in particular the relentless concentration on Haig. From the late 1970s onwards, a growth in military interest in the functioning of command, control and communications – C^3 as it became known – encouraged a study of the structures and techniques of command. Meanwhile, British military historians in particular began to approach the First World War in new ways, notably by analysing and making use of the huge quantity of material which had been declassified in the Public Record Office from 1968 onwards.[9] This not only gave some of them a newfound assertiveness in their defence of Haig, but encouraged a move beyond stale debates to a clearer focus on the structures of command and control, and a reconsideration of the war in less impassioned terms.

In the longer run this can be seen to have led, for example, to the excellent studies by Robin Prior and Trevor Wilson of the career of Sir Henry Rawlinson and the fighting at Third Ypres,[10] a mass of more in-depth studies of individual actions which have challenged some prevailing orthodoxies,[11] and the magnificent collection of essays *Passchendaele in Perspective,* which brings together a host of approaches.[12] Moreover, treating the First World War as an event within, rather than outside history, has begun to allow historians to work comparatively; most obviously by comparing the military history of the two world wars.[13]

More recently, historians have begun to work on even less fashionable aspects of military history, which have previously gone almost unconsidered despite their crucial influence on the fighting. The shining example is Ian Malcolm Brown's *British Logistics on the Western Front*, which makes clear the key part played by developments on the line of supply far behind the battlefront.[14] It should be apparent from its title that the present book is very much in this tradition, and seeks actively to examine the issues of command and control in a more modern, more conceptual, and better articulated light, expressing itself in a form which is less emotional or polemical than some previous works.

The second development is the degree to which study of the detailed history of the war has gained in strength outside the ranks of academia or professional historians. Popular interest in the First World War, in particular amongst the generation formed by the grandchildren of those who fought, remains high. Access to primary and secondary material is comparatively easy, and desktop publishing and the Internet have facilitated the reproduction and dissemination of research. The quality of this research remains highly variable, but at its best it is well written, painstakingly detailed and often informed by professional skills and experience that most full-time historians do not possess. Given the vast quantity of primary material available, the popularity of research into the war increasingly appears not merely an aid to further study, but a necessity.

This collection opens with Niall Barr's analysis of the shift from mobile to position warfare in the opening months of the war. Barr highlights the difficulties this posed for commanders, in particular in terms of communications, and points out the high levels of casualties amongst senior officers at the beginning of the war, a useful corrective for those whose image of the First World War commander is still of a château-bound Blimp. Dan Todman's chapter on GHQ provides a detailed preliminary investigation of an area that has been the subject of much polemic but little systematic study. The organisational charts Todman has been able to draw show in the clearest terms the huge developments that took place in GHQ over the course of the war.

Gary Sheffield examines the performance of Hubert Gough as commander of Reserve (later renamed Fifth) Army on the Somme in 1916. While acknowledging that Gough's conduct of the Battle of the Ancre in November 1916 was competent, Sheffield criticises Gough's 'thrusting', abrasive command style, impetuosity and propensity to micromanage operations.

Andy Simpson's contribution is an excellent chapter on the developments in corps command. This level of command has been somewhat neglected and Simpson presents evidence for the change in corps' roles, from an essentially administrative device at the beginning of the war, through a period of centralisation in 1916, to a remarkable level of flexibility by the end of the war. Moving down a level, John Lee examines divisional command at the highly successful battle of the Menin Road in September 1917. Lee demonstrates how much had been learned by this stage of the war, and applied in the Third Battle of Ypres. Peter Simkins examines command of brigades from the Somme to the 'building block' of the BEF's offensive operations. Moreover, he suggests that given the importance of this level of command in the mobile operations of 1918, it has not received the attention from historians that it deserves.

Chris McCarthy looks at the command, organisation and tactics of the infantry battalion, tracing its evolution from the relatively large and straightforward body of 1914 to the smaller but much more complex unit – in reality, a collection of semi-independent subunits – of the Hundred Days. One of McCarthy's themes is that the progressive devolution of command placed ever more responsibility on the shoulders of junior officers, NCOs and even privates. Sanders Marble's chapter on artillery command focuses on an individual, in this case Herbert Uniacke. Marble analyses the changes in one professional gunner's approach within a context where artillery as a whole gained more operational importance and freedom.

Reading these chapters, we can identify certain overall trends and suggest some conclusions. Without wishing to adopt the triumphalist tone that has characterised some 'bunking' histories, it is necessary to reiterate the huge problems facing the British army on the Western Front in the First World War, and the scale of its achievement in overcoming them. Many of these problems imposed profound limitations on the exercise of command and control.

The first problem was the sheer scale of the war. As Richard Bryson, following on from the work of many other writers, has pointed out, the loss rate for the British army in individual actions in the Second World War was often not much different from that of twenty years before (indeed, it was often higher):

> . . . what is markedly different is the scale of its commitment. At El Alamein, the eleven British divisions of the Eighth Army faced four weak German divisions and a further eight Italian divisions of varying strength and quality, at a time when 171 German and other Axis divisions were operating on the Eastern Front. The BEF of 1914–1918 deployed at its peak up to sixty-six divisions, in five armies, with a total manpower sometimes over two million. During the German offensives of March–April 1918 the British armies engaged a total of 109 German divisions, and ninety-nine divisions during the final offensive from August 1918 to the Armistice.[15]

The need to expand the army to enable it to meet this commitment – its growth from a few hundred thousand to over two million men – was a huge undertaking. It involved the formation of the largest single corporate body created by the British state up to that point. It meant not only recruiting, training, equipping and incorporating over a million new soldiers, but provision for their board, lodging, health and education in a foreign country for four years. To an extent, these issues of man management and logistics – the little considered side of command and control – were the primary concerns of senior commanders for the first three years of the war. It was only in 1917 and 1918 that adequate systems were in place to ensure the army's smooth functioning; and even then the BEF faced a struggle to ensure it was supplied with sufficient men.

A second, related issue was the totality of the conflict. The war was not only larger than its predecessors in terms of numbers of soldiers involved, but it involved the whole nation more fully. The Great War was the first time that Britain had participated in a modern, industrialised, total war. Casualties were no longer limited to combatant troops close to the front line; they might include civilians bombed in London or merchant sailors sunk at sea. Total war had its own logic: victory would go to the side that most successfully utilised the war-making capacity of the entire nation. There was a conceptual change involved here: for example the need to mobilise businessmen to bring their knowledge of forecasting and economies of scale to military logistical supply. The degree to which the military and civilian spheres should interact, and which, if either, should gain the upper hand, was a crucial issue for contemporaries.

The third factor to be emphasised is the influence of the particular battlefield environment within which operations were conducted. The strategic geography of the Western Front imposed much of its own logic on the way the war was fought. Large numbers of troops were concentrated in a comparatively densely populated area, which made dramatic strategic manoeuvring of the sort evident from the Eastern Front in both wars almost impossible. The Germans, having invaded France and Belgium, could choose to be on the defensive, and could therefore select terrain that favoured their positions.

The fourth and final factor was the impact of changing, and unchanging, technology. Seldom can a war have been fought during which the pace of technological change was so swift. As an example, although the tanks employed in Europe in 1945 were a huge improvement on those used in 1939, they remained a development of an established and recognised weapon. Elements in the weapon system available to the British commander of 1918 – tanks, gas, whirlwind bombardments on targets that were accurately predicted or located through sound-ranging, ground-attack aircraft, to name but the most obvious – had been unknown four years before. Although it has been criticised for rigidity or lack of imagination, the BEF in fact proved able to recognise and adopt many of these new technologies, and develop some of the tactics necessary to employ them efficiently. The combination of scale and rapid change in weapons technology may be seen to have led to a step-change in the nature of warfare. Jonathan Bailey has argued persuasively for the arrival, in 1916–18, of the 'modern' battlefield, deep and three dimensional, as opposed to the more linear battles of the nineteenth century. Crucially for Bailey, technological developments allowed the employment of effective indirect artillery fire, capable of a devastating impact on an opponent's organisation and morale.[16]

Yet at the same time as weapons technology altered and improved so rapidly, communications technology remained in its infancy. Radios were not employed at subordinate formation level until late 1917; even so they remained highly unreliable. At a tactical level, command remained a matter of voice, visual message or runner. Trench conditions obviously imposed profound restrictions on the effectiveness of any of these methods.

Even where communications could be provided and protected, this was usually only the case as far as the front line. In the assault, once troops had 'jumped the bags', communications with their superiors almost inevitably broke down. Sending messages back from an assault that by its nature became confused, across a no-man's land which was almost certainly under shellfire, was problematic in the extreme. Although attempts were made to improve the quantity and quality of the information available to senior commanders, their part in immediate combat command naturally tended to be limited to detailed pre-planning.

Bearing in mind the restrictions imposed by the factors outlined above, what developments can be seen to have taken place during the war? Given the professional ethos and experience of the Regular army in 1914, it should perhaps be unsurprising that there was a comparatively early (relative to popular conception) recognition of some of the essential problems of trench warfare. The army encouraged, to a degree, individual innovation and improvisation. 1915 seems to have seen a number of officers at different levels recognising and attempting to solve the tactical and operational conundrums of trench warfare. There is evidence that some officers moved towards the identification of the solution which would come to be widely employed two years later: the use of brief but heavy artillery bombardments to neutralise the enemy and allow fast-moving infantry to make an advance of limited extent which would leave them still under the protection of their own guns.

However, powerful obstacles existed which prevented the optimal employment of this approach. The British artillery lacked sufficient guns, and even more critically, appropriate shells, to allow them adequately to support the infantry. This was to be a persistent problem; even when sufficient numbers of shells became available in 1916, they were often of the wrong type (shrapnel rather than High Explosive) or simply defective. The army's reluctance to disseminate a prescriptive doctrine meant that tactical advances in one unit were not necessarily copied throughout the army. Although this allowed a mass of experimentation by subordinate units, mechanisms for recognising and spreading successful innovation were defective – although, as Albert Palazzo has recently argued, the British army's robust ethos proved a sound basis on which to construct battlewinning methods.[17] Of course, the huge growth in the army in 1915 led to a widespread lack of command experience at all levels. Throughout the army, newly promoted commanders from section upwards were learning on the job, with varying degrees of success.

From the end of 1916 there does seem to have been an effort to move on from the individualism and confusion of previous years and adopt a more consistent and cohesive approach. It is tempting to put this down, at least in part, to the disaster on the first day of the Somme: but it may also have been that the end of the initial period of massive expansion and the checking of German assaults allowed time for reflection and reorganisation. Certainly there were developments in the structures of command, particularly at Corps and GHQ level, which seem to suggest an attempt to recognise and react to the realities of modern warfare on the Western Front.

At the same time, however, the sheer obviousness of the immediate problem – the defences opposite the front line – seems to have led to what might be called a 'trench fixation'. In the course of late 1916 and 1917, the British army became adept, given the right circumstances, in creating and winning limited battles. But the quantity of effort required for the 'break-in' seemed to preclude detailed consideration of the transition to 'breakthrough'. On the other hand, this concentration of thought and effort seems hard to criticise. What other options were available, given the limitations already noted?

By 1918 the BEF not only had a selection of weapons which could contribute to breaking trench deadlock, it was able to integrate them into a highly effective, battle-winning, all-arms force whose approach was closer to that of 1939–1945 than 1914. At the same time, great competence and experience at all levels of command led to a decentralisation of command and control, despite the employment of conscript soldiers whose physique and morale seems to have inspired less confidence than the volunteers of 1915. Some historians, notably Tim Travers, have chosen to see this as an indication of the army escaping Haig's control, arguing that the success of the Hundred Days was achieved in spite of the Commander-in-Chief. We would prefer to represent it as the achievement of a remarkable operational and tactical flexibility that had been the aim of senior commanders – even if it was inadequately articulated – from an early stage. This flexibility, and the confidence placed in it by those at the top, played an essential part in the 'weapons system' that allowed the BEF to establish dominance over the German army in the last months of the war.

It is perhaps appropriate to conclude this Introduction by looking beyond this book, and asking where the study of command and control on the Western Front goes from here. Reviewing these chapters, it becomes possible to suggest not only some fruitful areas for future research, but also the approaches that should be adopted. For all that this Introduction has stressed the positive effects of the turning away from the cult of personality in the historiography of the First World War, further study of some individuals is still required. Our knowledge about commanders subordinate to Douglas Haig is sadly lacking. Detailed studies (particularly comparative studies) of the careers, experiences, command techniques and performances of individuals at Army, Corps, Division and Brigade level would help us to get an idea of the norm of command at various strata of the BEF.

1915 still forms a gaping chronological gap in the military history of the war. That year still awaits a detailed and systematic study using the techniques that have been pioneered with regard to the larger-scale battles from 1916 onwards. This was a period of enormous growth in the army, tactical innovation, some success but also disaster, during which the capabilities and flaws of the pre-war army were demonstrated to the full as it grappled with the problems of trench warfare at first hand. It deserves to be the subject of greater historical inquiry.

Finally, perhaps continuing and developing the areas studied in this book, there is still a great deal of work to be done on the practical details of the administration and technology of command. We still know little about matters such as the quantity of information available to headquarters at different levels at different points. What were the time constraints on decision making, and how swiftly were orders given out? The materials for such a study seem to be available within the Public Record Office (National Archive) and could surely provide some hard data to aid our understanding of command.

We would venture to make two recommendations about the approaches to be taken on research into command and control, and indeed all other new research into the military history of the war. The first is that there are huge advantages to be gained from any effort at comparative research, both between the different armies in the First World War, and between the armies of that war and previous and subsequent combatants, most obviously in the Second World War. Already there is evidence of the latter form of comparison gaining ground. The former will remain limited for many individuals by time, research funding and linguistic ability, but is still an ideal to be aimed for because of its potential utility. The pioneering work that has appeared comparing the experience of British and

Dominion elements in the BEF has demonstrated that this is a productive area of research, which certainly deserves further exploration.[18] A study of the interchange of ideas and innovations between the British and French armies is another obvious but as yet understudied topic.

Such trans-historical work might go further, for example by studying the army's organisation and innovation using the approaches of management science. The quotation from Rabindranath Tagore favoured by one of the best known poets of the First World War, Wilfred Owen: 'When I go from hence, let this be my passing word, that what I have seen is unsurpassable'[19] has all too often seemed to influence subsequent interpretations of the war. To treat the experience of the British army, state and nation in the First World War as an event somehow 'outside' of history, and thus beyond comparison with anything else, places wholly artificial limits on research and leads ultimately to a dead end.

Second, to return once more to the issue of personality, is the need to recognise the human factor in command and control. Myths of military incompetence and brutality are so deeply ingrained in British culture that it can still seem difficult for some to grasp that First World War commanders were not actively attempting to massacre their men: 'Yes, John, I'd like to think I did for them both with my plan of attack.' It is worth re-emphasising that those British commanders at all levels were men attempting to do their best, under extremely difficult circumstances, in jobs for which they often had little or no appropriate training. They were not automata. Some came up with brilliant, innovative solutions that eventually led to victory. Some made terrible mistakes that cost other men their lives unnecessarily. There is a paradox here with which military historians of the war must engage, whilst avoiding the temptation to romanticise the past. At times attempting to humanise, in modern terms, a generation which was Victorian in upbringing can appear impossible: their beliefs and actions so far away from our own as to inhibit comprehension. At others, their behaviour is so recognisably human that an instant recognition is felt across the years. This recognition of fellow human spirit – the thumb print in the prehistoric pot – is one of the pleasures of historical study: its possibility in connection with those who exercised command during the First World War should not be ignored.

NOTES

1   M van Creveld, *Command in War* (Cambridge, Mass. and London, 1985), 7, 5, 12–13.
2   Compare the unfavourable tone of Gibbs' comments on GHQ in *Realities of War* (London, 1920), pp. 200–1 with his generally uncritical treatment of staff officers and commanders in books such as *The Battles of the Somme* (London, 1917).

3   D Todman, '"Sans peur et sans reproche": the retirement, death and mourning of Sir Douglas Haig, 1918–1928', *Journal of Military History*, 67, 4 (October 2003), 1083–1106.

4   G A B Dewar and J H Boraston, *Sir Douglas Haig's Command*, two volumes (London, 1922); C Falls, *The History of the 36th (Ulster) Division* (Belfast, 1922).

5   For a critique of Edmonds' approach to writing the official history, see T Travers, *The Killing Ground* (London, 1987) pp. 203–49. For a more positive view, see A Green, *Writing the Great War: Sir James Edmonds and the Official History 1915–1948* (London, 2003).

6   H Strachan, 'Liddell Hart, Cruttwell and Falls' and I Beckett, 'Frocks and Brasshats' in B Bond (ed.), *The First World War and British Military History* (Oxford, 1991); R Prior, *Churchill's The World Crisis as History* (London, 1983); B Bond, *The Unquiet Western Front* (Cambridge, 2002).

7   See D Todman, 'Representations of the First World War in British popular culture 1918–1998', PhD thesis, University of Cambridge, 2003.

8   See, for example, the conspiracy-theory ridden D Winter, *Haig's Command: a reassessment* (London, 1992), or J Laffin, *British Butchers and Bunglers of World War One* (Stroud, 1989).

9   Notable early examples might be P Simkins, *Kitchener's Army* (Manchester, 1988) and D French, *British Strategy and War Aims 1914–16* (London, 1986).

10 R Prior and T Wilson, *Command on the Western Front* (Oxford, 1992); idem, *Passchendaele: the untold story* (New Haven, CT, 1996).

11 For example, J Walker, *The Blood Tub: General Gough and the Battle of Bullecourt, 1917* (Staplehurst, 1998); B Rawling, *Surviving Trench Warfare: Technology and the Canadian Corps 1914–1918* (Toronto, 1992); I Passingham, *Pillars of Fire: the battle of Messines Ridge June 1917* (Stroud, 1998).

12 P Liddle (ed.), *Passchendaele in Perspective: the Third Battle of Ypres* (London, 1997).

13 J Bourne, P Liddle, I Whitehead (eds), *The Great World War 1914–45*, Vol. I, *Lightning Strikes Twice* (London, 2000).

14 Ian Malcolm Brown, *British Logistics on the Western Front 1914–19* (Westport, CT and London, 1998).

15 R Bryson, 'The once and future army', in B Bond *et al*, *'Look to your Front': studies in the First World War* (Staplehurst, 1999), p. 28, using figures from J Terraine, *The Smoke and the Fire: Myths and Anti-myths of War 1861 to 1945* (London, new edition, 1992), Chapters III–V and Table F to Chapter VIII.

16 J Bailey, *The First World War and the birth of the modern style of warfare*, Occasional Paper 22 (Camberley, 1996). See also G Sheffield, *Forgotten Victory: The First World War – Myths and Realities* (London, 2001).

17 A Palazzo, *Seeking Victory on the Western Front – The British Army and Chemical Warfare in World War I* (Lincoln, NA and London, 2000).

18 See for example P Simkins, 'Co-Stars or Supporting Cast? British Divisions in the 'Hundred Days', 1918', in P Griffith (ed.), *British Fighting Methods in the Great War* (London, 1996) pp. 50–69; J Bourne, 'The BEF's Generals on 29 September 1918: An Empirical Portrait with Some British and Australian Comparisons' in P Dennis and J Grey, *1918: Defining Victory* (Canberra, 1999) pp. 96–113; G D Sheffield, 'How Even was the Learning Curve? Reflections on the British and Dominion Armies on the Western Front, 1916–1918' in Y Tremblay, *Canadian Military History Since the 17th Century* (Ottawa, 2001) pp. 125–34.

19 E Blunden, 'Memoir' in C Day Lewis (ed.), *The collected poems of Wilfred Owen* (London, 1972), 175.

CHAPTER II

Command in the Transition From Mobile to Static Warfare, August 1914 to March 1915

Niall Barr

When the British Expeditionary Force landed in France in August 1914, it marked the British army's first confrontation with a major European opponent since the Crimean War of 1854–5. Over the previous century, the British army's methods of command and control had been shaped not by major conventional wars, but by experience in colonial campaigns. The Boer War of 1899–1902, which had provided both the British army and the British government with many shocking revelations of deficiencies, had been the conflict which most shaped the nature of Britain's army before 1914. The far-reaching changes made in the army's establishment and organisation by the Liberal Secretary of State for War, R B Haldane, reformed the worst of the problems revealed by the Boer War but also prepared the British army to face a continental commitment with confidence. Haldane's main task had been to bring the army up to date while preparing an Expeditionary Force of six infantry divisions and one cavalry division – at no extra cost to the Treasury. Haldane was successful to a great degree, but the British Expeditionary Force which sailed to France had one major flaw: its size.

The BEF initially comprised just 100,000 men, and while this was a large force by British standards it simply could not be compared to the million-strong behemoths mobilised by France, Germany, Austria and Russia in 1914. Thus, in terms of size, if in little else, the BEF more closely resembled a Napoleonic army than a modern force. When they went to war in 1914, British commanders did not have to confront the problems of commanding vast armies in action and indeed, the broad outline of the BEF's systems of command and control would probably have been recognised by Wellington.

The organisation of the BEF in August 1914 was small, and traditional methods of command and control, supplemented with new techniques, were deemed sufficient. Yet, from the BEF's baptism of fire at Mons on 23 August 1914, to the Battle of Neuve Chapelle on 10 March 1915, British commanders experienced a very sharp increase in the need to control and co-ordinate units in the unprecedented situations which confronted them. The encounter battle at Mons and the subsequent retreat to save the BEF from destruction put enormous pressure and strain upon the BEF but nevertheless followed a pattern, however unwelcome, which was broadly familiar to most of its commanders. The advance to the Aisne differed only in the fact that the BEF's command and control was strained by the needs of an advance. However, the sustained battles fought on the Aisne soon confronted commanders with new problems of scale, scope and difficulty in commanding troops under modern conditions. The Battle of First Ypres in November was the greatest crisis for commanders and their staffs still struggling to come to terms with the power of modern weaponry and adapting as quickly as possible to the new conditions of trench warfare. The winter of 1914–15 saw a period of great experimentation and improvisation within British staffs and the signal service, at the same time as the BEF expanded beyond its original two corps structure. The Battle of Neuve Chapelle represented the British army's first attempt to mount a major offensive operation under these new conditions, but the problems of command and control which were revealed by this action were to bedevil operations on the Western Front for years to come.

There are a number of difficulties in examining the command and control of the BEF during this early phase of the Great War. Perhaps the most serious problem is the relative dearth of official evidence concerning staff work in the early months of the war.[1] The regular officers of 1914 had had many years' experience of command and took the information contained in the pre-war Field Service Regulations for granted. They carried out procedures almost instinctively and could be relied upon to make decisions and execute orders without the need for the myriad of pamphlets which were later produced to educate the citizen officers of the New Armies. The first battles of the BEF were also periods of exceptional stress which left no time to ponder the niceties of the Field Service Regulations. Staff officers understandably relied on the existing procedures and manuals as any part of the army's organisation which worked reasonably well had to be taken for granted as officers and men struggled with the new problems of trench warfare.

In fact, the pre-war Field Service Regulations were models of clarity which made the relationship between commanders and staff plain. Staff work continued to be divided into three sections: General Staff, Adjutant-General and Quartermaster-General. While the Adjutant-General's staff fulfilled his traditional functions in discipline, pay and medical services, and similarly the Quartermaster-General's staff dealt with supplies and billeting, the General Staff had been created to assist a commander in the execution of his orders.[2] The General Staff was to co-ordinate staff work as far as was delegated by the commander, while also issuing all operations orders. This was made explicit in the Field Service Regulations:

> An officer of the staff as such, is vested with no military command, but, he has a twofold responsibility; first he assists a commander in the supervision and control of the operations and requirements of the troops, and transmits orders and instructions; secondly it is his duty to give to the troops every assistance in his power in carrying out the instructions issued to them.[3]

Staff officers were also to ensure that orders were routinely sent by more than one means to ensure delivery. The regulations insisted that orders should be written 'whenever it is practicable to do so' as: 'In war, verbal messages are often incorrectly delivered, especially in the excitement of an engagement.'[4] With this emphasis on ensuring the delivery of orders, staff officers certainly had an important role to play in action. While the pre-war regulations were generally satisfactory, the BEF found that the initial engagements stretched the command and control arrangements to the limit.

The mobilisation of the BEF was remarkable in its efficiency and a real testimony to efficient staff work, but one factor which no set of regulations could ever have allowed for was the physical strain placed on the Force and its commanders. Within days of arriving in France, the BEF was fighting and marching for its life. It is a matter of legend that many of the reservist soldiers, recalled to the colours in August 1914, were unused to the rigours of route marching, and found the retreat from Mons an exhausting experience. The sad case of General Grierson, who died of a suspected heart attack on 22 August while on the train to take command of II Corps near Maubege, demonstrates that some of the officers were also not fully prepared for the sharp transition from peacetime soldiering to command in war. Indeed, the physical and mental stamina demanded from commanders and staff officers during the retreat from Mons was enormous.

Perhaps the most famous example concerns the BEF's Chief of Staff, General Sir Archibald Murray, who suffered a nervous breakdown on 26 August 1914 when confronted with the news that both British Corps might be overwhelmed. Lt Col. T W Sheppard later wrote: 'Historians and writers, in the comfort of their studies insensibly underestimate two immensely important facts – fatigue and moral effect.'[5] He was told by Sir Archibald Murray that:

> . . . late in the afternoon of August 26th 1914 (the day of Le Cateau) he arrived at the place selected for GHQ. He had had no sleep for 70 hours. Immediately he got in he was handed two messages. The first from Smith Dorrien, to the effect that the extrication of the Second

Army was well nigh impossible, but that he was doing all he could to pull it out; the second from Sir Douglas Haig that he considered the extrication of the First Army very problematical! i.e. The Whole British Army! Sir Archy told me that after getting these two messages he sat for over half an hour, incapable of thought or action, whilst the perspiration streamed off him.[6]

Edmonds, the official historian, was sceptical about this particular version of Murray's breakdown, writing in the margin that:

Smith-Dorrien's message reached GHQ St Quentin about 4.30pm (. . . Murray when awakened, read the message and fainted. He was revived with a pint of champagne).

GHQ moved in the afternoon to NOYON, and received no information there until shortly after midnight 26/27. When Smith Dorrien reported personally to Sir J. French who was in bed asleep.[7]

Sheppard's relation of Murray's breakdown illuminates the tremendous physical strain and mental stress loaded on to an individual who had not made the full transition from peace to war. Murray was not alone in finding wartime conditions overwhelming. Sir Douglas Haig made constant references to the marked fatigue displayed by commanders and their staff during the retreat from Mons. On 28 August Haig remarked: 'Staff officers as well as troops were so dead tired it was most difficult to get orders understood and delivered to troops and then carried out'.[8] The lack of reliable communications, combined with the atmosphere of confusion present in the early engagements, meant that commanders had to rely on frequent personal visits to ensure that orders were delivered. Commanders had to ensure that they were in contact with their higher headquarters as well as their subordinates, while sorting out lines of retreat, bivouacking and new headquarters for the next night – all while attempting to march their men away from the danger of German envelopment. Not surprisingly, this placed enormous strain on commanders and their staff. Almost every officer in the BEF found the transition from peace to war sharp and painful and it took some time before the punishing effects of this change had dissipated.

However, while past British commanders could only rely on the horse and verbal message for command, commanders in 1914 did have access to 'mechanical contrivances' which seemed to make command an easier prospect. The most personal was the motor car. Rather than riding on horseback, or relying on faulty telegraph wires, commanders could drive to their subordinates' HQs to give orders in person. Haig noted with satisfaction in his diary that his orders for retreat on the evening of 22 August were transmitted quickly:

Thanks to the motor I was able to give personal orders to all the chief commanders concerned in the space of an hour. Written orders reached them later but the movement was started on certain lines in a way which would have been impossible before the days of motors.[9]

While Haig, as a Corps commander, could expect motor transport whenever it was required, more junior commanders and staff officers often could not. In fact, many of the motor cars used by the BEF's staff officers in the early months were provided and driven by civilian volunteers. Specially enlisted drivers were asked to volunteer with their cars through the auspices of the Royal Automobile Club and report at Southampton for service in France. Unfortunately, it was found that:

Many specially enlisted motor car drivers arrived from LONDON a few hours after they had been enlisted, many had only a service overcoat and cap – neither underclothing, S.D. suit, necessaries, equipment, or documents were in their possession, and no reserve of any of these articles existed at the time in SOUTHAMPTON . . . Several of the cars brought by the specially enlisted M.T. drivers were found to be unworthy and had to be returned; none came provided with spares and tools which are indispensable to active service conditions.[10]

Nonetheless, these volunteers played a very important role during the first few months of the war.[11] Yet even with the assistance of motor cars, despatch riders and telegraph, Haig noted that it was: 'Impossible to command at a distance of 30 miles from the scene of action by HQ at Mauberge'.[12] With an unreliable signal service, commanders and their staffs were forced to place heavier reliance on drivers and despatch riders to get messages through to subordinate headquarters. Indeed, during the retreat from Mons the main difficulty for the volunteer drivers and their staff officer passengers was in locating the headquarters or units they had been sent to contact. Once the front became static and the signal service was able to provide more reliable communications, the volunteer drivers were increasingly replaced by ASC drivers and cars that continued to fulfil this important role behind the lines.

Another 'mechanical contrivance' which very quickly transformed the nature of command and control in the Great War was the aircraft. The fledgling Royal Flying Corps had an auspicious baptism of fire on 22 August when twelve RFC reconnaissance flights gave clear evidence of the advance of von Kluck's German First Army on Mons. The Cavalry Corps, which was often out of touch with GHQ during the retreat from Mons, did not function particularly well in its reconnaissance role and Sir John French and his two Corps commanders began to rely increasingly heavily on the RFC for reconnaissance.[13] When the Germans began their retreat from the Marne, Haig relied heavily on reports from aircraft. On 7 September he noted:

> I sent reconnaissances by aeroplane wide on the East and N E. They returned at 7 am and said fog in the valley prevented them from seeing. But by 10 am they gave me useful information showing the Germans all on the move northwards except some Cavalry & guns.[14]

On 9 September Haig noted that: 'I sent out special aeroplane reconnaissance and soon I was able to send word to Divisions to continue on the march and that the enemy seemed to be in full retreat.' These notes make it clear that Haig was relying almost solely on early aerial reconnaissance to determine his orders. In the heavy fighting which broke out along the Aisne, there was little or no scope for traditional cavalry scouting and as the front lines solidified into trench lines, commanders' reliance on aerial reconnaissance continued to grow.

Although aircraft and motor cars assisted command and control greatly, the most important element of technology lay with the Signal Service and its telegraph lines. While the British army's signal service of August 1914 was of undoubted technical efficiency, it remained small and ill equipped for the demands of a European war. Progress in developing the use of telephone and wireless had been slow and the Signal Service still relied on the telegraph for most communications. The pre-war regulations emphasised the need for 'constant maintenance of communication between the various parts of an army' but also cautioned that: 'The elaborate means of communication provided under modern conditions should not be used in such a manner as to cripple the initiative of subordinates by unnecessary interference'.[15] Even with the experience of the Boer War, where extensive use of the telegraph had been developed down to divisional level, commanders and their staff continued to rely on the traditional methods of mounted messengers and command.[16] This was just as well because the 'elaborate means of communication' available in 1914, far from stifling initiative, quickly broke down under the conditions of battle.

The enormous problems inherent in utilising land-line telegraphs during a war of movement were fully demonstrated during the first few months of the war. Just as the Signal Service was in the process of establishing a full telegraphic communications between GHQ, the Corps and Divisions, the BEF received orders to retreat. Much of the telegraphic cable was lost during the retreat, and no formal system of re-supply was established. Great use was made of the civilian telegraph network to ensure that GHQ was linked to each Corps at night, but telegraphic communication rarely extended to lower formations. Individual units also made use of the civilian telephone network and one of the most famous telephone conversations of this period took place on a civilian line with both generals having to travel from their HQs to make the call, when General Sir Horace Smith-Dorrien, commander of II Corps, informed Major-General Sir Henry Wilson, General Staff, of his intention to fight at Le Cateau.[17] By the end of the retreat, the Signal Service was becoming more efficient and on 4 September the Signal Company of GHQ handled 230 telegrams. However, during the retreat the main form of communications between headquarters and units remained despatch riders and staff cars.

The advance from the Marne brought a whole new series of difficulties in its train. Still short of cable, the signallers had to rely more heavily on the civilian network which had been heavily damaged by the retreating German troops. Although considerable effort had been made in building up three telegraph lines for an advance, it was reported on 11 September that 'all new lines [were] faulty'. Progress was made in clearing the faults until 16 September when it was noted that 'One line to Base working till 3 pm. and then cut by French working party which crossed the line. Sent all work by despatch riders in evening . . . Unable to construct any further forward owing to fighting'. It was not until 23 September, once the front lines had stabilised again, that it could be reported 'all lines working well'.[18] During the advance to Aisne, the Signal Service, no doubt in desperation, organised a system of mounted liaison officers to gather information from forward units and convey messages and information to their commanders. This was later noted as a useful innovation:

> The advantage of sending Staff Officers from the higher to the lower formations, to act as liaison officers, so far at any rate as between the Corps and Divisions is concerned, has been proved to be very great. During the fight, Divisional Commanders and Staffs are usually fully occupied; and, despite every intention of keeping the Corps fully informed, it has been found in practice that the latter does not as a rule get as much information as is desirable unless these liaison officers are provided.[19]

Although a forerunner of the GHQ Reporting Regiment which fulfilled an important liaison function throughout the war, in 1914 the mounted liaison officers were a throwback to the old days of the 'gallopers' because no other reliable form of communication existed. The BEF's Signal Service was simply not capable of providing the army with reliable communications during the periods of mobile warfare which the BEF experienced in 1914.

However, although the static conditions of warfare which descended on the Western Front during the Battle of the Aisne made it possible to lay greater lengths of telegraphic cable and establish reliable communications between GHQ, Corps and Divisional headquarters, the new static fighting imposed a whole new range of difficulties on tactical communications.

Commanders and their staff began to recognise the importance of the telephone as a rapid means of communication. The demand for telephones came especially from the artillery which found that better communications were vital in the new conditions they faced. It was noted in a paper concerning the lessons of the first few months of the war that:

> Perhaps the most unexpected feature of the present war has been the arresting power of modern artillery, and especially of howitzers and heavy artillery, both as regards their material and moral effect.[20]

The power of artillery was first noted during the Battle of the Aisne and its influence over the conduct of battles continued to grow during the war. While powerful artillery was an essential weapon in trench warfare, gunners had to cope with the fact that they could no longer fire over open sights at visible enemies. The artillery batteries had to be hidden or placed behind a reverse slope out of sight of the front line and sometimes deployed many thousands of yards behind it. It was noted that: 'The closest co-operation between infantry and artillery is an absolute necessity' mainly because:

> Even at moderate ranges, artillery commanders find it impossible to distinguish between our own troops and the enemy, and between our own trenches and those of the enemy. As a result, in the earliest stages of the war, fire was either occasionally directed on our own men or fire was withheld at important moments for fear of such consequences.[21]

While the BEF was relying on artillery officers observing from 'as near as possible to the infantry firing line', the lack of cable and equipment often made it difficult to link these artillery officers with their batteries by telephone. However, it was found that when this had been possible the results were 'eminently satisfactory'. It was further noted that:

> The telephone equipment is extremely valuable; but the instruments are very delicate and become unsatisfactory unless the greatest care is taken of them . . . observation posts have frequently to be at abnormal distances from the battery, and without telephones the service of the guns is unsatisfactory and slow. The equipment should, therefore, be treated as if it were made of glass, and as if it were as valuable as diamonds. Apparently it cannot be replaced.[22]

Thus, the artillery became the major voice in demanding more and more telephones to assist it in its new role during trench warfare.

Detailed instructions were soon disseminated to provide for the new conditions and communication needs of the artillery. It was noted that:

> With the development of telephone and telegraph communication in the field, duties are being thrown on divisional signal companies which are not included in any Manuals, but which require to be recognised.[23]

The divisional signal companies were duly increased in size: 'to enable the G.O.C. Division to provide adequate signal communication with all his units which may include a separate system for artillery fire control only'.[24] It is quite clear that the artillery had priority over the other arms of service in the development of dedicated telephone communications. Indeed, by November 1914, it was considered essential for an artillery commander 'who unites under his own orders batteries of all calibres, detailed to operate in the same sector of attack' to have:

> a highly developed telephone system connecting him either directly to or to the commander, the various artillery commanders under his orders, the observation posts and batteries; a telephone system can never be too elaborate and no precautions are too great to ensure its preservation.[25]

Although forward observation officers often still had to rely on despatch riders or visual signalling due to a lack of telephonic equipment, the system soon spread throughout the artillery. Such a system, combined with the use of a large-scale plan to mark out targets quickly, gave artillery commanders an unparalleled ability to direct fire. As artillery officers demonstrated the utility of the telephone, the BEF as a whole became an avid convert to the use of the telephone as the main means of communication. Increasingly, the telephone came to be seen as the essential form of communication at every level in the army.

This resulted in a race by units to procure telephones from any available source. During the winter of 1914/15, there was an ad hoc procurement of telephones from abandoned civilian networks, along with supplies of the official buzzer telephones, and crude exchanges were improvised to control the increasingly complex tangle of telephone lines. Unfortunately, the mud, damp and shellfire made the laying and maintenance of telephone lines particularly difficult and the reliable communications seemingly offered by the telephone often failed at critical moments. Because the telephone seemed to offer an answer to all of the army's communication needs, other forms of communication were ignored, shelved or dropped and the undue reliance on the telephone began to produce real problems. At Neuve Chapelle, this meant that when heavy German shellfire destroyed the forward telephone lines, all communications were gone as there were no alternatives in place.

Wireless equipment was still not reliable enough or portable enough to act as a serious competitor to the telephone. However, experiments with wireless aircraft in early 1915 were fruitful and this became the main focus of attention for wireless operation. One of the main problems, apart from the unreliability of the equipment, was the naïvete of the operators. Wireless stations had to be reminded forcibly that:

> One station is not to ask another in clear 'What is my Station Call'. Questions and answers of this sort give away the numbers used. Several cases of this between our stations have been overheard and also that cases had occurred of addresses being sent in clear: 'as "From Cavalry Division to G.H.Q." Even if the message has been authorised to go in clear, the address "to" and "from" is never to be so sent'.[26]

The BEF was certainly not alone in compromising wireless security, but such problems certainly limited the utility of wireless until proper procedures were developed and enforced.

While there were problems and difficulties in providing proper systems of communication at the higher levels of command, even greater dilemmas were faced at the tactical level. In 1914 battalion signallers were equipped with sixteen blue flags and sixteen white striped flags for semaphore messages, and eight heliographs, eight 'B' signalling lamps and eight signalling telescopes.[27] Unfortunately, all of this equipment was designed for visual signalling in open warfare. The combination of trench warfare and heavy artillery bombardments made visual signalling almost impossible. This left the battalion signallers without any viable means of communications, beyond the use of runners, as they had access to neither telegraph nor telephone equipment. Many battalion signallers abandoned their useless equipment and fought as infantry during First Ypres. These problems began a process of experimentation where many different forms of communication were evaluated in an attempt to provide reliable tactical communications. In September 1914 fifteen pigeons were donated by the French to British Intelligence which marked the beginnings of a great expansion in the use of pigeons by the British Signal Service.

These difficulties meant that in the opening phase of the Great War, tactical command and control of troops in the field remained very similar to the methods used by Wellington one hundred years before. Even with the various means of visual signalling, the most common form of communication remained the runner and the method of command remained personal; officers, on horseback or in a motor car, delivered orders and messages in person or by means of a staff officer, despatch rider, cyclist or runner. The BEF certainly tested these forms of command and control to their very limits during the retreat from Mons and the advance to the Aisne. It is certain that these very demanding movements were only possible due to the high quality of the British regular soldiers – and the high level of training and experience of the officers who commanded them. The rearguard action fought by Brigadier General Ivor Maxse's 1st Guards Brigade at Etreux on 27 August 1914 provides a textbook example of just how such an action could be fought under pressure but also demonstrates that even with good staff work and clear orders, events could still go badly wrong.

On 27 August 1914 Maxse was ordered to cover the retreat of both the 1st and 2nd Divisions with his 1st Guards Brigade reinforced with the 26th Brigade RFA, 23 Field Coy RE, two troops of the 15th Hussars, and one battery of howitzers. Maxse was ordered to hold a line on the north edge of Fesmy in contact with the French near Wassigny. At a hurried and impromptu meeting with Major General Lomax, his Divisional Commander, it was impressed on Maxse that he had to hold his position until both the 1st and 2nd Divisions had cleared the town of Etreux. Both divisions were to march through that town and would have supplies issued to them there. It was essential for Maxse's force to hold on to the Fesmy–Wassigny position to prevent the Germans from shelling Etreux while it was crowded with troops. However, Lomax left it to 'Maxse's discretion to fix the hour for starting the retirement of both the rearguard and the 2nd Brigade at WASSIGNY'.[28]

Maxse decided to wait until Etreux was cleared of troops before issuing orders for the retreat, but he wrote out his orders for the 'retirement leaving out the time for subsequent insertion'. These orders were read out at 12 noon to mounted officers who had been sent from their units to the Brigade Headquarters and they then 'returned to their battalions to explain the retirement orders to C.O.s'.[29] Thus, each battalion was properly warned of the need to withdraw although with no clear indication of when the retreat would take place. When Maxse's HQ received the message from 1st Division stating that '"ETREUX is now clear of impedimentia. GOC says you can march to ETREUX now" dated 12.20pm 27th August 1914 at ETREUX station', the written orders for retirement were sent out to all units at 12.45pm 'with the time filled in as "at once"' and delivered by cyclists.[30]

While most of Maxse's units received their written orders in good time and were able to begin an unhurried withdrawal, the 2nd Battalion, Royal Munster Fusiliers was not so fortunate. The Munsters had been engaged by German infantry since 10.30am but had successfully driven off every attack. While Major Day reached his battalion with the verbal orders and

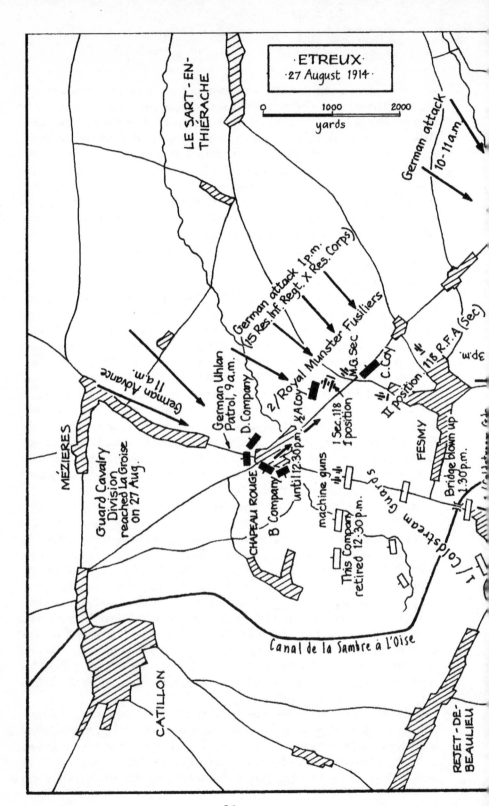

·ETREUX·
·27 August 1914·

0   1000   2000
yards

German attack
10-11 a.m.

German attack 1 p.m.
(15 Res. Inf Regt. X Res. Corps)

2/Royal Munster Fusiliers

LE SART - EN - THIÉRACHE

German Advance 11 a.m.

German Uhlan Patrol, 9 a.m.

D. Company

A Company until 12.30 p.m.

M.G. Sec

C. Coy

II position

118 R.F.A (Sec)

3 p.m.

FESMY

1 Sec. 118 position

MÉZIÈRES

Guard Cavalry Division reached La Groise on 27 Aug.

CHAPEAU ROUGE

B Company

machine guns

This Company retired 12.30 p.m.

1/Coldstream Guards

Bridge blown up 1.30 p.m.

1/Coldstream Gds

Canal de la Sambre à L'Oise

CATILLON

REJET - DE - BEAULIEU

24

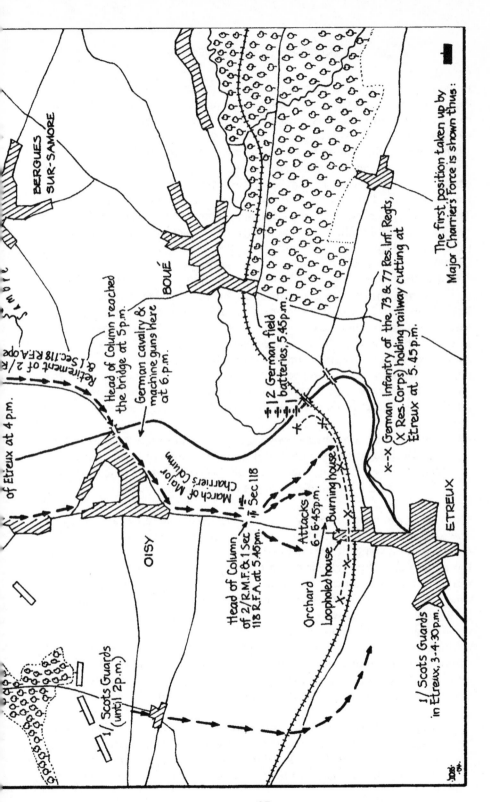

BERGUES-SUR-SAMORE

Samore

BOUÉ

OISY

ETREUX

of Étreux at 4 p.m.

Retirement of 2/R.M.F. & 1 Sec.118 R.F.A.ope

Head of Column reached the bridge at 5 p.m.

German cavalry & machine guns here at 6.p.m.

March of Major Charrier's Column

1 Sec.118

‡ 2 German field batteries, 5.45p.m.

Head of Column of 2/R.M.F. & 1 Sec. 118 R.F.A. at 5.45pm.

Attacks 6-6·45p.m.

Orchard

Burning house

Loopholed house

x—x German Infantry of the 73 & 77 Res. Inf. Regts, (X Res. Corps) holding railway cutting at Étreux at 5. 45 p.m.

1/ Scots Guards (until 2p.m.)

1/ Scots Guards in Étreux, 3-4·30p.m.

The first position taken up by Major Charrier's Force is shown thus:

25

then returned to Brigade Headquarters for further orders, the cyclist who carried the written orders at 12.50pm was unable to reach the battalion due to enemy fire. He was only able to deliver his written message to Major Day many hours later.[31]

Meanwhile, still waiting for orders to retire, the Munsters were fighting an increasing number of German troops. The last message received by Maxse's headquarters at 1.30pm from the battalion was carried by Major Day and reported that the battalion was 'heavily engaged with the enemy'. The written message from the Munsters' commander, Major Charrier, reported that the battalion was 'fighting and killing Germans and seemed to be opposed by 2 Regiments and some guns, that he had taken prisoners from the 15th German Regiment, and was getting on very well'.[32]

Due to the uncertainty of the Munsters' position, there was a long delay in the retirement of Maxse's rearguard. Eventually, Maxse ordered an immediate withdrawal of the rearguard 'in spite of the inability of the Royal Munster Fusiliers to extricate themselves from the grip of superior forces of the enemy'. The Munsters, isolated and under heavy attack, continued their resistance until 9.15pm when the survivors of the battalion were forced to surrender. However, the 1st Coldstream Guards and the 1st Black Watch delayed their retirement until after 4pm in an attempt to help the Munster Fusiliers. Maxse later wrote that:

> they compromised the safety of themselves and the whole force by their prolonged delay, but I cannot for one moment blame either of them in view of the fact that they took this risk for the whole purpose of succouring their comrades of the Royal Munster Fusiliers.[33]

This was a clear example of the nature of tactical command and control as it existed in 1914. Maxse had to rely on officers on horseback and cyclists to deliver his orders and inevitable delay and confusion could result from these methods. Although Maxse had prepared his units for a subsequent retreat order, the inability of a cyclist to deliver one set of orders led to the loss of an entire battalion. At the same time, under certain circumstances, battalion commanders were prepared to exercise their initative and take it upon themselves to ignore or delay acting on unpalatable orders.

Similar experiences of failed communications and mislaid orders were common throughout the BEF during the first few months of the war, although they did not always have such tragic consequences. One Colonel, fighting his battalion at Le Cateau on 26 August 1914, noted:

> Firing began between 8 and 9am. Rode up with Lloyd to cemetery on en.[emy]'s side of village to reconn[ai]tre. Bullets striking around and over our heads. Rode back, telling Lloyd to follow soon., so as to est.[blish] H.Q. at X r[oa]d n[ea]r Chateau to be able to receive any

message coming from B[riga]de., as no orders had been rec[ei]v[e]d since last night and B.H.Q. were not where they had said they would be.[34]

Command and control certainly broke down at Le Cateau and considerable confusion reigned. Officers and men were often thrown back on their own resources and initiative in such situations. James Jack's experiences as a Staff Captain at Le Cateau illuminated the anodyne comment in Regulations that it was the duty of staff officers 'to give to the troops every assistance in his power in carrying out the instructions issued to them',[35] when, as a Brigade staff officer, he had to singlehandedly visit units to ensure their withdrawal as orders had failed to reach the units.[36]

When the BEF faced its greatest crisis at Ypres on 31 October 1914, staff officers were still playing the same role. When Haig realised that the lst Division was in real peril and issued an order that the line 'FREZENBURG – WESTHOEK – bend of main road – KLEIN ZILLEBEKE – bend of canal' was 'to be held at all costs', he ensured that: 'These orders were taken personally by staff officers to divisional headquarters. At the same time a staff officer was sent to inform General FOCHE [sic] and GOC 9th Corps of the situation'.[37] Personal contact and transmission of orders was still an important part of command and control in the BEF of 1914. During the early battles commanders and their staff continued to operate in traditional ways. Commanding from horseback, or the seat of a car, they were never more than a few miles away from the fighting itself.

However, during First Ypres, the BEF also began to learn the high cost in lives paid by commanders and staff who remained near the front. Casualties amongst staff officers were high, particularly as the old habits of selecting crossroads, haystacks or farmhouses as the site of headquarters died hard.[38] When the fighting began to stabilise around Ypres in late October 1914, such prominent headquarters became high-value targets for German gunners. Staff Captain Jack noted in his diary that:

> We have had to change our residence twice . . . At our second headquarters on the following day three shells burst in the yard, wrecking part of the farm walls and roof, but again wounding neither man nor beast. All the same, we departed forthwith, grooms, horses and carts, servants with kits, orderlies with documents, Hodgkinson clasping his typewriter, the General and staff laden with despatch-cases, swords, accoutrements and mackintoshes. A quaint flitting![39]

Not all headquarters were so lucky. On 31 October 1914 the commanders and staff of both the 1st and 2nd Divisions were crammed into a room at Hooge Château, not far from Ypres, discussing the critical situation which was developing around Ghelevelt. Halg had just vacated the château the day before to give Monro and his staff more space than the cramped quarters in a small house they had been using. Unfortunately, no one in or around the château seems to have noticed a German reconnaissance plane which flew overhead and clearly recognised the château as a probable headquarters. One hour later, at 1.15pm, two salvoes of shells from a German battery killed six of the staff officers and mortally wounded General Lomax, commander of 2nd Division.[40] This misfortune left the two divisions essentially leaderless for over an hour before Generals Bulfin and Cavan were able to re-establish a new command chain.

As late as 29 December 1914, the commander of I Corps was reiterating the:

> urgent necessity of rendering Headquarters of Divisions (and Brigades) as inconspicuous as possible, particularly as regards observation from above. Care should be taken to prevent collections of motor cars, horses, orderlies etc. And sentries should be kept as far as possible under cover.[41]

The danger of losing an important headquarters to shellfire was too great to risk their placement in the immediate front line. Under the impact of high explosive, headquarters were forced to move away from the front, while those which had to remain near the front became less conspicuous. Losses amongst staff officers had been heavy. The Official History notes that fifty-six Staff College graduates were killed in 1914[42] and the table of staff officer casualties shows clearly the scale suffered by the BEF during the early months of the war.[43] Up until 30 November 1914, casualties amongst the staff had been very heavy, amounting to an average of 22%. The toll amongst divisional staff had been even greater at 36%, a total of thirty-three officers. While the total number of officers killed was much smaller than in the fighting units themselves, these statistics represented a critical loss of experienced and trained staff officers. Because the Staff College had closed on the outbreak of war, such men were very difficult to replace.[44] It was noted at the time that:

> It is not possible to make a comparison between officers of the staff and regimental officers in regard to casualties. The duties of each are distinct and involve risks which can hardly be compared. Under certain conditions a Staff officer may be obliged to run greater risks than the Regimental officer and vice versa . . . Further the well trained Staff officer is a valuable asset who cannot be readily replaced, and it is not his duty to expose himself unnecessarily.[45]

While casualties amongst staff had fallen by 1915 with the advent of trench warfare and more careful measures to protect HQs from bombardment,

Table 1: Staff Officer Casualties from the Outbreak of War to 31 May 1915

Outbreak of War -30th November 1914

Formation	Number in Country	Total Personnel	Total Casualties	Casualties as % of strength
Corps	4	40	2	5%
Cavalry Divisions	4	36	10	28%
Cavalry Brigades	11	44	2	4.5%
Divisions	10	90	33	36.6%
Brigades	31	93	20	21.5%
Total		303	67	22%

1st December 1914 -28 February 1915

Formation	Number in Country	Total Personnel	Total Casualties	Casualties as % of strength
Corps	7	70	1	1.5%
Cavalry Divisions	5	45	-	-%
Cavalry Brigades	14	56	3	5.3%
Divisions	13	117	3	2.5%
Brigades	40	120	2	1.6%
Total		408	9	2.2%

1 March 1915 -31 May 1915

Formation	Number in Country	Total Personnel	Total Casualties	Casualties as % of strength
Corps	9	90	1	1%
Cavalry Divisions	5	45	1	2%
Cavalry Brigades	15	60	9	15%
Divisions	21	189	7	3.6%
Brigades	64	192	26	13.5%
Total	-	576	44	7.6%

Taken from 'Staff Officer Casualties', French Papers, Imperial War Museum, JDPF 7/2(1).

the BEF continued to lose many experienced and capable staff officers. Haig lost Sir John Gough, VC, his very talented and capable Chief of Staff, on 20 February 1915, when he was mortally wounded by a stray bullet while on a visit to the front line.[46] Not surprisingly, Sir John French began to make it increasingly difficult for staff officers to visit the front line unless they were on vital business. Thus, the division between the front line and staff which developed during the war occurred for a very good reason. The cost in trained staff officers had simply been too high to allow their continued presence in the front lines.

Even as the BEF was struggling to deal with the very heavy losses incurred in fighting, and coming to terms with the problems of trench warfare, its commanders were turning their attention to the arrangements for the expansion of the Force. Although the BEF had been a finely honed instrument in August 1914, there had been no immediate plans or procedure for its expansion. When Kitchener rejected the idea of reinforcing the Army through an expansion of the Territorial Force in favour of his 'New Armies' it made plans for a logical and phased expansion of the Army in France difficult. Unsurprisingly, this led to a lively debate between Kitchener and French concerning the introduction of the Army level of organisation between GHQ and the Corps.

It is clear that French wished to delay the introduction of Armies for as long as possible, fearing that:

> Another channel of inter-communication interposed between Corps and G.H.Q. would mean more delay in the transmission of important messages, largely increased signalling establishments, and an in-elastic organisation which might hamper the execution of the C.-in-C's plans.
>
> In the conduct of a battle it is as well that the C.-in-C. should not delegate his responsibilities more than is rendered absolutely necessary by the size of the force he commands.[47]

French also advanced a number of valid reasons why there was no need for an Army organisation *just* yet. He mentioned the fact that each division was administratively self supporting, but also that the existing structure of ten divisions grouped into five Army Corps of two divisions each was not the optimum organisation. While he admitted that the five Army Corps, with the British and Indian Cavalry Corps was 'just about the limit they [GHQ] are able to control', he argued that:

> Corps of two Divisions are perhaps over-staffed and not best organized for tactical purposes. Experience has sometimes shown that two Divisions fighting abreast have not sufficient depth: on the other hand, two divisions one behind the other may not have sufficient front.[48]

Instead of expanding the Army's organisational structure, French argued that more expansion should be absorbed by adding an extra division to each Corps as: 'A third Division might increase the fighting efficiency of the Corps, and would not necessitate an increase in Corps staff.' French also admitted, revealingly, that: 'there are some Corps Commanders who are quite capable of handling two Divisions, but to whom I would rather not entrust the control of three'.[49] It was only after this avenue of expansion had been exhausted that French favoured the introduction of the Army level of organisation. French's arguments do suggest that he was attempting to delay the inevitable. French does not seem to have understood that his role as CinC would need to change as the BEF expanded. He feared a loss of control over his units – something he had already experienced with Smith-Dorrien's stand at Le Cateau – and he obviously believed that elevating Haig and Smith-Dorrien to the status of Army commanders could only make the problem worse.

Two weeks later, French had agreed that Armies should be introduced, but was now attempting to ensure that the Army level remained an administrative unit rather than a fighting organisation. He wrote to Kitchener that there would be 'no difficulty from an administrative point of view' in forming Armies, 'provided it is clearly understood that only the same administrative powers will be vested in Army commanders as are now vested in Army Corps Commanders'. French argued that: 'The only change involved, therefore, by the army organization will be that general questions will be referred to GHQ by Army Headquarters instead of by Army Corps Headquarters, as heretofore'.[50]

The Army organisation was finally adopted at 12 noon on 26 December 1914, with two Armies, one under Sir Douglas Haig and one under Sir Horace Smith-Dorrien. The Cavalry Corps remained a separate entity. Haig lost no time in emphasising his view of the new organisation to the troops under his command. In a note regarding staff duties written on 28 December 1914, he noted that: 'It is important to avoid turning the Army Headquarters into a "Post Office" pure and simple. GHQ will, therefore, deal direct with Corps on practically every subject except "operations"'. This was a quite different concept of the Army organisation. In a rhetorical question, Haig emphasised what he saw as the importance of the Army:

> What information are the Corps to send to the Army? – The answer to this is 'Everything that affects operations, and which the Army Commander should know in order to command his forces in action'. Corps staff should be able to judge for themselves what to send to Army Headquarters bearing the above principle in view.[51]

The interposition of the Army organisation between GHQ and Corps level was a significant one. Haig was determined not to be a mere postmaster but instead a commander in charge of his units. The battles which followed in 1915 were increasingly planned by the Army and Corps staffs rather than GHQ. Certainly, while Haig was in command of First Army, he made the Army level the most important operational command in the BEF. Ironically, many of French's concerns about his loss of control over operations were to be realised over the controversies about the positioning of reserves during the Battle of Loos which eventually saw Haig supplant his former Commander in Chief.[52]

Just as the BEF began to expand, so methods of command and communicating the commander's intent took on different forms. Conferences or 'Councils of War' between commanders and subordinates had been commonplace throughout the history of warfare, and it was noted by December 1914 that: 'Conferences of the Administrative Staff should be held twice daily where possible. The Senior Supply Officer should attend in order that all may be au courant with the general situation'.[53] However, although the BEF's supply officers were the first to regularise such arrangements, the habit of holding regular conferences soon spread. Haig held his first Corps conference with his Divisional Commanders on 23 November 1914 to 'review the future conduct of operations'.[54] These conferences became a very important method of command in the BEF due to the static nature of the operations. It would have been inconceivable to hold such a Conference during the retreat from Mons when every commander had to desperately keep hold of his subordinate units through personal command. But with the much slower tempo, and static nature of trench warfare, commanders had the time to come together to discuss common problems and work out the best way of progressing against fixed defences. This first Conference discussed a number of issues including the suitability of the trenches occupied, the utility of loopholes, the nature of communication trenches, and the opportunities for offensive action in each of the divisional areas under Haig's command. Staff conferences came to be widely used throughout the BEF as a means of disseminating important information and sharing knowledge about the new problems confronting commanders at all levels

While there were numerous trench raids and minor actions throughout the winter of 1914–15, the first major British attack undertaken in the spring of 1915 was the Battle of Neuve Chapelle. Lessons and methods derived from this battle formed the model for most of the British attacks for the rest of the war. The problems of command and control which were revealed by this battle, and their impact on the fighting, continued to confront British commanders for most of the war.

Neuve Chapelle was 'based on the conception of penetrating the enemy's front by a violent attack pressed continuously till the desired result was achieved'.[55] With the support of a heavy bombardment of short duration, it was hoped that the assaulting infantry of IV Corps and the

Indian Corps would be able to seize Neuve Chapelle village and the heights of Aubers Ridge which lay beyond it in one attack.

The success of the short artillery barrage which opened the battle has often been attributed simply to the element of surprise, but the level of co-ordination and control achieved through the use of a detailed artillery timetable which gave precise targets and length of bombardment to each battery was also very important. The timetable:

> was carefully prepared beforehand and issued to all concerned. This programme was the result of many conferences and much delibera-tion, and the result was gratifying. After fire was once opened, the Major General R.A., Commanding the Artillery of the 1st Army, hardly found it neccessary to issue any orders regarding the control of fire.[56]

While the timetable ensured that the initial artillery fire programme was effective, the division of the artillery batteries into two groups and the use of an extensive telephone network, gave unrivalled flexibility and rapid artillery response to infantry requests for fire support.

The commanding Major-General of the Royal Artillery was linked by telephone to each of the Corps involved in the operation and both artillery groups. The groups were, in turn, linked to each other, the divisional headquarters and the artillery brigades, and in wireless communication with the Royal Flying Corps. The information received from aircraft allowed commanders 'to direct the fire of their batteries on to hostile active batteries and other targets that were at the time important tactical objectives'. Each of the brigades was of course linked to its batteries, 'and the batteries again with their forward observing officers'. With such a comprehensive communications network: 'the Major General was able to obtain satisfactory information as to the progress of the attack till the capture of NEUVE CHAPELLE'.[57] During the initial phase of the attack, Brigadier General Pinney was able to request artillery support which arrived soon afterwards from 8th Division to bombard an uncaptured section of trench.[58] However, after the capture of Neuve Chapelle, the system of communications and the co-ordination began to break down. Information became:

> intermittent owing to the constant breakages of the telephone wire between forward observing officers and their batteries by hostile Artillery fire and the numerous casualties among the forward observing officers themselves. These are incidents of a big battle which cannot be provided against.[59]

While such problems could not be prevented in 1915, the breakdown in communications had very serious implications for the rest of the battle. Without effective communications, the higher commanders had to wait for news and this delayed the exploitation of the initial success. General Rawlinson, commander of IV Corps, refused to allow the 7th Division to advance until he was certain that one defended locality, known as The Orchard, had been confirmed as taken. In the event, The Orchard was not heavily defended, but news of its capture did not reach Rawlinson for over an hour.[60] By the end of 10 March IV Corps had penetrated the German defences to a maximum depth of 1,200 yards on a frontage of 4,000 yards and taken 748 prisoners. This was a considerable success given the novelty of the conditions being faced. However, by the end of the day, the British attack had effectively been played out. Even though Haig ordered a continuation of the attack for the next day, without effective communications and an increasingly stiff German resistance, any chance of further success was slim.

On 11 March the command and control arrangements of 1st Army fell apart. German batteries put down a heavy bombardment along the whole of the British front for over three hours. This bombardment cut all of the telephone lines between the infantry battalions and the brigade head-quarters, and almost all of the battery links as well. The curtain of fire also made it very difficult for runners with the average time taken to reach brigade headquarters being between two and three hours. In this situ-ation, divisional and corps headquarters could take no effective action during the morning. At the same time, artillery batteries could no longer be directed accurately or swiftly to support attacks. In the confusion of battle, even battalion commanders could no longer be sure of their company positions and the British attacks broke down into unco-ordinated actions. By the end of the day, Corps and Divisional head-quarters could not even disentangle the mass of conflicting situation and position reports which had arrived during the day. Fighting continued into 12 March and although Haig had, at 3.06 pm, ordered an all-out attack in the belief that the Germans had become demoralised, further efforts to make ground against increasingly stiff German resistance failed. Haig decided to call off further attacks late on 12 March. Even though the British had not seized the Aubers Ridge, Neuve Chapelle had been a minor success for the British First Army, but the problems of command and control which were revealed by the battle were serious indeed.

Unfortunately, much of the subsequent analysis of Neuve Chapelle was too optimistic. It was noted that:

> The result of the recent fighting at NEUVE CHAPELLE has not changed the strategical situation, but by that fighting we have gained certain definite tactical and moral advantages. We have proved that trench warfare has not affected adversely our offensive powers, and

that in spite of wire and trenches we can break the enemy's line given adequate numbers and preparation. We have inflicted heavy loss on the enemy, have upset his plans and forced him to conform to ours.[61]

While Neuve Chapelle did indeed prove that, with sufficient preparation, a British attack could 'break the enemy's line', the real problem inherent in an attack only began after this initial success. The breakdown in command and control became progressively worse as the battle went on, which meant that any chance of exploitation – and thus real success – evaporated. One far sighted staff officer noted this problem, and realised that:

> When the first assault had been delivered the troops got beyond the scope of this system of communications. The leading of the infantry was therefore dependent on the initiative of the subordinate commanders, and the system of artillery observation broke down to a considerable extent. The intervention of fresh troops of the enemy prevented this elaborate system being restored, with the result that isolated bodies of infantry that found themselves unopposed pushed on while other bodies found themselves confronted by strongly fortified localities. Vigorous assaults were delivered on these localities, but in some cases they were not preceded by an artillery bombardment and failed.[62]

British attacks for the next two years tragically echoed this description of Neuve Chapelle, as the BEF struggled to deal with the problems of trench warfare and the enormous difficulties created in command, control and communications.

The growth in the BEF, combined with the need to keep headquarters behind the lines, and the new emphasis on telephonic communication – forced by the dearth of alternative reliable tactical communications – all conspired against the traditional forms of command and control as envisaged by the pre-war regulations. There were very good reasons why divisional and even brigade headquarters had to be located in safe positions behind the lines. The BEF had experienced the cost of 'forward command' at First Ypres and would not repeat the mistake. The growth of the BEF from six divisions and a cavalry division into a much larger force necessitated the development of Army Headquarters to control the units involved. Inevitably, this added more administration and bureaucracy which appeared unnecessary to the fighting troops but was essential to run the expanded organisation. Since all other forms of communication had been found wanting, and as the distances between headquarters and units, units and artillery batteries, artillery batteries and the front line all increased, the demand for telephonic communication spiralled as well.

Even by the time of Neuve Chapelle the main outline of command and control for the rest of the war had been set. Commanders sat at headquarters by their telephones anxiously waiting for news from the front line which – as soon as the battle began – often did not arrive because the telephone lines had been cut by hostile shellfire. While commanders and their staff at higher levels had to adopt 'command by remote control' and an increasingly technological and managerial solution to the problems confronting them, at the tactical level, methods of command and control remained primitive and restrictive. These intractable problems of command and control would confront the commanders of the BEF for years to come.

NOTES

1   Brian Bond, *The Victorian Army and the Staff College* (London, 1972), 305.
2   *Field Service Pocket Book* (London, 1914), 25.
3   *Field Service Regulations, Part II Organisation and Administration* (London, 1909), 35.
4   *Field Service Regulations, Part I Operations, Reprinted with Amendments* (London, 1914), 55.
5   Extract from Private Diary of Colonel T W Sheppard, 1/King's (Liverpool) Regiment, Public Record Office (PRO), WO 95/1.
6   *ibid.*
7   *ibid.*
8   Field Marshal Sir Douglas Haig's Diary, 28 August 1914, National Library of Scotland, Edinburgh, Haig Papers (NLS).
9   Haig's Diary, 22 August 1914, NLS.
10 'Notes on the Working of the Mobilization Scheme of General Headquarters, 1st and 2nd Echelons, August 1914', PRO, WO95/1.
11 For accounts written by volunteer drivers see F Coleman, *From Mons to Ypres with French* (London, 1916), and A Rawlinson, *Adventures on the Western Front: August 1914–June 1915* (London, 1925).
12 Haig, 22 August 1914, NLS.
13 P Mead, *The Eye in the Air: History of Air Observation and Reconnaissance for the Army I 785–1945* (London, 1983), 51–8.
14 Haig, 7 September 1914, NLS.
15 *Field Service Regulations, Part I Operations, Reprinted with Amendments* (London, 1914), 14.
16 R F H Nalder, *The Royal Corps of Signals, A History of its Antecendents and Developments (circa 1800–1955)* (London, 1956), 48–9
17 J Terraine, *Mons: The Retreat to Victory* (London, 1960), 142.
18 Director of Army Signals, War Diary, September 1914, PRO, WO95/57.
19 'Notes Based on the Experience Gained by the Second Corps during the Campaign', PRO, WO95/629.
20 *ibid.*
21 *ibid.*
22 *ibid.*
23 Director of Army Signals, Circular Memorandum No.27, PRO WO95/57.
24 *ibid.*

25   'Instructions regarding the Employment of Artillery', GHQ, 9 November 1914, Imperial War Museum Department of Documents (IWM), French Papers, JDPF 7/2 (1).
26   Director of Army Signals, Circular Memorandum No.17 A, Wireless Procedure in the British Army, PRO, WO95/57.
27   *Field Service Manual, 1914 Infantry Battalion, Expeditionary Force* (London, 1914), 55.
28   Major General I Maxse, 'Rearguard Action ETREUX 27th August 1914', PRO, WO95/1261; see also J E Edmonds, *History of the Great War Based on Official Documents* (Official History), *Military Operations France and Belgium 1914*, Volume I (London, 1928), 206–13.
29   *ibid.*
30   *ibid.*
31   *ibid.*
32   *ibid.*
33   *ibid.*
34   Copy of Col. Hancox's Diary, 26 August 1914, PRO, CAB45/196.
35   *Field Service Regulations, Part II, Organization and Administration* (London, 1909), 35.
36   J Terraine (ed.), *General Jack's Diary 1914–1918: The Trench Diary of Brigadier-General J L Jack, DSO* (London, 1964), 36–40.
37   Narrative of 1st Corps Operations on 31 October 1914, PRO, WO95/589.
38   'Notes Based on the Experience Gained by the Second Corps during the Campaign', PRO, WO95/629.
39   Terraine, op. cit., 74.
40   1st Division, War Diary, 31 October 1914, PRO, WO95/589.
41   I Corps to 1st and 2nd Divisions, 29 December 1914, PRO, WO95/589.
42   Edmonds, *Official History*, France and Belgium 1914, Vol. 11, 465.
43   See Table 1, taken from 'Staff Officer Casualties', IWM, French Papers, JDPF 7/2 (1).
44   Bond, *Staff College*, 303.
45   'Staff Officer Casualties', IWM, French Papers, JDPF 7/2 (1).
46   I F W Beckett, *Johnnie Gough VC: A Biography of Sir John Edmond Gough V.C., K.C.B., C.M.G.* (London, 1989), 203–6.
47   Sir John French to Field Marshal Sir Herbert Kitchener, GHQ, 1 December 1914, IWM, French Papers, JDPF 7/2 (1).
48   *ibid.*
49   *ibid.*
50   French to Kitchener, GHQ, 17 December 1914, IWM, French Papers, JDPF 7/2 (1).
51   'Notes regarding Staff Duties', 28 December 1914, 1st Army, PRO, WO95/589.
52   I F W Beckett, 'Haig and French', in B Bond and N Cave (eds), *Haig, A Reappraisal Seventy Years On* (London, 1999); R Holmes, *The Little Field Marshal: Sir John French* (London, 1981), 305–13.
53   'Notes Based on the Experience Gained by the Second Corps during the Campaign', PRO, WO95/629.
54   1st Army, 2nd Division, Operations Section, 23 November 1914, PRO, WO95/589.
55   To CGS, 15 March 1915, IWM, French Papers (notes on Neuve Chapelle), JDPF 7/2 (1).
56   'Control of fire during the operations 10th–16th March 1915', PRO, WO95/154.

57   'Organisation of the artillery of the 1st Army for the Operations 10th–16th March 1915', PRO, WO95/154.
58   Edmonds, *Official History*, France and Belgium 1915, Vol. I (London, 1927), 98, 100.
59   'Control of fire during the operations 10th–16th March 1915', PRO, WO95/154.
60   Edmonds, op. cit., 101–2.
61   General Staff Note on the Situation 14.3.15, IWM, French Papers, JDPF 7/2 (1).
62   To CGS, 15 March 1915 (notes on Neuve Chapelle), IWM, French Papers, JDPF 7/2 (1).

CHAPTER III

The Grand Lamasery revisited: General Headquarters on the Western Front, 1914–1918[1]

Dan Todman

Introduction

The day-to-day organisation of an army for modern war is neither glamorous nor exciting. It does not fit well with traditional representations of martial skill or valour. It carries with it tremendous responsibilities, particularly if the army involved is Britain's largest ever expeditionary force, fighting a war of unprecedented scale and casualties which confronts a nation with the horrific logic of modern industrialised warfare. Given the interaction of these factors – incompatibility with accepted military stereotypes and perceived responsibility for carnage – it is perhaps unsurprising that the highest level of headquarters on the Western Front has been the subject of bitter polemic but little actual study.[2]

This began with the opinions held by subordinate officers during the war, and often expressed after it in autobiographies or memoirs. These tended to portray the officers of GHQ as isolated from the realities of terrain and combat and out of touch with front-line experience.[3] This was not merely an attitude of junior officers in the trenches far away from GHQ: J F C Fuller, an officer with extensive experience of staff work and GHQ, described it as a 'grand lamasery', a military monastery in which doctrine, order and tradition were the religion. Although its senior officers were inadequate, if well intentioned:

> . . . the real weakness of GHQ did not lie in the character of any of these individuals, but in the lamaistic system which prevailed . . . Haig worked there like a mechanical monk . . . There was little or no contact with reality – with the circumstances which surrounded the cutting edge of the army. Hence time and again this edge was blunted, jagged or even broken.[4]

However, for a body which excited such comment, GHQ was curiously understudied. Major A F Becke, the officer who painstakingly composed the volumes of the Official History detailing British orders of battle, was moved to remark in 1945, in his introduction to the work dealing with *The Army Council, General Headquarters, Armies and Corps* that:

> Whereas in the compilation of the divisional orders of battle considerable assistance could be obtained from published divisional histories, there exists little similar material for the compiler of this volume to use.[5]

The study of GHQ has been complicated by the fact that many of its papers, in particular those of the Military Secretary's branch, were destroyed by enemy bombs during the Second World War.

As the Introduction to this volume has described, the historiography of the Western Front during the middle years of the twentieth century was dominated in Britain by debates over the standard of senior command; in particular the abilities or otherwise of the British Commander-in-Chief from late 1915, Sir Douglas Haig. As those involved became increasingly polarised in their views, and more strident in their opinions, the organisation which had existed around Haig tended to be subsumed into him, rather like the figure presented in the 1963 stage production of *Oh! What a Lovely War*. Such an attitude – Haig as symbol rather than individual – has been a problem for historians as well as playwrights. That amorphous body 'HaigandGHQ' has constituted a serious barrier to further research.

More recently, scholars have focused more tightly on the systems and processes of command and organisation in the BEF. This is symptomatic of changing fashions in military history and society more widely, as well as historians gradually becoming aware of and working through a mass of archival material declassified in the 1960s. The publication of Ian Malcolm Brown's *British Logistics on the Western Front* represents a major step forward not only in the understanding of the less glamorous functions of GHQ, but in wider approaches to the way the war was fought.[6] Brown highlights the importance of an 'ad hoc' system in the maintenance of British administration in the early years of the war, the key reforms instituted by Sir Eric Geddes in the army's transport network and the vital role played by logistics in the tactical and operational development of the British army. However, it is also apparent that Brown's study leaves substantial areas still to be analysed in detail, in particular the structure of the General Staff and its relationship to the developing administrative system.

At the most basic level, the story of GHQ equates to that of the BEF as a whole: tremendous difficulties overcome with differing degrees of success, huge growth, eventual victory. The total expansion of GHQ in officers and men matched that of the BEF, thirteen times bigger at the end of the war than its beginning, almost exactly.[7] This chapter aims to flesh out that story, by serving as an introduction to the role and structure of GHQ as a whole, and describing how it developed in the course of the war and how officers experienced life there. It attempts a preliminary analysis of the reasons behind the development and expansion of GHQ, and some assessment of its performance. It aims to combine an analysis of the GHQ's structure with more traditional personal and social factors. It interacts with two recent interpretations of British command and control at the highest level on the Western Front: the theories of 'command paralysis' or 'vacuum', and of a 'learning curve'.

The structure of GHQ

GHQ was responsible for supplying the army with all it required to function: men, equipment and supplies, information, orders and training. Its structure had been set out in the 1912 *Staff Manual*.[8] Although various developments took place in the course of the war, the hierarchy and basic division of labour were to remain constant throughout. GHQ in 1914 is shown in Diagram 1. It was relatively small, made up of about thirty staff officers. It consisted of three branches, each under the command of a senior officer and sub-divided into two sections. The Quartermaster-General (QMG)'s branch (Q) had responsibility for providing the army with supplies in the field. Qa dealt with transport, post and accommodation for troops, Qb dealt with supplies, ammunition, equipment, clothing and animals. The Adjutant-General (AG)'s branch (A) had responsibility for the personnel of the army. In the 'First Echelon', based with the main body of GHQ, two sections of A branch, AG (a) and AG (b), dealt with the supply of personnel, casualties and medical services, and discipline, prisoners of war and promotions respectively. In addition, another sub-branch of A, under the command of the Deputy Adjutant-General, was located at the base, separate from GHQ, and formed the so-called 'Third Echelon', responsible for the personnel and personal requirements of the army away from the front.

The General Staff branch (G) was widely considered the most prestigious of GHQ. It was responsible for the planning and implementation of operations in the field and the collection and handling of intelligence. Its head, the Chief of the General Staff (CGS), although he might rank equally with the QMG and the AG, was in fact first amongst equals, and it was he who was presumed to have most influence over and contact with the C in C. G was divided into Operations and Intelligence Sections. Operations consisted of two sub-sections, Oa and Ob. Oa dealt with planning operations, writing orders and liaison. Ob acted as a registry, primarily for records of communication. Intelligence consisted of four

Diagram 1: GHQ autumn 1914

Compiled from Becke, *The Army Council, GHQs, Armies and Corps 1914-1918*, 11-16, War Office, *Staff Manual*, 34, Robertson, *From Private to Field Marshal*, 214-5, Military Secretary, GHQ, *Composition of Headquarters*, Nov 1914.

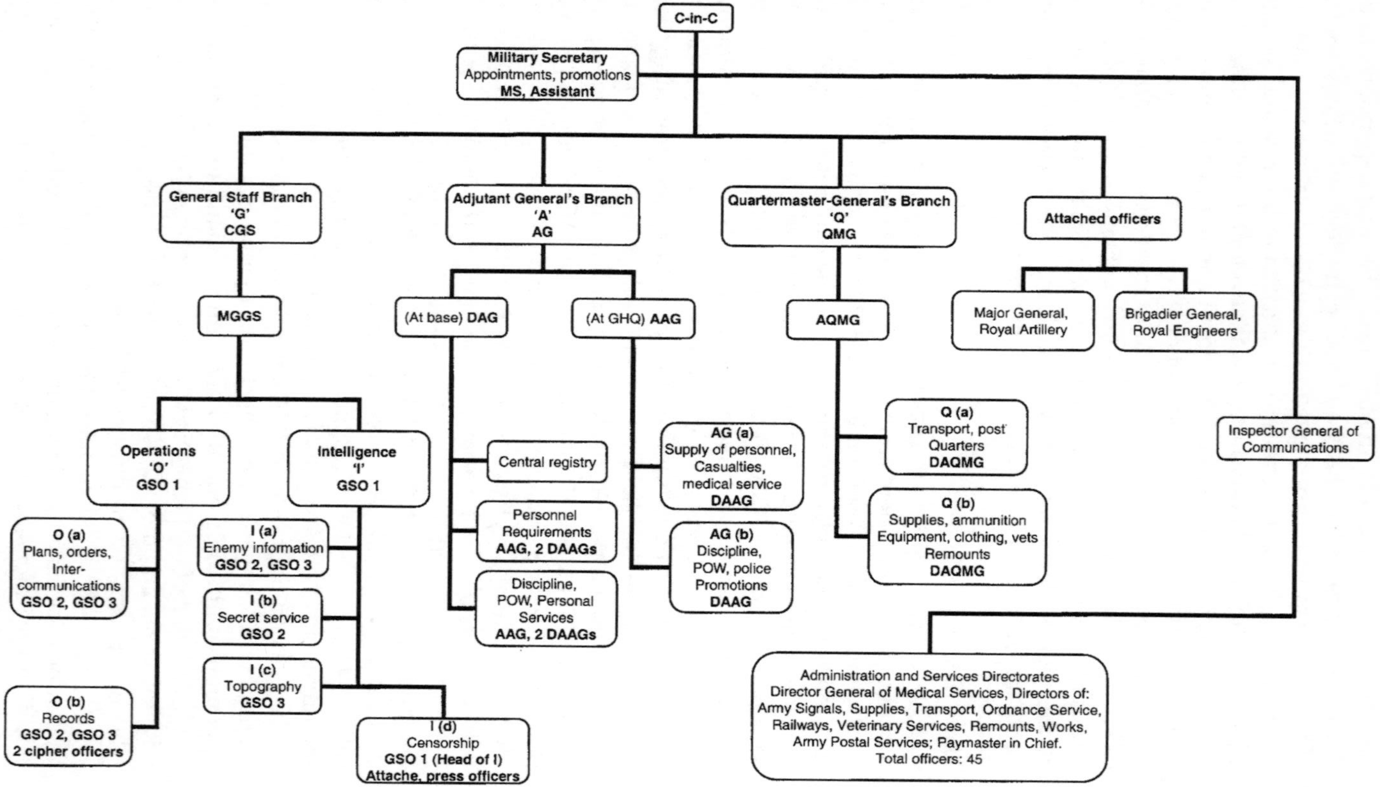

C-in-C

Military Secretary
Appointments, promotions
MS, Assistant

Attached officers

Major General,
Royal Artillery

Brigadier General,
Royal Engineers

Inspector General of Communications

Quartermaster-General's Branch 'Q' QMG

AQMG

Q (a)
Transport, post'
Quarters
DAQMG

Q (b)
Supplies, ammunition
Equipment, clothing, vets
Remounts
DAQMG

Adjutant General's Branch 'A' AG

(At GHQ) AAG

(At base) DAG

AG (a)
Supply of personnel,
Casualties,
medical service
DAAG

AG (b)
Discipline,
POW, police
Promotions
DAAG

Central registry

Personnel
Requirements
AAG, 2 DAAGs

Discipline,
POW, Personal
Services
AAG, 2 DAAGs

General Staff Branch 'G' CGS

MGGS

Intelligence 'I' GSO 1

I (a)
Enemy information
GSO 2, GSO 3

I (b)
Secret service
GSO 2

I (c)
Topography
GSO 3

I (d)
Censorship
GSO 1 (Head of I)
Attache, press officers

Operations 'O' GSO 1

O (a)
Plans, orders,
Inter-
communications
GSO 2, GSO 3

O (b)
Records
GSO 2, GSO 3
2 cipher officers

Administration and Services Directorates
Director General of Medical Services, Directors of:
Army Signals, Supplies, Transport, Ordnance Service,
Railways, Veterinary Services, Remounts, Works,
Army Postal Services; Paymaster in Chief.
Total officers: 45

sub-sections, Ia, dealing with information about the enemy; Ib, the secret service; Ic in charge of topographical studies and maps, and Id, dealing with censorship and the press. In addition to these branches, a number of officers were attached to GHQ to act effectively as technical advisors on specialist areas. In 1914 these consisted of a Major-General Royal Artillery, and a Brigadier-General Royal Engineers.

The staff officers in the three branches were able to implement their aims through the work of a number of administration and services departments and directorates. The 'Second Echelon', located at GHQ, consisted of a number of advisors from the Directorates and Services who needed most regular contact with the main branches of the staff, as well as officers responsible for the organisation and administration of GHQ itself.[9] The situation was further complicated by the existence of another officer, the Inspector General of Communications (IGC), located at the base, who was effectively equivalent to one of the senior officers at GHQ without being officially part of it. He had responsibility for the provision and movement of supplies in the rear areas and along the lines of communication until they were taken over by Q branch. Many of the administration and services departments not only seemed to be required to work with the IGC, they had their main offices close to his at the base.

This organisation encouraged a more or less logical distribution of responsibilities between administration and operational duties, with the intention of freeing the Commander-in-Chief to concentrate on the advice and information provided by G branch so that he could direct the army's operations effectively. On the other hand, there were clear areas of confusion of responsibility in terms of administration, not only between A and Q, but between Q and the IGC. In particular, it was unclear to what degree supplies should be 'pushed' up by the IGC, or 'pulled' by the units closer to the front line. That these had not been resolved prior to the outbreak of war can be put down to the concentration, in pre-war exercises, on prestigious G branch roles, to the neglect of administration. Indeed, the very structure of GHQ encouraged 'departmentalism' and could allow, or even encourage, senior officers to ignore potentially serious administrative problems until they reached crisis levels.[10]

GHQ was staffed by officers drawn from the regular army. Those who had passed through the Staff College, or later in the war, shorter staff course, were ranked on a structure ranging from Staff Captain, through three grades of General Staff Officer (3 to 1) to Staff Colonel, Brigadier-General and Major-General, General Staff.[11] In A and Q branches, intermediate ranks were named with regard to their relation to the senior officer – Deputy, Assistant, Deputy-Assistant. It is difficult to describe an equivalency, as the different arms of the staff seldom interacted to this degree. Whilst the, insufficiently stated, intention of the *Staff Manual* was that officers should have experience of all arms of the staff, in practice a mixture of specialisation and snobbishness limited such movement. Where it did occur, it was insufficient to prevent each branch of the staff developing a strong, and somewhat exclusive, corporate identity.

British officers did have the benefit of a wide breadth of service in a variety of situations as a result of their imperial role. This had tended to create a professional ethos which valued adaptability, improvisation and above all pragmatism. Yet this potential range of employment combined with a generally anti-intellectual attitude to militate against the articulation of doctrine or detailed thought about the way the army was run. The General Staff had only been founded in 1906; in its short life, it had greatly improved the standard of staff work in the British Army. However, it was difficult for headquarters units to gain practical experience of their craft before the outbreak of war. The officers who would staff GHQ in 1914 participated in the 1913 summer manoeuvres, but their principal role was to organise, and in the case of senior officers, umpire, the participation of subordinate units, rather than replicate the challenges that war would impose.[12]

1914

The principal testimony to the success of the pre-war General Staff was the remarkable speed and efficiency with which the BEF mobilised in August 1914. However, the process of mobilisation also revealed a number of intellectual shortcomings in the staff as a whole, and in particular amongst the senior officers at GHQ. The suggestion by Field Marshal Sir John French, the C-in-C, that the army should concentrate around Antwerp, rather than near Mauberge, as had been planned, displayed a worrying tendency for vacillation and disregard for staff work.[13] French's selection of GHQ staff was also suspect. Excited by the outbreak of war, General Staff qualified officers sought to leave Britain en masse for France, seeking service without thought to their suitability. This not only left a gaping hole in the Staff at the War Office, it led to the employment of a number of officers in France who were simply too old, or too unfit, mentally or physically, for the rigours of active campaigning.[14] Despite this, GHQ was still somewhat understaffed by the standards of the *Staff Manual*. GHQ managed to leave London without the necessary code-books, and so was temporarily unable to decipher messages from London.[15]

It rapidly became apparent that, as well as difficulties caused by overlapping duties, the principal problem for Q and A was the unwieldiness of the BEF's supply chain. Fortunately for the army, the officers involved worked together to overcome these difficulties. In particular, the IGCs – first Lieutenant-General Robb, then Lieutenant-General R C Maxwell – were willing to informally subordinate themselves to the command of Major-General Sir William Robertson, the QMG. However, a solution to the problem based on personal compromise meant that there was no need to reorganise the senior administration of the army so as to resolve its contradictions. This kind of ad hoc solution typified the BEF's response to administrative and organisational problems over the next two years. Born out of the army's pre-war experience, it was a mixed blessing, permitting continued service but obscuring the need for more fundamental change.[16]

G's primary problems were those experienced by senior command on both sides of the Western Front. Whilst weapons technology had massively increased the weight of firepower it was possible to deploy, in particular the destructive power of artillery, communications technology had not moved forward to the same degree. It was extremely difficult for senior levels of command to do more than plan a battle: once it had begun, keeping track of the movements of friend and foe was problematic. These problems, detailed in Niall Barr's chapter in this book, were to prove a continual difficulty for officers. G also suffered from an unwieldy structure which restricted the flow of information. G contained two information gathering sections, I and Ob. Both were regarded as immediately subordinate to the officer in charge of Oa. In practice, this led to a double-bottleneck, slowing down the passage of information as it was passed first through Operations to the Sub-Chief, then to the CGS, and then to the Commander in Chief.[17]

The situation was undoubtedly exacerbated by the personalities of officers at GHQ. Sir John French, though he was popular with his troops, was temperamentally unsuited to the task of commanding a modern army in war. He was indecisive, emotionally volatile, and had little regard for the niceties of staff work. He might have been aided by a firm CGS, able to guide his mercurial nature. As it was, he chose Lieutenant-General Sir Archibald J Murray, far from the strongest character either emotionally or intellectually. Murray was to collapse under the pressure of the retreat. In the absence of a firm CGS, the Sub-Chief of Staff, Major-General Sir Henry Wilson, was able to exercise considerable influence. Wilson has tended to divide commentators; he has been seen as either a brilliant and relaxed wit, or an unreliable schemer, too clever by half. In truth, his character probably lay somewhere between these two; he was undoubtedly an intelligent man, but he did little to steady his Commander's emotions, and was not consistent or single-minded enough to make an effective Chief of Staff. It is easy to see how his behaviour during the Great Retreat, standing around in gown and slippers whilst GHQ packed up to flee, dispensing 'sardonic little jests to all and sundry within earshot',[18] could be reassuring for some, but profoundly irritating for others.

The events of autumn 1914 created a hysterical atmosphere at GHQ. Senior officers became convinced that the BEF had been routed, issuing orders to troops to leave all encumbrances behind and hasten away from the enemy. It is ironic that an army which had placed considerable emphasis on the need for moral ascendancy as a tactical instrument should suffer from such a collapse at a senior level, although it should be noted that officers in other armies were also undone by the emotional stresses of the early days of the war. However, G branch's inadequacies went beyond a tendency to panic; orders were consistently poorly worded and information was poorly analysed and distributed. Wilson, when he took over after Murray's collapse, failed to pass on crucial information about French plans to his Commander-in-Chief.[19]

Taken as a whole, the performance of GHQ during 1914 might be judged barely adequate. The impressive performance of Q and A branches in supplying the army during the Great Retreat, and subsequently re-equipping it with men and equipment, must be balanced with the almost farcical performance of senior elements of G branch. Perhaps inevitably, the stresses of a new sort of war revealed a variety of problems with the organisation of GHQ. The degree to which these problems could be dealt with successfully depended largely on the quality of the personnel involved.

Robertson as CGS, 1915

Fortunately, opposition from both army and politicians prevented French promoting Wilson when he sent Murray home in early 1915. Instead, he turned to Robertson, who accepted with heavy reservations, and became CGS on 25 January 1915, being replaced as QMG by Maxwell.

Aided by the greater systematisation and stability which were encouraged as the Western Front set into trench warfare, and with GHQ firmly established in the French town of St Omer, Robertson introduced three key changes at GHQ. Firstly, he altered the structure of G, introducing three separate sections: Operations, Intelligence and General Staff Duties. The latter took on responsibility for British policy and organisation, training, and the incorporation of new units. The heads of these sections, whilst expected to keep in contact, were each made individually responsible to Robertson. Although individual officers had been added to all three branches, or promoted within them, as it became clear that GHQ's workload was larger than anticipated, this was the first formal change in its structure. It is shown in Diagram 2. It removed the bottleneck that had existed and relieved some of the pressure of work from Operations. It dealt with three areas which Robertson had rightly identified as key: the rapid growth of the army required some decentralisation of staff work; the lack of training of many new arrivals at all levels had to be addressed before they went into action, and trench warfare itself demanded a knowledge of new techniques of warfare.[20]

Secondly, Robertson brought in fresh personnel. At a senior level he appointed Colonel Frederick Maurice to head Operations, and took Colonel Edward Perceval as his Sub-Chief of Staff and head of Staff Duties

Diagram 2: GHQ late summer 1915, showing effect of Robertson reforms and ad hoc expansion 'A', 'Q' and IGC simplified to fit.

Compiled from Becke, *The Army Council, GHQs, Armies and Corps 1914-1918*, 11-16, Robertson, *From Private to Field Marshal*, 219-22, Military Secretary, GHQ, *Composition of Headquarters*, July, Oct 1915.

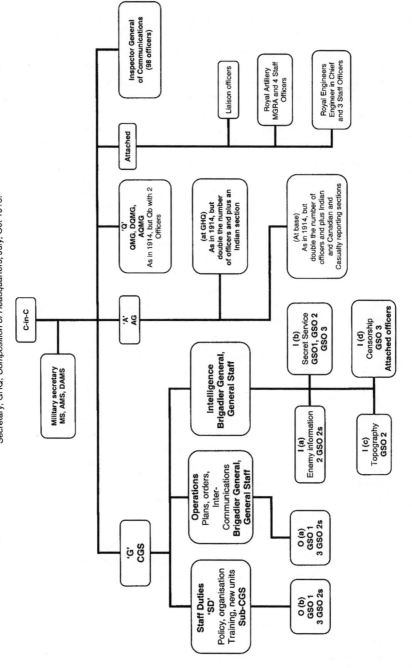

section. Perceval was replaced by Colonel 'Kitten' Whigham in July. Both Perceval and Whigham represented an improvement over their predecessor, Brigadier-General Harper, in terms of approachability and focus.[21] Robertson also brought in a host of new junior officers. These were men whom he had encountered whilst he was Commandant at the Staff College; as such he knew they were able and loyal.[22]

Thirdly, Robertson sought to introduce a new attitude to GHQ generally. Personally, he was more forceful with his military and political superiors in London than Murray had been, emphasising to them the primacy of the Western Front.[23] This represented a degree of strategic thought about the war that had not previously been evident. GHQ remained, even after the line had settled to a degree, an extremely high-pressure environment, with massive responsibilities and a large work-load, with fourteen-hour days not uncommon. The physical compactness of GHQ, with sections occupying single houses within St Omer, could add to the tension.[24] During major battles a smaller group of officers moved to a forward HQ with French. For those involved, these periods were even more stressful.[25] Whilst emphasising the innovating and energising role the Staff had to play, Robertson attempted to create a more effective working environment, encouraging his officers to take some limited time off for exercise. This was a welcome change from the headless chicken school of command practised by Murray and Wilson. At the same time, Robertson advised GHQ staff to take every opportunity to establish friendly contact with fighting formations and junior ranks, in an effort to dispel the sense of separation which he feared would grow up between the two. Further to this, he sought to establish a network of liaison officers to keep GHQ informed of events and problems at the front.[26]

Whilst Robertson was CGS the BEF made two major steps forward. The most obvious at the time was the initial expansion of the BEF from the tiny pre-war regular force. As Ian Malcolm Brown has described in glowing terms, it underwent a rate of growth no modern business could aspire to, with a 320 per cent increase in ration strength:

> Approximately one million men, 220,000 animals, 460,000 tons of forage, 305,000 tons of food, 120,000 tons of ammunitions and hundreds of thousands of tons of other stores had been landed and moved forward from the base ports to the front. That the administration accomplished this without great hardship for the soldiers and animals being moved and supplied is a credit to the men working on the lines of communication.[27]

The tremendous strain and host of problems which were created by this increase in personnel and logistical throughput were handled in the same improvisational, ad hoc fashion seen the previous year.[28] The areas of conflict between the three senior administrative officers and the demands of forward units continued to be resolved on the basis of a series of personal compromises, which did little to address the underlying faults of the organisation. Additional officers were added to existing organisations as their workload increased. They were not necessarily best suited to the jobs they were allocated to. A civilian later brought in to assist the War Office with transport suggested that:

> Military officers are supposed to be acquainted with a great variety of subjects, and they are. The 'Contemptibles' experience at home, in India and elsewhere, made them adaptable in all sorts of situations, but it could scarcely be expected that a captain of a regiment of the line wounded in the retreat from Mons would excel in an attempt to allocate freight to a ship . . . the freight consisting of ammunition and guns, groceries and medicines, road rollers and railway materials, aeroplanes and carrier pigeons, clothing and motor-cars, together with a miscellaneous collection of material necessary to keep the soldier in good fighting form.[29]

Moreover, the departmentalism encouraged by the structure and staffing of GHQ tended to mean that, whilst improvised solutions prevented a breakdown in the army's administration and logistics system, the C-in-C and officers in G branch were not forced to pay any attention to these areas. Instead, they took the functioning of the systems for granted and did not factor their needs into operational planning or actions.[30]

This improvisational, and often inconsistent, approach was also apparent in training and the creation of solutions to the military conundrum of the Western Front. Brigadier-General C D Baker-Carr, who had come out to France as a staff chauffeur in 1914, was responsible for the setting up of a GHQ machine gun school in 1915:

> The chief trouble at GHQ was that there was no one there who had time to listen to any new idea. Everybody was busy writing 'Passed to you', 'Noted and returned', or 'For your information', etc, etc, on piles and piles of 'jackets' that no one had a moment to consider any proposal for altering the existing condition of affairs.[31]

However, told to get on with forming a school without help or guidance, Baker-Carr found that his improvisation was allowed considerable leeway:

> It is more than likely that this lack of 'establishment' was of the greatest value to me. If, in the early days, I had tried to put the school on an official footing, it would have been on a ridiculously small basis

49

and every increase in staff, etc, would have been strenuously opposed
... As it was, by hook or by crook, I gathered, without sanction from
anybody, fatigue men, assistants for 'Slushy' in the cookhouse,
additional instructors from the Artists, and a large amount of equipment.[32]

During the battles of 1915, elements within the BEF began to develop a
tactical and operational system that could function well within the
restrictions of trench warfare. This was based on the use of brief but
overwhelming artillery bombardments to neutralise enemy defences,
followed up by a fast-moving and aggressive infantry advance aimed at
capturing strictly limited objectives within the range of British artillery.
Operational analysis is visible at GHQ, which in hindsight can be
suggested to have groped towards this solution. This is most apparent in
the papers produced at GHQ by the MGRA, J P Du Cane, and the
Operations Staff after the Battle of Neuve Chapelle. Although their
intention was still to provide the opportunity for a breakthrough battle,
these documents came close to articulating the tactical approach that
would eventually be adopted.[33]

However, these techniques were not to be widely understood and imple-
mented until the summer of 1917. There were a number of reasons for this,
organisational, psychological and technical. The absence of an established
doctrine, a belief in the decentralisation of planning and training, and the
lack of experience of many new officers and men all meant that the BEF did
not necessarily recognise the solution it had come up with. They also mili-
tated against these techniques gaining widespread acceptance, as may
have their departure from a military tradition that emphasised decisive
and immediate victories. A belief in pragmatism and flexibility did not
encourage the identification and imposition of successful doctrine from
above. Technical and logistical factors also limited their employment. To
work well, these tactics required technological developments, in particular
effective heavy artillery, instantaneous fused shells, predicted targeting of
guns, and sound ranging for counter-battery work which the BEF could
not yet provide. Above all, these tactics, and the experimentation required
to perfect them, demanded a massive number of artillery shells. The British
Army suffered more than most on the Western Front in 1915 from a dread-
ful lack of shells of all sorts, a fault of production in the United Kingdom,
rather than of the BEF's logistical services. This led to day-to-day restrictions on the number of shells guns could fire. In these circumstances, the
BEF had to seek alternative solutions which diverted it from its more
promising innovations. The supply of artillery ammunition was to be a
decisive factor in the BEF's tactical success. Even when sufficient numbers
of shells were delivered in 1916, they were often of poor quality and inadequate type. As Brown has suggested, however, the inadequate supply

of shells in 1915 may have been a blessing in disguise. Under tremendous strain from the expansion of the army, it seems likely that efforts to handle greatly increased quantities of ammunition might have caused the logistical and administrative system of the army to collapse at a crucial moment.[34]

1916–17. Sir Douglas Haig, the Somme and Third Ypres

Over the winter of 1915–16, changes once again took place amongst the senior personnel at GHQ. Sir John French was replaced by Sir Douglas Haig in mid-December 1915. Robertson left to become Chief of the Imperial General Staff at the War Office. In February 1916 the AG, Lieutenant-General Sir Neville Macready, also moved to London, being replaced by Lieutenant-General Sir George Fowke.

It is extremely difficult for the modern historian to pick his way through the vast minefield of works on Haig and come to some assessment of the man and the general. It seems fair to present him as a man of fixed views and extreme determination. Although this represented an improvement on French's inconstancy, it brought its own problems, not least a tendency to become fixated on objectives for their own sake, and a certain inflexibility of approach. Whilst far from an unfeeling monster, unconcerned for his men, Haig's judgement was much less affected by the sight of their suffering than French's had been. It is clear that Haig was not at his best in verbal discussion; descriptions of his inarticulate nature can verge on caricature.[35] It was perhaps less that he was absolutely incapable of communication, and more that the combination of Haig's lack of verbal facility and forbidding personality tended to allow misunderstandings and incoherences of approach to exist between him and his subordinate commanders.

In the course of his military education, Haig had developed a theory of command that was strongly 'hands off'; it emphasised responsibility and decision-making at a lower level. To a degree this was in line with the unarticulated doctrine of the army, of adaptability and ad hoc solutions, based on its experience of small unit actions in colonial wars, and with the relatively small size of GHQ, particularly its planning section. However, it was somewhat incompatible with the rigid and strongly hierarchical attitudes displayed by many senior officers. These tended to prevent the free communication necessary for this style of command to succeed. In fact, faced with the reality of command on the Western Front, Haig was seldom able to avoid a more 'hands on' approach. He remained keen to fight a decisive battle, inevitably involving a breakthrough of the enemy line. Haig was relatively distrustful, at least for the early part of his command, of the abilities of his Army commanders and the New Armies. He was also faced with a situation in which new methods and weapons of war had constantly to be considered and possibly utilised.[36] As a result Haig often felt obliged to intervene in subordinates' plans or operations.

The application, at differing times, of both these approaches to command led to confusion over objectives and methods.[37]

Haig brought with him a new set of senior officers for G branch, most of whom had served with him at the headquarters of First Army.[38] His Director of Military Operations, Brigadier-General John 'Tavish' Davidson, was initially naïve about the requirements of operational planning at this level,[39] although he was to learn on the job, and eventually display a clear understanding of the developments in British operational and tactical practice. Davidson was not able to bring consistent influence on operational planning at Army level. In part this may have been because he was too much in awe of Haig, more substantially it was because, as has been suggested, Haig's concept of command tended to sideline operational input from above.

Haig's head of Intelligence, Brigadier-General John Charteris, was strongly career-minded, enjoyed the opportunities for departmental politics and aggrandisement presented to him by his position at GHQ, and actively competed with Davidson for Haig's favour. He has in the past been portrayed as an evil genius behind Haig's throne. Although he showed little aptitude for intelligence work, this is to misjudge his motives. He shared Haig's optimism, and took it upon himself to support his C-in-C in what he knew to be difficult choices. This affected his direction and assessment of intelligence. Under his command, I section was to undergo a vast expansion.[40]

Haig's Chief of Staff at First Army, Brigadier-General Butler, was considered too junior to take on this role at GHQ, instead becoming Deputy Chief (an equivalent position to Sub-Chief). Lieutenant-General Sir Launcelot Kiggell took his place as CGS. Although Kiggell was an able administrator, who sought to enforce 'intellectually efficient staff methods' at GHQ, he did not have sufficient strength of character for the role.[41] He was ineffective as a senior manager over Davidson or Charteris, but also incapable of representing the views of G branch as a whole with a coherent and strong voice, important inadequacies when faced with a man as determined and forbidding as Haig could be. These faults would become more apparent as time went on.[42]

Shortly after Haig and his team took over, GHQ moved from St Omer to Montreuil, another small French town, although this time with better communications and perhaps a more pleasant setting. This was to be GHQ's main location for the rest of the war. Haig was based in a château some two miles away. The central units of GHQ were based in the barracks of Montreuil's Ecole Militaire. Officers were billeted in houses in or close to the town. Later in the war, additional hut encampments were added to provide extra accommodation. Despite the still comparatively small size of GHQ as a unit, most of its more junior officers had little contact with the C-in-C:

One rarely saw 'the Chief'. He seldom had occasion to come to the offices in the Ecole Militaire, and it was only the highest officers who had to go to confer with him ... When 'the Chief' did appear at Montreuil all felt they had the right to desert work for five minutes to go to a window to catch a glimpse of him as he passed from one side ... to the other, or stopped in the courtyard to chat for a moment with one of his officers.[43]

The workload remained extremely hard, with most officers working from 9 am until at least 10.30 pm with only short breaks. The sense of responsibility was undoubtedly stressful. However, post-war claims by GHQ officers, aware of their reputation with front-line troops, that: 'compared with conditions at GHQ regimental work was care-free and pleasant',[44] are somewhat undermined by descriptions of an officers' club for which:

The subscription was five francs per month, and for that and a ridiculously small sum per day the Club gave members three square meals a day and afternoon tea. The Club kept up a good cellar, and to the very last, when good wine was almost unprocurable in London or Paris except at exorbitant prices, the Officers' Club, Montreuil, could sell a vintage claret or burgundy at nine francs a bottle, a decent wine at five francs a bottle, and champagne at fifteen francs a bottle.[45]

GHQ was still unpopular as a posting for many officers, however, because of its perceived separation from action. Brigadier-General Burnett Stuart wrote of it that in 1916 it: 'was a depressing place, remote from the battle, and packed with officers who applied at regular intervals to be released from it.'[46] Officers were separated, not only from the front line and their C-in-C, but all too often from colleagues in other branches. In this new location, under the command of new officers, GHQ and the BEF girded their loins to fight the Battle of the Somme in the summer of 1916.

Tim Travers has suggested that the BEF in 1916 suffered from a 'paralysis of command'. He argues that faced with the task of directing the Somme battle, terrified by Haig, the staff at GHQ and the Army commanders were unable to act decisively.[47] Whilst in Haig's own case, the problem seems to have been inconsistency of command – too much or too little – rather than paralysis, for G branch, there does seem some justification for this view. In planning for the campaigns of 1916, Haig's staff at GHQ displayed a willingness to be bound by the restrictions imposed on them by problems of supply and alliance warfare. There is a mood of inevitability about the papers produced by Oa sub-section at this time: of choices made because of a lack of viable alternatives rather than as a result of active analysis and decision making.[48] The story of the planning for the opening moves of the Somme, with its confusion in intentions between Haig and his Army commander, General Sir Henry Rawlinson, shows the ways in which communication between senior officers and also between their staffs could break down. This has properly been seen as a coincidence of personalities and military-social factors. Although the Somme undoubtedly saw some British units, from battalion to army level, develop in reaction to their experience of combat, GHQ's resistance to Rawlinson's subsequent plans for a dawn assault on 14 July, an assault which proved successful, can be cited as evidence of its continued conservatism and lack of trust in the capabilities of the New Armies. However, the problem for the administrative and logistics branches was anything but paralysis: both were stretched to the limit, working frantically to prevent an overloaded system ceasing work altogether.

On the other hand, Travers ignores the developments that took place in the months after the Somme battles, when GHQ improved the logistical services, forming the basis for better tactics, established and disseminated a tactical doctrine, and developed its own structures in an effort to improve its performance. The sheer scale of the Somme fighting, the enormous quantity of men, equipment and ammunition it used up (in particular shells), and the employment for the first time in a major offensive of the men of the New Armies made a number of points startlingly clear to GHQ, and resulted in changes in the winter of 1916–17. The effects of these are shown in Diagram 3.

Firstly, as Brown has pointed out, the logistical requirements of the Somme campaign brought the ad hoc system that had previously been used close to the point of collapse. Not only had the size of the army as a whole increased, but the availability for the first time of sufficient quantity, if not quality, of ammunition to meet the demands of the artillery led to a massive increase in the throughput of shells. Although as the Somme fighting went on, supplies to the battlefield were increasingly affected by the condition of the ground and German interdiction, these factors only served to compound problems existing farther back in the supply chain. It was apparent that a reorganisation was necessary, particularly as tactical trends made it likely that even more ammunition would be necessary for the next year's offensives.[49]

In the early autumn of 1916, Sir Eric Geddes, then Director-General of Military Railways at the War Office, was asked to report on the state of the BEF's transport. Geddes was a civilian. Before the war he had been General Manager of the North Eastern Railway, and after its outbreak he had served in the Ministry of Munitions. Geddes recommended the need for a coherent overall administrative policy, and the placing of the whole transport system under a single commander. Geddes himself was appointed to this position, as Director-General of Transport (DGT), on 3 December 1916. The DGT was subordinate to the CGS, AG and QMG,

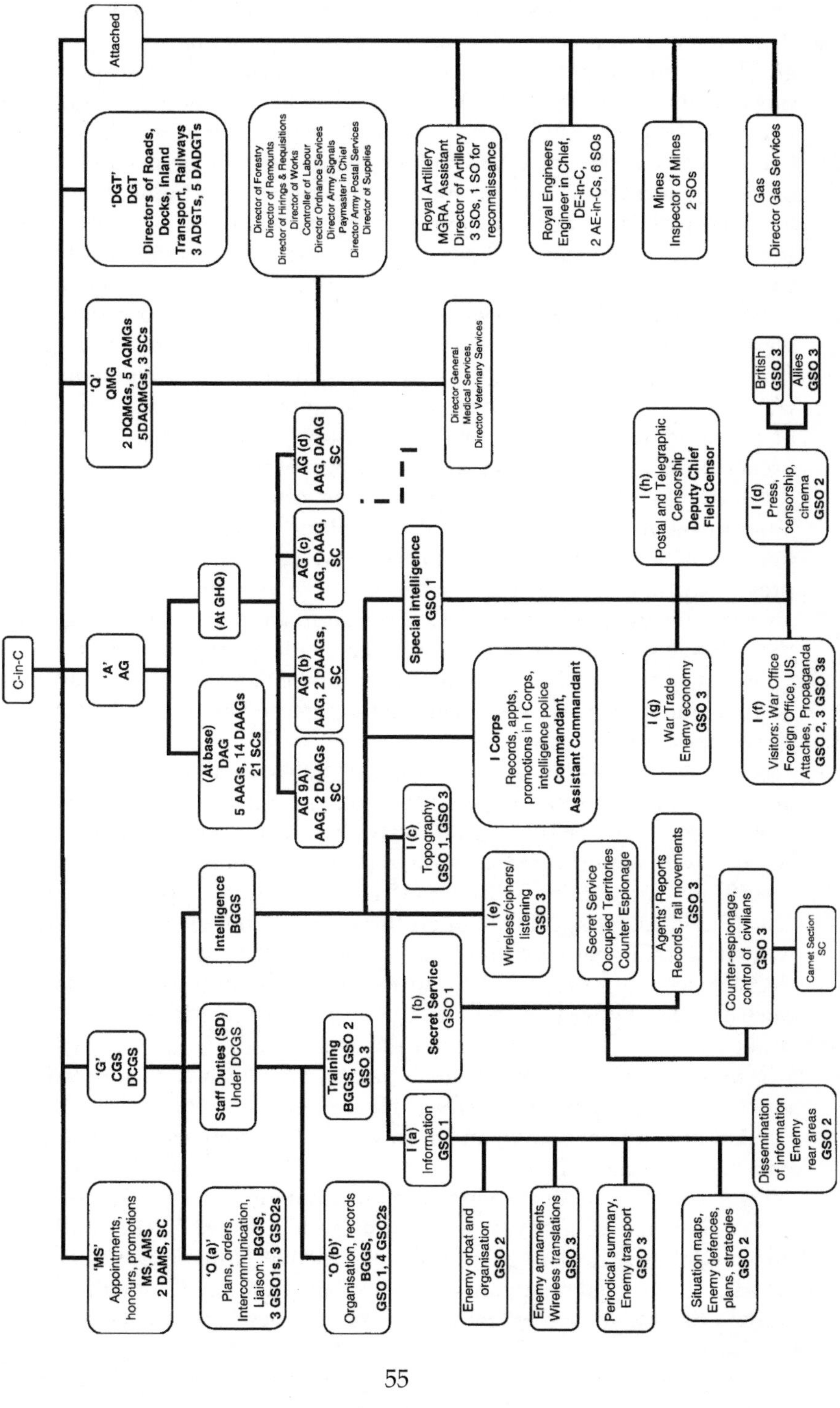

Diagram 3: GHQ Summer 1917, showing expansion of I section and DGT

Compiled from Becke, *Army Council*, 11-16, Military Secretary GHQ, *Composition of Headquarters*, April, Aug 1917, 'I branch, July 1917', PRO, WO 106/359

C-in-C

Attached

'DGT'
DGT
Directors of Roads, Docks, Inland Transport, Railways
3 ADGTs, 5 DADGTs

Director of Forestry
Director of Remounts
Director of Hirings & Requisitions
Director of Works
Controller of Labour
Director Ordnance Services
Director Army Signals
Paymaster in Chief
Director Army Postal Services
Director of Supplies

Royal Artillery
MGRA, Assistant Director of Artillery
3 SOs, 1 SO for reconnaissance

Royal Engineers
Engineer in Chief,
DE-in-C,
2 AE-in-Cs, 6 SOs

Mines
Inspector of Mines
2 SOs

Gas
Director Gas Services

'Q'
QMG
2 DQMGs, 5 AQMGs
5DAQMGs, 3 SCs

Director General Medical Services,
Director Veterinary Services

'A'
AG

(At GHQ)

AG (d)
AAG, DAAG
SC

AG (c)
AAG, DAAG
SC

AG (b)
AAG, 2 DAAGs
SC

(At base)
DAG
5 AAGs, 14 DAAGs
21 SCs

AG 9A)
AAG, 2 DAAGs
SC

Special Intelligence
GSO 1

I Corps
Records, appts, promotions in I Corps, intelligence police
Commandant,
Assistant Commandant

I (h)
Postal and Telegraphic Censorship
Deputy Chief Field Censor

I (d)
Press, censorship, cinema
GSO 2

British
GSO 3

Allies
GSO 3

I (g)
War Trade
Enemy economy
GSO 3

I (f)
Visitors: War Office Foreign Office, US, Attaches, Propaganda
GSO 2, 3 GSO 3s

'G'
CGS
DCGS

Intelligence
BGGS

I (c)
Topography
GSO 1, GSO 3

I (e)
Wireless/ciphers/ listening
GSO 3

Secret Service
Occupied Territories
Counter Espionage

Agents' Reports
Records, rail movements
GSO 3

Counter-espionage, control of civilians
GSO 3

Carnet Section
SC

Staff Duties (SD)
Under DCGS

Training
BGGS, GSO 2
GSO 3

I (b)
Secret Service
GSO 1

I (a)
Information
GSO 1

'MS'
Appointments, honours, promotions
MS, AMS
2 DAMS, SC

'O (a)'
Plans, orders, Intercommunication, Liaison: BGGS,
3 GSO1s, 3 GSO2s

'O (b)'
Organisation, records
BGGS,
GSO 1, 4 GSO2s

Enemy orbat and organisation
GSO 2

Enemy armaments, Wireless translations
GSO 3

Periodical summary, Enemy transport
GSO 3

Situation maps, Enemy defences, plans, strategies
GSO 2

Dissemination of information
Enemy rear areas
GSO 2

although in effect he operated under the command of the QMG, and his department was classified as a branch of GHQ. Under him were gathered all those directorates and departments dealing with transport and movements. With the DGT taking responsibility for the BEF's transport network, the post of IGC lapsed, the IGC's other military responsibilities being taken over by the QMG and a General Officer Commanding Lines of Communication. This streamlined the system of administration and logistics. Geddes brought further improvements to the system through the implementation of methods he had used in business, notably centralisation and forecasting. The use of civilian techniques and expert personnel met with some resistance,[50] but the most visible aspects of this were quickly overcome, not least because of the strong support he enjoyed from both Haig and Lloyd George. It quickly became obvious that his techniques worked, and that the DGT had improved almost every aspect of transport for the BEF, from the quantity of stores moving through French ports to the construction and running of the railways.[51]

Geddes' reforms were accompanied by other improvements in the administrative arms of GHQ. The Military Secretary, who had responsibility for officers' appointments and promotions, and who had previously operated as part of the C-in-C's personal staff, had been awarded his own branch of GHQ in the summer of 1916; this recognised the massive growth in his workload as a result of the army's expansion. Q and A branches also grew, and the number of officers employed in administrative and services departments increased by more than fifty per cent from late 1916.

Secondly, the disparity in performance between different units of the army, evidence of differing tactical awareness and doctrine, made it clear that it was no longer sufficient to leave the majority of responsibility for training with junior formations. Instead, Haig created a new department specifically for training within Staff Duties Section, appointing Arthur Solly Flood as its BGGS. Although the structure for such a position had existed since Robertson's reforms to GHQ in the spring of 1915, the decision to use a section of GHQ to create and disseminate a tactical doctrine, as opposed to merely attempting to co-ordinate training at different levels, was an important departure. Solly Flood's department was to produce pamphlets on small-unit tactics which were adopted and practised by many units in early 1917, and have been hailed as a British version of the famed German 'stormtrooper' techniques which were to gain such success in 1918.[52]

As a result of these developments in training and logistics, the BEF could make use of a developed tactical system in 1917. At its best this meant a coherently planned, closely integrated all-arms set piece battle, in which well trained infantry, aided by increased small-unit firepower, utilised fire and movement tactics against emplaced opponents, preceded and supported by an adequate weight of artillery fire using shells appropriate to the target. The infantry would consolidate an objective within the effective range of their own guns, allowing them to break up the likely counter-attack. These tactics were used and refined in the course of the major offensives of 1917. Although the circumstances of trench warfare made even successful attacks costly in lives, such limited assaults inflicted much heavier casualties on the Germans, and played a key part in the wearing down and eventual destruction of their army. They would not have been possible without the input of administrative and training units of GHQ.

Other developments at Montreuil over the winter of 1916–17 were not so successful. Oa expanded for the first time since 1915, doubling in size and appointing officers specifically for planning and liaison duties. The sub-section developed its own plan for offensives in Flanders during early 1917. However, this plan, drawn up by two comparatively junior officers, had little impact on the operations eventually proposed by the army commanders involved in the Third Ypres offensive. Worse, repeated warnings by the Head of Oa, Davidson, that the opening attack by Fifth Army had over-ambitious initial objectives, beyond the reach of British artillery even if they were attained, went unheeded.[53] Oa seemed unable to act as a centralised planning unit for army operations. As has been noted, Haig's concept of command emphasised the need for subordinate commanders to plan and fight battles for themselves, even if his inclination was often to interfere. This could tend to negate any input from his own staff. Arguably, Oa's comparatively small size and relative inexperience made it unsuitable for such detailed planning in any case. Davidson's attempts to influence Fifth Army's plans, however, were appropriate, and his inability to do so should be seen as a combination of his own failure to argue sufficiently strongly against his superiors, and failure to appreciate the tactical realities of the battlefield.

Similar factors were in operation later on in the battle when Oa became aware of the appalling state of the ground around Passchendaele. These conditions were preventing the implementation of the battle system described above. Liaison officers within GHQ visited the battlefield and attempted to report back on conditions there. However, these reports were not awarded the priority they deserved:

> From all he saw, he reported repeatedly that it was no good – he remembered saying in particular that even the guns could not find a firm platform. When he told Davidson so the latter told him he had better tell Haig for himself. This he did. But the trouble he found was that the effect of these unfavourable reports that the Liaison Officers made, was counteracted by the reports that came back through the ordinary channels, especially from Second Army Headquarters.

Knowing Haig's determination to press on at all costs, the sub-ordinate commanders were inclined to send him the reports he wanted, rather than risk setting their opinion in opposition to his.[54]

In contrast, I branch enjoyed considerable influence over the C-in-C. It had grown substantially, doubling in size from ten to twenty officers in the year from summer 1916. This expansion can be seen in practical terms: officers were added on an ad hoc basis to deal with new techniques of war such as radio intercepts or cinema censorship. However, expansion also represented and reinforced Charteris' own influence within GHQ. Sharing his C-in-C's optimism, and enjoying a close professional relationship with him, Charteris sought out information which would reassure Haig about the validity of his operational inclinations. Separated by Robertson's changes from the control of O section, I was free to expand its interests towards strategic and grand strategic intelligence.

As a result I branch became increasingly unwieldy. Its responsibilities included not only operational military intelligence, but also counter-intelligence, enemy communications intercepts, secret service agents, maps, censorship, relations with foreign dignitaries, and assessment of the state of Germany's economy. These are functions that would now be handled by at least four separate organisations: MI5 and 6, GCHQ and the Intelligence Corps.[55] I's large size and various responsibilities brought it into conflict with the Intelligence Branch at the War Office in London.[56]

In part, this shift towards wider intelligence was dictated by the logic of total war; in the *materialschlact*, Germany's economic status did affect its battlefield performance. But this was also information that could be manipulated to provide a further measure of battlefield success when more traditional methods were not encouraging. Whilst relevant in global terms, such information was unhelpful in the context of this campaign. Not only was this an inappropriate use of intelligence resources at this level of command, it was not integrated with the information coming in from Operations' liaison officers, which presented a conflicting impression of apparent success on the ground. With the organisational structure of GHQ separating O and I, and without a combative Head of Operations or a strong CGS to maintain a balanced flow of data, it was possible for I section, like the Army HQs, to provide information which encouraged Haig to continue fighting a battle which should probably have been halted, rather than being integrated into a decision-making process involving all arms of the staff.

That this could occur was indicative of the continuing problem that the expansion of GHQ, combined with its well-established location, tended to isolate it from its front-line units. This was particularly likely when senior members of staff had been in position for some time. Burnett Stuart reported that, when he returned to GHQ in 1917 as Deputy Adjutant General:

I did not like GHQ any more than I had done a year before. It was even further away from the war; and I got the impression that several of the senior officers had been there so long that they developed an inferiority complex vis à vis the forward troops, and were shy of visiting them . . . The Adjutant General was . . . a most capable man and knew the work of his department inside out, but he has the complex badly and practically [never] left GHQ even to visit Army Headquarters.[57]

Similarly, W N Nicholson wrote that:

'Q' was completely out of touch with the war below; Maxwell did not favour visits to formations – he condemned them as 'joy rides'. His outlook, they say, was limited to the clean white sheet of paper on which in his own fair hand he transcribed his ideas, orders and instructions. Moreover for his 'Q' staff he ordained that once at GHQ always at GHQ; and the result of such a system must be real bad.[58]

This feeling was shared, with considerably more animosity, by many of the troops closer to the firing line, and the result was a breakdown of trust between the Staff and those they directed and supplied, which was to form the basis for many representations of the Staff in years to come. It is to GHQ's credit, however, that many of these faults were to be addressed in the course of the next year.

Winter 1917–November 1918
The final months of the Third Ypres campaign had caused considerable controversy at home. In light of this, and of the existing tensions between the C-in-C and the Prime Minister, Lloyd George, it was almost inevitable that there would be changes in the High Command. In the end, probably because of able manoeuvring by Lord Derby, neither Haig nor Lloyd George resigned or brought down the other.[59] However, there were major changes around Haig. Charteris was replaced by Lieutenant-General the Honourable Sir Herbert Lawrence on 31 December 1917. Twenty-four days later, Lawrence replaced Kiggell as CGS, where he remained for the rest of the war. Kiggell's physical and emotional health was beginning to waver under the stress of his position. Whilst the accuracy of the tale of him crying in the mud at Passchendaele remains uncertain, the atmosphere of apparent isolation from reality and personal instability which this implies seems to have reflected a broader truth.[60]

Lawrence was well aware of his predecessor's inadequacy. When Clive questioned him about whether he would be CGS, he said that he: '. . . was not sure he could get on with DH, and would certainly refuse to act on the same lines as Kiggell, who had become rather like a senior ADC and was unknown to the army.'[61] Lawrence was certainly more direct and more self-confident than Kiggell. Having been in the same regiment as Haig at the start of his military career, he had left to pursue a successful business career. Returning to service, he had commanded a division in France. Charteris suggested that his background gave him a greater degree of independence of action than other senior staff officers:

> He has one very strong asset. He has a very big job in civil life to go back to whenever he may wish to go, so he is absolutely independent. It is difficult for any regular professional soldier not to be influenced to some extent by considerations of his own future prospects. Lawrence has the independence of a civilian and the training of a soldier.[62]

The place Lawrence had temporarily occupied as Head of Intelligence was eventually taken by Brigadier-General Cox, an extremely able officer who had served in Intelligence, first at GHQ and then in London, throughout the war. The Deputy Chief of Staff, Butler, was also removed. Slightly before Lawrence's arrival, Maxwell, the QMG, had been replaced by Lieutenant-General Sir Travers E Clarke. The ostensible reason for this was Maxwell's injury following a fall from his horse. In fact, it seems likely that his lack of contact with the troops, his tendency to treat Q branch as a personal fiefdom, and his criticisms of London had led to his unpopularity at the War Office.[63]

In the following months significant changes took place in the personnel, structure and atmosphere of GHQ, effectively revitalising it as an institution, renewing its links with the armies, and allowing it to play a central role in the eventual advance to victory. Whilst these must be seen predominantly as a result of the influx of new senior officers, eager to improve GHQ and with a mandate for change, it does appear that Haig participated in this process and was content to see it take place.

Firstly, G branch was reorganised and a number of new officers brought in. In the course of March and April, G was divided into two sections, O(perations), headed by Davidson, promoted to Major-General, and S(taff) D(uties), headed by Major-General Guy Dawnay. O consisted of Oa, headed by Brigadier-General John Dill, and I, headed by Cox. SD consisted of sub-sections concerned with Ob, Training, Machine Guns and Anti-Aircraft.

A further set of changes followed in June, abolishing the Machine Gun sub-section of SD, and moving those officers responsible for administration and Censorship and Publicity from I sub-section to SD. This change provides an example of the different interpretations the officers involved could put on changes around them. Colonel Lee was sure that this shift resulted from demands from the newspaper barons to make C and P less

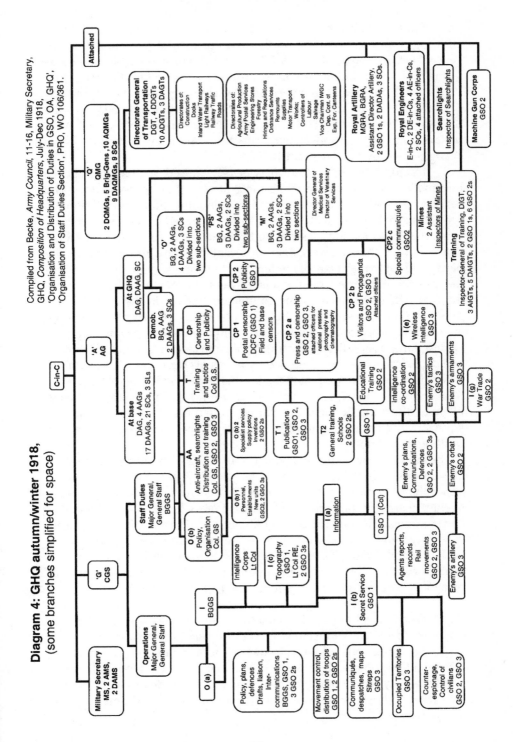

Diagram 4: GHQ autumn/winter 1918,
(some branches simplified for space)

Compiled from Becke, *Army Council*, 11-16, Military Secretary, GHQ, *Composition of Headquarters*, July-Dec 1918, 'Organisation and Distribution of Duties in GSO, OA, GHQ', 'Organisation of Staff Duties Section', PRO, WO 106/361.

powerful. Lytton saw this as a move by Cox to reduce his responsibilities, allowing him to concentrate on the real business of operational intelligence.[64] Finally, the position of DGT as subordinate to the QMG alone was formalised, streamlining the supply process. A final raft of changes in July 1918 saw the creation of an Inspectorate of Training, attached to GHQ and headed by Lieutenant General Sir Ivor Maxse. Simultaneously, the Brigadier-Generals who had commanded the sub-sections of SD were replaced by Staff Colonels with the title 'Assistant Director'. These changes are shown in Diagram 4.

In structural terms, G branch was reorganised so that intelligence information would once more be integrated with operational data. The reduction in size of I sub-section from its monolithic status in 1917 allowed further specialisation, with officers being awarded much more specific roles. Such information was crucial to the BEF's developing operational ability. Other changes were also representative of a recognition of the need to adapt to the needs of modern warfare, for example the increase in the number and variety of specialist officers attached to GHQ. Although the first half of 1918 saw some confusion, evident in the creation of a Machine Gun sub-section in SD, then the shift of its staff to become attached advisory officers, these can be interpreted as positive signs of experimental adaptation. The creation of an Inspector General of Training and department has been criticised by James Mythen, and it was certainly less influential in creating new tactics than was claimed by Maxse at the time and after the war, but it did recognise the real problems that were likely to affect the BEF had the war continued into 1919, with a mass of younger soldiers still requiring training in the tactics of mobile and positional warfare.[65]

The influx of new personnel which went along with this re-organisation also improved GHQ's performance, its relationship to the troops, and its atmosphere. In part this was the result of the appointment of genuinely talented staff officers, such as Dill and Travers Clarke, whose ability had been recognised in their rise through the system. The arrival of new officers re-invigorated GHQ, releasing it from the moribund state it had reached under Kiggell. These officers were determined to establish better links with front-line units. They travelled more widely, and there was an insistence on a more regular turnover of officers at GHQ. As Nicholson put it:

> Now, we tried to keep in touch by means of officers who constantly toured; while all our senior 'Q' staff officers had, like me, experience of the formations below . . . In such an organisation as GHQ an officer might become a first class office man; but he tended to grow hideously hidebound by procedure, regarding delays as inevitable. The only hope was that all should serve constantly at the business end of the stick.[66]

This went alongside a renewed desire for professionalism, in particular the use of the statistical and graphical methods introduced by the DGT that was partly based on the need to ensure proper employment of ever more scarce resources. 'Every matter great and small had searching attention, and the British Army began to be run like an up-to-date competitive business.'[67]

The beginning of this quite complex process of change may have affected GHQ's ability to deal effectively with the German offensive of March 1918. As Travers has pointed out, there was a widespread confusion in the BEF about the implementation of the 'defence-in-depth' tactics introduced in early 1918. GHQ's own lack of clarity on this point did not assist its efforts to establish a universal doctrine. Although I section identified the likely date and location of the German assault, it failed to determine adequately its scale and tactics.[68] It took GHQ some time to recognise the seriousness of the attack. Brown has suggested that in fact A and Q branches realised what was happening before G, as a result of the demands on their resources and the impact on supply depots. In contrast, however, G realised much earlier that the tide had turned, and some logistics plans to divert traffic and destroy railways continued to operate when they had been rendered redundant by events. It was evident that the departmentalism that had affected GHQ throughout the war still existed.[69] GHQ made preliminary moves to evacuate in the event of a German breakthrough, and it appears that there was a degree of panic reminiscent of 1914, leading to further disruption.[70]

However, GHQ's eventual ability to co-ordinate, and critically supply, the BEF to stop the German attack, and then to move directly into the even more difficult work of planning and supporting counter-attacks which developed into an ongoing continuous offensive is worthy of praise. Travers suggests that following the traumas of the German offensive in 1918, Haig's Army commanders took advantage of a command vacuum to establish their own power, and that the successful offensives of that summer can be seen as a result of a state of creative anarchy.[71] Again this seems unfair to GHQ. Haig had, after all, aspired to a more decentralised style of command throughout the war. More experienced army commanders and staff finally made this possible in 1918, even if Haig did still interfere unduly on occasions. GHQ branches made a significant contribution to the Allied successes in 1918. The Operations staff sequenced a series of major Army offensives; this role in fact suited the section's size and structure much better than more detailed planning for subordinate formations. I section co-ordinated information on enemy artillery which was vital to operational success. Most impressively, the administrative and logistics branches kept the army supplied throughout the Hundred Days advance, in particular with the vital quantities of shells. Although he was able to take a more 'hands-off' role, Haig himself played a key part in

63

persuading Foch to order an ambitious offensive in the summer, and persisting with a belief that victory was attainable before the end of the year.[72]

The Australian Corps commander, Lieutenant-General Sir John Monash, described his battles in terms of a musical composition, in which each arm had to play its part precisely to contribute to the general harmony.[73] To continue the metaphor, what GHQ staff were able to do in late 1918, as never before, was to select a concert hall for Monash's orchestra, direct his players to it, give them their instruments, and allow them and their conductor to get on with the performance. These were all vital, if subsequently somewhat obscured, roles. Although at the time, GHQ officers were frustrated by a lack of public realisation of their achievements, even those subordinate officers who criticised it recognised that its performance in terms of liaison and supply had improved by mid 1918.[74]

Conclusion

This chapter has proposed a division of the history of GHQ into four parts. The first, up until the end of 1914, saw administrative improvisation and adaptability, and operational inadequacy. The second, from then until the end of 1915, saw very limited re-structuring and efforts to adapt to the demands of trench warfare, mostly on an ad hoc basis. Although these allowed the army to remain in the field whilst undergoing dramatic expansion, and removed some of the operational faults of the previous year, failure to consider the underlying flaws of, or potential difficulties for, GHQ's structure laid up trouble for the future. In the third stage, from 1916 to the end of 1917, the shock of the Somme battle forced GHQ to reorganise the supply and training of the army. Whilst these changes allowed tactical and operational improvements the following year, their impact was reduced by operational and intelligence failures, for which the personnel and structure of GHQ were at least partially responsible. In the final stage, from the winter of 1917–18 to the end of the war, some of these faults were addressed in a series of reforms which improved the structure and behaviour of GHQ and played a part in the BEF's advance to victory. In terms of administration and supply, the performance of GHQ through-out was admirable. Bearing in mind the requirements of an expanding army, the fact that its ad hoc system did not break down was a testament to the efforts of its officers. As the BEF's supply and administration system improved after 1916, it fulfilled an essential pre-condition for tactical and operational success, and eventual victory. In operational terms, GHQ's record was less impressive, with real improvement only coming in 1918.

Perhaps the most viscerally unappealing charge against GHQ is that it allowed itself to become isolated from the 'reality' of the front line. This is also the best enduring representation of high command in the First World

War: 'château generalship'. Although its longevity might be predicated on misconceptions about the role and duties of modern commanders, and its coincidence with a popular image of First World War soldiers as victims, it has its basis in fact. Particularly towards the end of 1917, it is apparent that many senior officers at GHQ allowed themselves to lose touch with the experiences and emotions of the units at the sharp end. What has seldom been credited is the degree to which this situation was recognised and rectified in the early part of 1918.

This points towards the first of two issues, which might be drawn out of this study: the seasonal pace of change at GHQ. Officers such as Fuller and Baker-Carr criticised GHQ for being unable to see the wood for the trees, being too wrapped up in minutiae to contemplate new ideas. Whilst it is apparent that what they thought was nit-picking was often the concern for detail which was the very basis of good staff work, it is also clear that GHQ found difficulty in breaking away from its day-to-day concerns to consider wider issues. Changes in GHQ's own personnel and structure tended to occur over the winter. It was only when the campaigning season was over that time existed to take stock of what had been achieved and what needed changing. If GHQ's seeming intellectual inflexibility was a problem that was worsened by structural, personal and social factors, it also derived from the massive scale of the war itself.

The slow pace of change complicates the application of a 'learning curve' theory to GHQ. Although some individuals and departments did learn from experience – Davidson and the DGT's branch are good examples respectively – such a process was not necessarily replicated universally, or reflected in GHQ's organisation. The rigid hierarchy that existed in most elements of the British army often acted against the effective implementation of individuals' knowledge and experience. It is important, even whilst stating that GHQ improved its performance over the course of the war, to avoid a determinist view which sees every development in structure as part of an inevitable smooth progression towards an optimum in 1918. Instead, structures tended to function until they approached collapse or had clearly failed, at which point dramatic change occurred. Not every change was for the better. It might be more accurate, though perhaps less pleasing in terms of metaphors, to posit a variety of different developmental processes, which if represented graphically would be seen as a number of lines whose gradients and direction were not only different, but changed at different times.

Secondly, the importance of effective management by and between the heads of different branches. The division of the staff into separate operational and administrative branches was justly criticised after the war. It reduced communication between officers whose work should have been inseparable, encouraged strong departmental interests which did not coincide with those of the army as a whole, and allowed some individuals to become isolated from battlefield realities. Given their importance to the final victory, it is clear that throughout the war G should have been much more concerned than it was with the needs of A and Q.

On the other hand, in the high-pressure and heavy workload environment of GHQ, officers often did not have time to consider other departments. The complexities of total war encouraged and rewarded specialisation to a degree which would not necessarily have been possible for perpetually peripatetic officers. It was appropriate that officers who were good at particular tasks should continue to perform them. As importantly, GHQ had to recognise its own limitations. Its success in 1918 was related to greater specialisation and an avoidance of role overload through insufficient command decentralisation that had affected it in the past.

However, such an organisation relied on the personalities of its branch chiefs. Their role combined numerous responsibilities. They had to keep tight control of their own branches, and enforce a chain of information that prevented one section becoming predominant over the others. They had to be aware of other branches' situations and demands, and be ready to co-operate or to resist them. Above all, effective management had to be exercised by a strong-minded and independent CGS. If there are heroes to be discerned in the story of GHQ, they are Robertson and Lawrence. The CGS's role was crucial firstly because of his influence over the atmosphere of GHQ as a whole. The C-in-C did not have the time to exercise command over GHQ itself – in Haig's case, he remained geographically isolated from it. The CGS was the representative face of headquarters, not only to the Staff but to the men of the army as well. Secondly, the CGS had a vital role as a manager within G branch. He not only had to control the heads of sections under him – with their wide breadth of concerns and responsi-bilities – but act as a conduit for information between them and the C-in-C. Although structures could be put in place to assist the CGS this was essentially a matter of personality, as was apparent to officers at the time. Despite Fuller's condemnation, mechanical monks often made excellent staff officers; but they needed magisterial management if they were to function effectively.

NOTES

1   I am grateful to Dr Stephen Badsey, Dr Gary Sheffield and Bob Evans for their advice and comments during the production of this paper, to Ms Barbara Taylor for her assistance in the creation of the organisational charts, and to the staff of the Liddell Hart Centre for Military Archives, King's College London, and the Department of Documents, Imperial War Museum, London, for their help during my research.

2   See however Simon Robbins' excellent recent study which contains much material of relevance to this debate: 'British Generalship on the Western Front in the First World War, 1914–1918', PhD, University of London, 2001.

3   See, for example, R C Sherriff, *Journey's End* (London, 1929); A G Macdonell, *England, their England* (London, 1933).

4   J F C Fuller, *Memoirs of an Unconventional Soldier* (London, 1936), 141–2.

5   A F Becke, *History of the Great War, Order of Battle Part 4, The Army Council, General Headquarters, Armies and Corps, 1914–1918* (London, 1945), ii.

6   I M Brown, *British Logistics on the Western Front 1914–1919* (Westport CT, 1998) 187–8.

7   I am grateful for Bob Evans of the Army Historical Branch, for making these figures available to me. In the case of certain departments based at GHQ, the expansion was much greater than this. For example, as Brigadier E M Jack recorded: 'When the Expeditionary Force left England in 1914, Maps GHQ consisted of one officer and one clerk at GHQ, with another on the Lines of Communication to look after map reserves. By the end of the war this total of four had expanded to 215 officers and about 4,600 other ranks.' (E M Jack, 'Maps, GHQ', *Reveille*, 1 Dec, 1936 (6), 32. Liddell Hart Centre for Military Archives, Kings College, London (hereafter LHCMA), LH 15/21).

8   War Office, *Staff Manual* (London, 1912), PRO, WO 32/4731, 34.

9   In the course of the war, the Second Echelon was absorbed into Directorates or the 'Special Appointments' section of GHQ, but the First and Third Echelons retained their names.

10 Brown, *British Logistics*, 46–8.

11 On the development of the General Staff and its performance in the first part of the war, see B Bond, *The Victorian Army and the Staff College* (London, 1972), 230–332.

12 R Holmes, *The Little Field Marshal: Sir John French* (London, 1981), 164; Brown, *British Logistics*, 43.

13 Holmes, op. cit., 197–8.

14 This was criticised by the post-war Kirke Report: *Report of the Committee on the lessons of the Great War* (London, War Office, October 1932), 6. LHCMA, Kirke 4/30. For the evidence before the committee, see 'Lessons of the Great War Committee, report by Maj-Gen A E McNamara, Lessons from the Great War on the Western Front', 1, LHCMA, Kirke 4/9.

15 Holmes, op. cit., 206.

16 Brown, op. cit., 48–59. For an example of the tensions that could arise, see letters between Cowans and Robertson in December 1914, LHCMA, Robertson Papers 2/2/26, 28, 30, 60.

17 W R Robertson, *From Private to Field Marshal* (London, 1921), 220.

18 C D Baker-Carr, *From Chauffeur to Brigadier* (London, 1930), 29.

19 Holmes, *The Little Field Marshal* 217–18, 225.

20 Robertson, op. cit., 220.

21 For an example of Harper's character, see Baker-Carr, op. cit., 73–8.

22 Robertson, op. cit., 221–2.

23 'Government Military Policy, Note by CGS', March 1915, PRO, WO 158/17.

24 For French's GHQ routine, see C Repington, *The First World War* (Aldershot, new edition, 1991), 27–9. For a slightly later date (2 Jan 1916), see J Charteris, *At GHQ* (London, 1931), 130.

25 Extracts from the letters of Brigadier-General Cox (then a junior officer in I), 7 May, 14 June, 25 Sept 1915, Department of Documents, Imperial War Museum, London (hereafter, IWM), Cox papers, 99/56/1.

26 Robertson, op. cit., 225–7.

27   Brown, op. cit., 103.

28   *ibid*, 103–4.

29   S Fay, *The War Office at War* (London, 1937), 41.

30   Brown, op. cit., 46, 104.

31   Baker-Carr, op. cit., 89.

32   *ibid*, 79.

33   'GS Notes on Operations 5 Feb to 7 Oct 1915', 'Du Cane's memo on Neuve Chapelle', PRO, WO 158/17.

34   Brown, op. cit., 104.

35   Sir Desmond Morton's account of Haig's ADC's having to learn a shorthand of grunts has been much quoted, but may have grown rather in the telling before Morton wrote to Liddell Hart with it in 1961. (LHCMA, LH 15/2/45, Morton to Haig, 17 July 1961). Both Repington and Fay found him calm and coherent in speech. (Repington, *The First World War*, 265; Fay, op. cit., 188.)

36   Contrary to received opinion, Haig was a keen advocate of any new technology that might aid the war effort. His enthusiastic use of a specially equipped train as a forward GHQ is often cited as an example. Repington disagreed: 'Most inconvenient, very hot, and the noise of trains passing murders sleep and prevents telephoning.' *(The First World War*, 363).

37   J Terraine, *Douglas Haig, the educated soldier* (London, 1963); G J De Groot, 'Ambition, Duty and Doctrine, Haig's rise to High Command'; J Hussey, 'Portrait of a Commander-in-Chief'; P Simkins, 'Haig and his Army Commanders', all in B Bond and N Cave (eds), *Haig, a reappraisal seventy years on* (London, 1999), 37–50, 12–36, 78–106 respectively.

38   The scale of upheaval this seemed to represent to those at GHQ was considerable. Clive Diary, 21 Dec, 1915, PRO Cab 451201/1.

39   'Comparison of the results obtained from the British attack at Loos with possible offensive operations on Fourth Army front', Davidson to Haig, 15 April 1916, PRO, WO 153/19.

40   J Marshall-Cornwall, *Haig as Military Commander* (London, 1973), 214, M Occleshaw, *Armour Against Fate: British Military Intelligence in the First World War* (London, 1989), 325–53. See also G De Groot, *Douglas Haig, 1861–1928* (London, 1988), 220, 291–2.

41   See Kiggell's obituary from *The Times*, 25 February 1954, collected by Edmonds. LHCMA, Edmonds, V2.

42   De Groot, op. cit., 220.

43   GSO (F Fox), *GHQ (Montreuil-sur-Mer)* (London, 1920), 37.

44   *ibid*, 36.

45   *ibid*, 53.

46   J T Burnett Stuart, Unpublished memoirs, LHCMA, Burnett Stuart, Chapter 7, 77.

47   Travers, *The Killing Ground*, 110, 190, 252.

48   See, for example, the General Staff paper, 'General factors to be weighed in considering the allied plan of campaign during the next few months', 16 Jan 1916, PRO, WO 158/19, especially points 6 and 7. However, that GHQ was working towards some coherent definition of its strategy seems evident in Haig's note demanding clarification of the concept of 'The wearing out fight', February 1916, in the same file.

49   Brown, op. cit., 133.

50   As described by a young regular of the Railway Operating Division.

And here assembled every kind
Of intellect alive:
They combed the army out to find

The fittest to survive.
And, hearing from their English lairs,
Thus Rank plus Safety could be theirs
Experts on Roads and Rails and Docks
Came out in Flocks.
. . .
By merely reading through their files,
One could advance for miles and miles,
– Or so it seemed to everyone,
– Except the Hun.
(Fay, op. cit., 94).

51 Brown, op. cit., 140–50; K Grieves, 'The Transportation Mission to GHQ,
    1916' in B Bond *et al*, *'Look to your front': Studies in the First World War*
    (Staplehurst, 1999), 63–78; and more generally, K Grieves, *Sir Eric Geddes.*
    Business and Government in war and peace (Manchester, 1989).
52 This paragraph draws extensively from J Mythen, 'The revolution in British
    battle tactics July 1916–June 1917: the spring and summer offensives during
    1917', unpublished M.Phil. Thesis, University of Cambridge, 2000, 26–28,
    39–41, 44–50.
53 J Davidson, *Haig, Master of the Field* (London, 1953); 26–33; J R Colville, *Man*
    of Valour, the life of Field Marshal the Viscount Gort (London, 1972), 28–9;
    Davidson to CGS, 26 June 1917, PRO, WO 158/20; I F W Beckett, 'Operational
    Command: the plans and the conduct of battle', in P Liddle (ed.),
    Passchendaele in Perspective: the Third Battle of Ypres (London, 1997), 102–116.
    (Beckett suggests that Macmullen and Gort's plan was unrealistic); R Prior
    and T Wilson, *Passchendaele the untold story*, (London, 1996), 76–7, 100.
54 'Note on letter from Sir Edward Grigg, 15/5/36', LHCMA, LH 11/1936/63.
    See also notes on letters from other liaison officers Brigadier Anderson,
    13/5/36 (LH 11/1936/60), Lord Gort, 14/5/36 (LH 11/1936/61) and Major-
    General C C Armitage 15/5/36 (LH 11/1936/62), which suggest that no
    regular system for liaison duties and visits existed.
55 Again, I am grateful to Bob Evans for making this point to me.
56 Occleshaw, *Armour against Fate*, 359–72.
57 Burnett-Stuart memoirs, LHCMA, Burnett-Stuart Chapter 7, 80.
58 W N Nicholson, *Behind the Lines: an account of the administrative staffwork of the*
    British army 1914–18 (Stevenage, 1990), 302–3.
59 De Groot, op. cit., 360.
60 B Bond, 'Passchendaele: verdicts, past and present', Liddle, *Passchendaele in*
    perspective, 482–3.
61 Clive Diary, 5 Jan 1918, PRO, Cab 45/201/3.
62 Charteris, *At GHQ*, 286.
63 Brown, op. cit., 180–1.
64 Lytton, *The Press and the General Staff*, 141–2.
65 Mythen, The revolution in British battle tactics', 96–102.
66 Nicholson, op cit., 301–2, 303.
67 Fox, op cit., 230.
68 T Travers, *How the war was won: command and technology on the Western Front*
    1917–1918 (London, 1992), 54–6, 64–5.
69 Brown, op. cit.
70 Note of conversation with Dill 8/9/1936, LHCMA LH 11/1936/76.
71 Travers, *How the war was won*, 175, 177–8. Travers' interpretation has con-
    siderable precedents. Repington put it to an anonymous staff officer in 1918:
    'X. would not have it that the GHQ was now only a post office and that the

Army Commanders did the fighting, as I suggested. He thought that Haig, Pershing or Petain could make or mar an operation.' Repington, *The First World War*, 371.

72   Simkins, 'Haig and the Army Commanders', 95–97. R Prior and T Wilson, *Command on the Western Front* (Oxford, 1992), 305.

73   J Monash, *The Australian victories in France in 1918* (London, 1993), 56, quoted in G Sheffield, *Forgotten Victory: the First World War, myths and realities* (London, 2001), 197.

74   Fuller, *Memoirs*, 243, describes Dill's efforts to maintain contact with the Tank Corps.

CHAPTER IV

An Army Commander on the Somme: Hubert Gough

Gary Sheffield

On 18 July 1916 Major General H B 'Hooky' Walker, the British Regular officer commanding 1st Australian Division, met with Lieutenant General Sir Hubert Gough, commander of Reserve (later renamed Fifth) Army. According to Charles Bean, the Australian official historian, Gough told Walker, 'I want you to go into the line and attack Pozières tomorrow night!'[1] Walker was appalled at these 'Scrappy & unsatisfactory orders from Reserve Army', writing in his diary: 'Hope shall not be rushed into an ill prepared . . . operation but fear I shall'. He had good reason to be concerned, for I Anzac Corps headquarters had not yet arrived on the Somme, and little more than a day was hopelessly insufficient time for preparation for an attack on a heavily defended, strategically vital village which had already been the target of a number of unsuccessful assaults.[2] Walker, 'the sweat on his brow', argued with his Army commander, as did Brudenell White, the chief of staff of I Anzac Corps. Gough eventually gave in. After proper preparation, the attack eventually went in on 23 July and was highly successful.[3]

Apparently, this was not the only battle that Walker had to fight against Gough before the attack of the 23rd. In 1928 Walker recorded how he had to seek more artillery, as the initial allocation was insufficient. Moreover, Walker was strongly in favour of attacking from the south-east, rather than the south-west, the route of previous and unsuccessful assaults by British divisions. Walker only gained permission to do this after taking 'Moses' Beddington, a Reserve Army staff officer whom Gough trusted, up to the front, to show him the ground. Walker's post-war verdict on Gough was scathing: 'the very worst exhibition of Army commandship [sic] that occurred during the whole campaign, though God knows the 5th army was a tragedy thoroughout'.[4]

After the war Gough angrily rejected this version of events. He was shown a draft of Bean's Australian official history, in which Bean claimed that Gough was 'temperamentally' inclined towards rushed attacks. 'I can hardly believe a word of this story about my meeting with General Walker,' Gough wrote. 'I was not "temperamentally" addicted to attacks without careful reconnaissances and preparation . . .'[5]

In Gough's 1931 memoir, *The Fifth Army*, ghosted by the novelist Bernard Newman, we find this passage:

> No subordinate was ordered to attack before he was ready, if the reports of his unreadiness reached Army Headquarters. On the contrary, many attacks by subordinates were prevented or postponed by the Army because the preparations were not complete, the front too narrow, or the numbers engaged inadequate.[6]

This passage, and several others, seem to be a direct rebuttal of Bean's 1916 volume of the Australian official history, which had appeared in 1929. Gough's omissions in *The Fifth Army* are equally interesting. He says nothing about the argument with Walker on 18 July, and in a passage which praises several Australian officers, including divisional commanders, omits any mention of Walker.[7]

Gough's alleged behaviour at Pozières acts as a microcosm of the charge-sheet against his performance as an Army commander. He was a 'thruster', prone to launch hasty, ill-prepared attacks, often on a narrow front; he bullied his subordinates; and the staff work in Fifth Army was deficient. Gough and Fifth Army stand in sharp contrast to the commander of Second Army, General Sir Herbert Plumer, and his staff. They became renowned for methodical and successful conduct of operations under the conditions of trench warfare, and earned a favourable reputation among officers and men quite at odds with Gough's.

Yet Gough also had his defenders. Beddington, in summing up the Somme campaign, referred to Gough as 'a great commander'.[8] Much more surprising was the verdict of that scourge of Great War generals, Basil Liddell Hart. Liddell Hart, who was instrumental in reconciling Gough and Lloyd George in the 1930s[9] stated that Gough 'was unlucky' in that the First World War cramped his 'dynamism and acute sense of mobility'. In an earlier war, or in the Second World War, Gough might have emerged as 'one of the outstanding figures in military history . . . Even under the extraordinary cramping conditions of the Western Front . . . his performance was a lot better than was generally recognised'.[10] A more moderate view was the verdict of Sir Charles Bonham-Carter, the respected head of GHQ's training branch in 1917–18. He opined that Gough 'had greater qualities than any of the other Army Commanders if the conditions of war suited him . . . If only he had had a good staff he might have done great things. He was too impatient and did not realise that infantry attacks took time to prepare'.[11] These are views that cannot be ignored.[12] This chapter examines Gough's career, and especially his performance as an Army commander on the Somme, in an attempt to discover the accuracy of such judgements.

Hubert Gough's Career

Hubert de la Poer Gough was born in London in 1870, of a distinguished Irish military family. His father and his uncle won the Victoria Cross, as did John Edmond Gough, Hubert's younger brother. A contemporary, General Sir George Barrow, described 'Johnnie' as 'one of the most soldierly-minded men I have ever come across and a twentieth century Chevalier Bayard ... Had he lived he might have gone to the top of the Army'.[13] Hubert was educated at Eton and the Royal Military College Sandhurst and was commissioned into the 16th Lancers in 1889. He saw service in one colonial 'small war', the Tirah expedition of 1897–8. In January 1899 he went to the Staff College, Camberley, as a student, but following the outbreak of the Second Boer War, Gough went out to South Africa at the very end of 1899. On the whole Gough was an effective regimental officer and commander, and the high point of his war was leading the party that relieved Ladysmith in February 1900.[14] The nadir came on 17 September 1901. He led a composite mounted regiment, without adequate reconnaissance, towards a tempting target of Boers at Blood River Poort, only to find that they were merely the advance guard of a numerically far superior body, who promptly captured Brevet Lieutenant Colonel Gough and his entire force. In his sympathetic biography, General Farrar-Hockley commented that Gough 'had made a judgement and a decision that led to the death, injury or capture' of his command.[15] Lord Anglesey, a leading authority on British cavalry, attributes the incident to 'A combination of vague intelligence and youthful impetuosity (or, as some might say, a misapplication of "the cavalry spirit") . . .'[16] Gough emerged from this fiasco with his reputation more-or-less intact. Kitchener expressed his 'deepest sympathy'. Farrar-Hockley is probably correct to surmise that the excess of zeal displayed by Gough at Blood River contrasted favourably with the timidity that had characterised most previous defeats in South Africa. To his credit, Gough treated this episode at some length in his memoirs.

In 1904 Gough was posted as an instructor to Staff College, Camberley. He took over command of his regiment, 16th Lancers, at the end of 1906. In 1911 Gough was promoted to command 3rd Cavalry Brigade, and he took this formation to war in August 1914.[17] Thereafter his rise was swift. Gough commanded, as a major general, 2nd Cavalry Division at the First Battle of Ypres. In spring 1915 Gough assumed command of 7th Infantry Division, and moved up to lead I Corps in July of that year. Gough was appointed in March 1916 as commander of the Reserve Corps for the imminent operation on the Somme. His force was renamed Reserve Army in May 1916, although until late June Gough was effectively under the command of Rawlinson's Fourth Army.

Relations with Fellow Officers

The pre-war officer corps was a small body, divided into the inevitable cliques. By the time war broke out in August 1914, Hubert Gough had already established relationships, for good or ill, with many of the men with whom he would work at the highest level of command on the Western Front. When Gough was instructing at the Staff College, the Commandant was Henry Rawlinson, who was to command Fourth Army on the Somme in 1916. Gough's fellow instructors included Richard Haking and John du Cane, who both became Corps commanders during the First World War, and 'Tommy' Capper, whom Gough succeeded in command of 7th Division in 1915.[18] Another instructor was Launcelot Kiggell, later Haig's chief of staff at GHQ. In later life Gough was to describe Kiggell, not without reason, as a weak and indecisive man.[19] One of the students was Hubert's brother Johnnie Gough.

In 1914 the Curragh Incident divided the Army. Many officers, with those of 3rd Cavalry Brigade, based at the Curragh Camp near Dublin in the vanguard, threatened to send in their papers rather than face the possibility of being used to coerce Protestants into accepting Home Rule for Ireland. The Gough brothers were prominent among the protesters. 'Wully' Robertson, a future Chief of the Imperial General Staff (CIGS), gave support of a less strident nature.[20] A number of officers were on the other side, including Field Marshal Sir John French, and Major Philip Howell of the 4th Hussars. Gough was glad when French was sacked as Commander-in-Chief (CinC) British Expeditionary Force (BEF) at the end of 1915, describing him as 'an ignorant little fool'.[21]

Perhaps the most significant breach in the Gough brothers' personal relationships over the Curragh was with Henry Wilson. Their former friend played an 'equivocal' role in the affair.[22] In October 1916 Wilson, as commander of IV Corps, came under the orders of Gough's Reserve Army. Although Wilson was to mount no major action, Gough, no doubt with some relish, 'haul[ed] him over the coals' because of the state of Wilson's command. In later life Hubert Gough blamed 'his own ill-repute' and his scapegoating for the Third Battle of Ypres on 'stories spread by Henry Wilson'.[23] Gough's resentment against Wilson did not diminish with time. He devoted a chapter of his memoirs to denouncing Wilson, and shortly before his death in 1963, Gough lambasted Wilson in a television interview: 'Had him under my command once. Out-and-out crook. Never did a stroke of work. Sat in his office writing to his lady friends in high places'.[24] But in comparison to Henry Wilson, one of the most 'political' soldiers that the British Army has ever produced, Hubert Gough's skills as a political in-fighter were limited. In March 1918, by which time he had leap-frogged Gough to become CIGS, Wilson had his revenge.

Three future Army commanders, Gough, Byng and Birdwood, worked together in the South African War in 1900. At this time, Gough wrote in an uncomplimentary fashion about Julian Byng in his diary. This led Byng's biographer later to comment on Gough's 'prickly and suspicious nature', which made it difficult for him to become friends with his peers.[25] Certainly, the view that Gough was jealous of Byng seems to be borne out by some views expressed privately some years after the Great War. Byng's strength, Gough insisted, lay in 'appealing to colonials' (a reference to the former's successful command of the Canadian Corps in 1915–17) but he lacked 'military ideas' and had 'no brain'.[26] As Third Army commander, Gough opined, Byng's conduct of the 1918 March Retreat was 'damned incompetent'.[27] In 1916 Byng's Canadian Corps had served under Gough's command on the Somme, and the relationship was not particularly happy.[28] Brainless or not, Byng's conduct of the attack on Vimy Ridge in April 1917 was highly successful, and his handling of operations in 1918, although not immune from criticism, was sound enough. Byng's successes led to honours, financial rewards and the governor-generalship of Canada, which in the 1920s must have been wormwood and gall to the disgraced Gough.[29]

Gough had an equivocal relationship with another cavalryman and future fellow Army commander, 'the Bull', Edmund Allenby. Gough and Allenby shared the characteristic that they frightened their subordinates; John Bourne has described them as 'demanding tyrant[s]'.[30] Gough served under Allenby before the war, and while he admired the man's character he had no great respect for his brains. Gough claimed that on the Western Front Allenby 'would apply orders rigidly without reasoning'. However Allenby was 'very just – never bore malice against subordinates who disagreed'. At least Allenby came off better than another contemporary who achieved success as a cavalryman in the Great War, Philip Chetwode, whom Gough denounced as a 'crawler' and a 'funk'.[31] Gough also criticised Lord Dundonald, his superior in South Africa. Anglesey has suggested that this was 'probably unfair'.[32]

As Gough admitted, his rapid promotion at a relatively early age (an Army Commander at 46; Rawlinson was seven years older) caused him problems. As a Corps commander, Gough bridled when Kitchener made what he perceived as a sneering reference to his youth.[33] One is tempted to apply a little amateur psychology and see Gough's managerial style as an attempt to compensate for his lack of years when dealing with subordinates who were his contemporaries or who were older. In fairness, one should mention that a junior officer recorded that on the Western Front he met Gough while out riding and they 'talked very civilly, which I appreciated'.[34] Although Gough's post-war comments should be seen in the light of his disappointment and anger at being removed from command in 1918, the overall picture that emerges is not an attractive one to modern eyes.

Gough and Haig

Unquestionably, the major figure in Gough's rise was General Sir Douglas Haig, the commander of I Army in 1915 who became CinC BEF in December 1915. Haig and Gough had served together as far back as the Boer War, and again at Aldershot. Haig was deeply affected by the death of Johnnie Gough, his Chief of Staff, in January 1915. Hubert to some degree replaced his brother as Haig's 'confidant and sounding-board'.[35] Clearly, mutual respect was high. Haig's views of Gough's qualities are indicated by a remarkable passage in a book co-authored by Lieutenant Colonel J H Boraston, Haig's private secretary. Boraston's views can safely be assumed to reflect those of his chief, who gave 'tacit approval' to the project.[36] This passage amounts to a spirited defence of both Gough and Haig's championing of his subordinate. Boraston argued that Gough's 'fine record of service' in 1914–15 made him the obvious man for the job of commander of Reserve Army. Gough's performance on the Somme 'amply justified the selection of this young but brilliant general' and in the semi-mobile fighting of February–March 1917, Gough

> showed a mastery of tactical manoeuvre, and of the skilled use of ground and artillery in support of infantry attack, which, it is submitted with respect, would establish his right, had he no other claim, to rank among the most able of the many competent generals that the war brought into positions of high command.[37]

Before the Somme, Reserve Army was under the control of Haig's GHQ. The details of the scheme for its employment are still fairly obscure, but in the opinion of Stephen Badsey, who has pieced together the evidence, the formation's

> training and structure clearly suggest that the embryo Reserve Army plan was for 25th Division to exploit any success by Fourth Army, closely followed by two or more of the [three available] cavalry divisions . . . and then by the infantry of [the three division-strong] II Corps following up.

In the event, Rawlinson's breakthrough did not occur; in any case, the Fourth Army commander subverted the whole concept.[38] Thus Gough never had the opportunity of open warfare in which Liddell Hart believed he would excel.

Gough's elevation may also have owed something to Haig's relationship with Rawlinson. Haig may have seen Rawlinson as a rival. In April 1915 Haig had appointed Gough to command of a division in Rawlinson's IV Corps. In doing so, to use modern political parlance, Haig briefed Gough against his new corps commander.[39] Haig's appointment of Gough to take over part of Fourth Army's front on the second day of the Somme offensive perhaps owed something to the CinC's desire to use his protégé as a counterbalance to the well-connected Rawlinson.[40] In terms of age, seniority (at the beginning of the Somme Gough was a lieutenant general, Rawlinson a general) and function Gough was the junior Army commander on the Somme, but of the two he had a greater rapport with Haig. The whole Gough–Haig–Rawlinson triangle would certainly repay further research.

Gough emerged from the Somme with his reputation riding high. In March 1917 Lord Bertie, the British Ambassador in Paris, noted that Gough was being 'mentioned in French quarters as a possible successor to Haig'. Nivelle seems to have been the instigator of this rumour.[41] Nevertheless, Rawlinson rather than Gough (or Plumer) was Haig's initial choice in January 1917 to lead the forthcoming 'big push' in the Ypres salient.[42] By July 1917 things had changed. Gough was placed in command of the main assault at the beginning of the Third Battle of Ypres. However, in late August, after disappointing results, Haig gave Plumer responsibility for the main part of the battle. Even after Gough's sideways move he retained much of Haig's confidence.

The German breakthrough on Fifth Army's front on 21 March 1918 fatally undermined Gough's credibility. Foiled in his desire to remove Haig, Lloyd George 'chose to move against Derby [the Secretary of State for War and a Haig supporter, pushed sideways to become Ambassador to France in April 1918] and Gough . . . [who] became the army's sacrifice to appease the government's critics'. Passchendaele had already undermined Gough's position with the government, if not with Haig.[43] The CIGS, Henry Wilson, was not unwilling to wield the knife. On 26 March, at the Doullens inter-allied conference, Wilson 'discussed removal of Gough, and told Haig he could have Rawly, and Rawly's old Fourth Army staff from Versailles, to replace Gough'.[44] Haig tried to retain Gough's services. He ignored the suggestion of Lord Derby, who wrote to Haig on 5 March recommending that Gough be appointed Governor of Gibraltar.[45] On 24 March, three days after the beginning of the German offensive, Bertie noted that 'the Army wanted General Gough to be "ungummed" [sent home] and that Haig saved him'. Three days after that Bertie wondered whether there would have to 'be a scapegoat for the disaster', and that 'if Haig cover [sic] Gough' whether both men would have to go.[46] Indeed, on 26 March and 3 April Haig argued with Lloyd George on Gough's behalf.[47] Ultimately, Haig realised that if Gough did not go his own position was under threat, and Haig said privately, 'I was conceited enough to think that the army could not spare me'.[48] Haig had sympathy for Gough's plight after his dismissal but advised him not to make a fuss; Byng took a similar view.[49] This has been interpreted as Haig 'cold shoulder[ing]' Gough from selfish motives,[50] but a more generous reading is possible. Gough might have suffered an injustice, but the efficient conduct of the war at a crucial moment was more important than one man's reputation. An Army commander could be sacked without too many repercussions. The removal of Haig might have created more problems than it solved.

Reserve Army's Operations on the Somme

By the evening of 1 July 1916 Haig had recognised that the frontage held by Fourth Army was too big for one headquarters and commander to handle. On 2 July Gough took command of X and VIII Corps, although still under Fourth Army's aegis, and on 3 July Reserve Army formally assumed command of the northern sector of the Somme battlefield.[51] For most of the campaign, Reserve Army's operations were subsidiary to the main effort being undertaken by Fourth Army. Moreover, in 1916 the shell shortage was by no means over. To feed the enormous bombardments on Fourth Army's front, there was a need to economise on other sectors. These two factors restricted Gough's freedom of action from the outset.

In discussions on 2 July, Rawlinson and Haig agreed that Gough should attack with two brigades towards the Schwaben Redoubt, where survivors of the assault of the previous day were believed to be holding out. Kiggell reported that Haig wanted Gough to 'damp down his operations to the lowest limit in order to secure that result' and clearly Rawlinson was of a similar mind. Gough, however, wanted to attack an enemy salient south-east of Thiepval with two divisions (32nd and 49th). When he met Kiggell on the evening of 2 July, Gough agreed to use six battalions (i.e. less than two brigades) 'early' on the following day. Ominously, Gough 'said that he could not guarantee success with that force, but thought the prospects good enough to justify the attempt'.[52] Gough thus came up against the realities of his position, that his role was subordinate to Rawlinson's. He also showed his willingness to gamble, by committing small forces to carry out a difficult and demanding operation.

In the event, the attack was a complete shambles. Originally timed for 0315 to coincide with an attack on Ovillers, at 0255 Gough contacted III Corps to tell them that Reserve Army's attack had had to be postponed until 0600. Even this extended preparation time was hopelessly unrealistic for the two brigades of 32nd Division (14 and 75 Brigades, the latter attached from 25th Division) to prepare. Messages were delayed in reaching subordinate commanders and artillery support was grossly deficient. This was partly because batteries did not receive news of the new start time until they had already begun the preliminary bombard-

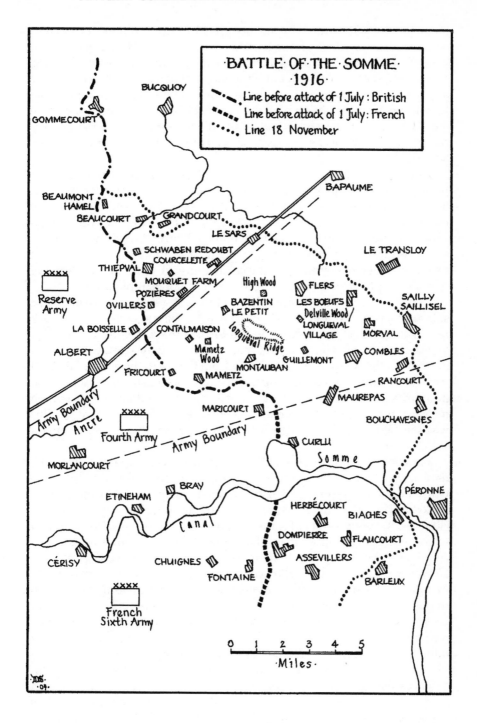

Battle of the Somme 1916

ment for the 0315 attack, using up precious ammunition. It was also because 32nd Division's frontage of attack was increased from 800 to 1,400 yards. The attack was thus carried out on an objective nearly twice as long as that originally envisaged, but with only half of the anticipated artillery ammunition available. Not all of this was Hubert Gough's fault; Haig, Rawlinson and X Corps all bore a share of the blame, and the attack bore the hallmarks of the chaos that typified the beginning of the Somme campaign. But it was an inauspicious start to Gough's command on the Somme.[53]

Gough's attempt to expand the scope of operations in his sector can perhaps be seen as an attempt to flex his muscles as an Army commander. If so, it was unsuccessful, and Kiggell on behalf of GHQ laid out the parameters of future Reserve Army operations. In a 'Note' of 4 July Gough was instructed to keep in touch with units of Fourth Army, and to pin the enemy on Reserve Army's front by threatening attacks. These objectives were, however dependent on the availability of ammunition. Reserve Army's supply of shells was finite and would not be replenished.[54]

Haig still envisaged a wider role for Gough should Fourth Army make substantial progress. On 15 July, the day after the successful dawn attack on Bazentin ridge, Third Army was informed that when Rawlinson had seized the Ginchy–Flers–Le Sars line, Reserve Army would then strike north from the Ancre valley, attacking from the south the enemy on Third Army's front.[55] Three days later, Haig's optimism had somewhat diminished and in view of the Fourth Army's difficulties in getting forward, the assault on Pozières was entrusted to Reserve Army.[56] This was the first time that Gough had been given anything approaching a starring role.

A major and valid criticism of British operations on the Somme was that they were often characterised by lack of co-ordination between formations, and that forces were used in inadequate numbers or 'penny-packets'. Too often, by attacking on a narrow front the British gave the Germans the opportunity of concentrating their defensive fire on a limited sector, with devastating effects. By contrast, an attack on a broad front could force the enemy to split their artillery fire, thus reducing its effect.[57] However Gough, who told Birdwood (commander I Anzac Corps) in July that Reserve Army had attacked often, with, in modest numbers, to keep the Germans 'off balance'. 'Once we allow him to get his breath back,' said Gough, 'we shall have to make another of these gigantic assaults by which time all the German defences will have been repaired and strengthened. I think our way keeps down casualties and brings the best results'.[58] Such a view was not unreasonable in July, when it appeared that the German defences might be on the point of crumbling. They made less sense in August, when it was clear, as Haig pointed out to his Army commanders at the beginning of the month, that the Germans had 'recovered to a great extent from the disorganisation' of early July and their positions could not be attacked 'without careful and methodical preparation'.[59]

Haig's instructions of 2 August to Gough and Rawlinson designated the struggle on the British right flank as the main effort, along the boundary with the French. Once again, Reserve Army was assigned a subsidiary role, to make 'careful and methodical progress' in the Pozières–Mouquet Farm–Ovillers area 'with as little expenditure of fresh troops and of munitions as circumstances will admit of.'[60]

The BEF's attack of 15 September 1916 was intended by Haig to achieve a breakthrough and have decisive consequences. On 28 August Gough submitted to GHQ a fairly ambitious plan for operations on his front, including the capture of Courcelette. However, on 4 September Kiggell told Gough that Haig was opposed to large-scale operations on Reserve Army front 'for the present'. Instead, Gough was to stick with his previous methods. For the 15 September offensive, Gough was to 'secure' Fourth Army's left flank and hold the Germans on Reserve Army's front 'by the usual means' which precluded a major attack. Courcelette should not be attacked until Martinpuich – which Rawlinson did not regard as a primary objective – was assaulted by Fourth Army. Kiggell went on to say that if Fourth Army did well, it would be able to threaten Thiepval from the rear. If Fourth Army did not succeed in this, there was unlikely to be a 'further decisive attack this autumn' and men and guns would 'probably' be sent to Gough to take Thiepval 'so that we can establish ourselves there for the winter'.[61] In issuing appropriate orders, Reserve Army informed Corps commanders that they 'were free to undertake any minor operations for the improvement of their positions and, whenever possible, they will dig forward towards the enemy'.[62]

In the event, Reserve Army was given a more active role in the attack of 15 September. On the afternoon of the previous day, Haig intervened to order that Martinpuich was to be captured as soon as Flers fell, which would allow Gough's Army 'to come into action with full effect at the earliest possible moment'. Reserve Army was to be ready to attack Courcelette on the afternoon of 15 September and 'directly Courcelette and Martinpuich were in British hands both Armies should begin a combined advance northward'. As the Official Historian commented, Gough 'had, in effect, anticipated the eleventh-hour instructions' issued by Haig.[63] In the event, Reserve Army secured its objectives but Fourth Army's limited progress did not permit this northbound push to occur.

On 26 September Reserve Army began its biggest operation so far: the battle of Thiepval Ridge. Fourth Army on the previous day had mounted another major and fairly successful push, and Gough used four divisions of Canadian and II Corps on an attack frontage of 6,000 yards, from Courcelette to the Schwaben Redoubt. Haig hoped that following successful operations by Gough, Third Army would attack at Gommecourt to protect Reserve Army's left. In the event, although Thiepval, an objective of the 1 July assault, was taken on 27 September, the offensive became bogged down, with fighting continuing well into November, and little advantage being gained. The British Official History's comments on the situation at the end of September are, for all their measured tone, damning of the higher command of Reserve Army:

> The attack was not conducted as an operation of semi-siege warfare, so all depended upon infantry *elan* allied with the usual destructive bombardment and creeping barrage; yet on the slopes of the ridge in the confused fighting along trenches and around shell-craters and dugouts, it was often impossible for the artillery to provide close support to the assaulting troops. In the later attacks, a greater degree of coordination along the whole front might have increased the prospects of success.[64]

Although attacking on a larger scale, Reserve Army soon reverted to penny-packeted, narrow front attacks. On 28 September Gough ordered that Stuff and Schwaben Redoubts were to be taken by the following day. Yet on 29 September very small numbers of troops were used. 3rd Canadian Division used only one battalion, which co-operated with three companies of a battalion of 11th Division to capture Hessian Trench. 18th Division, probably wisely, cancelled a proposed attack by an exhausted battalion, 7/Queen's, while another battalion became involved in a fierce bombing fight. This was the sum of Reserve Army units in action that day. Stuff Redoubt was not captured in its entirety until 9 October, and the Schwaben on the 14th.[65]

Haig entrusted Gough with the BEF's last major attack on the Somme.[66] Gough's offensive was launched on either side of the River Ancre on 13 November. This area had not been heavily fought over since 1 July, with the result that the terrain, although sodden and muddy, had not been as heavily shelled as that in the southern part of the battlefield. Thus supplies could be brought forward over relatively short distances on roads superior to those in Fourth Army's sector. Gough's plan was essentially limited, with the assaulting troops given realistic objectives. He was able to field a respectable concentration of artillery, including 282 heavy guns, and a moderately complex creeping barrage was designed to support the infantry. The staff work, planning and preparation for the attack was of a generally high standard, and the assaulting troops were able to draw upon the hard-won tactical lessons of the previous five months of fighting. There were failures, but the battle, fought in two phases, was a modest success, the villages of Beaumont-Hamel and Beaucourt being the most notable gains. Gough had forced the Germans out of some strong defences, and gained good positions for launching subsequent operations. As Haig went to the inter-Allied conference in Chantilly with a victory under his belt, he might have reflected that Gough had amply repaid his confidence.

Gough's Command Style

However, the CinC's high opinion of Gough and Fifth Army was not widely shared in the BEF.[67] Gough's biographer placed much of the blame for the unpopularity of Fifth Army on its chief of staff, Major General Neill Malcolm. According to Farrar-Hockley, while Gough went round jollying his commanders along, Malcolm 'exceed[ed] his powers' by verbally beating them up, and some thought that this was a variation on the 'nice policeman, nasty policeman' routine beloved of interrogators. Moreover, Farrar-Hockley argues that these problems mostly occurred in 1917, after Beddington had left Reserve Army staff.[68] Beddington had acted as a buffer, for instance in relations with the BGGS of V Corps, who always telephoned Beddington rather than Gough or Malcolm.[69]

This gives only a part of the true picture. Certainly, Malcolm was disliked; by October 1917, Haig had got to hear of Malcolm's unpopularity.[70] In the following month Major-General G S Clive discussed the 'unpopularity of the Fifth Army command' with Malcolm. Clive noted that Malcolm 'is only beginning to hear of it, although it has been common talk for perhaps three months'. Malcolm claimed that '"doubtful" officers' were dispatched to Fifth Army in the belief that Gough would sack them if they were not up to their job.[71] Beddington, if his memoir is to be believed, in December of that year told Malcolm to his face of his unpopularity, although Malcolm does not mention it in his diary.[72] After the war Gough – no doubt eager to shift the blame – privately admitted the truth of some of the complaints, saying that although Malcolm had a 'good brain, he had not been an ideal chief of staff . . . too impatient with those who are slow, and showed it.'

He also admitted that he had been wrong in having Malcolm accompany him on trips to corps and divisions, because this stopped his subordinates from frankly discussing their problems with Malcolm, a view he also aired publicly in *The Fifth Army*.[73]

But as Michael Howard commented in his review of Farrar-Hockley's biography, there was more to Fifth Army's 'malaise' than just that.[74] There is a considerable body of evidence of problems in Gough's command during the Somme.

Command in the BEF can been characterised as only a partially successful version of what today would be described as 'mission command'. In principle, this means higher commanders setting objectives but then giving their subordinates the latitude to work out the best methods of achieving those objectives. On some occasions on the Western Front this 'hands off' approach was ineffective because of a combination of insufficiently trained subordinate commanders, the British army's lack of a culture of mission command, and the inclination of higher commanders to interfere in operations. There is certainly some truth in this picture, although it can be overdrawn. In Gough's case, things were rather different. He was a practitioner of the opposite: prescriptive, 'top-down' command. His 'hands-on' approach is reflected by Reserve Army's dealings with Corps.[75]

In 1916 the Corps level of command had several main roles. Thanks to its static position in the line, it could perform an administrative function, it controlled artillery; and it planned operations. During the Battle of the Somme, Rawlinson's Fourth Army devolved much power and responsibility to Corps in allowing them to conduct battles. By contrast, Gough used a highly prescriptive approach, using Corps as little more than 'postboxes'; that is, as methods of passing down to division detailed orders drawn up by Army – orders that were far more detailed than those issued by Rawlinson's Fourth Army. Farrar-Hockley argued that Gough liked to miss out the Corps level of command.[76] Michael Howard suggested that Gough was quite simply over-promoted, and he certainly seems to have been happiest while commanding, sometimes by remote control, low level formations.[77] Gough's almost personal control of 32nd Division during the Ancre fighting is a case in point.[78]

During the fighting on the Ancre in October–November 1916, Gough issued a memorandum 'written by the Army Commander for the guidance of Divisional and Infantry Brigade Commanders'.[79] Gough, in effect, went over the heads of his Corps commanders and told his subordinates at divisional and brigade level how to do their jobs. Gough's 'hands-on' approach was an attempt to master the dilemma well expressed by Malcolm two days before the opening of the Somme battle. Malcolm identified the problems inherent in issuing orders that would cover all eventualities in the complex operations ahead. Subordinate commanders needed to be allowed to exercise initiative, but Army had to be able to direct operations. Unfortunately, events were to prove that Malcolm's view that Reserve Army had struck the right balance was inaccurate, as this formation's style of command and control caused a good deal of friction between Gough and his subordinates.[80]

However, if his post-war comments are to be believed, Gough believed in a collegiate style of command. In 1936 he commented that GHQ

> left [Army commanders] alone and rarely came to see them. It should have treated the Army Commanders as a battalion commander treats his four company commanders, conferring with them regularly, and thrashing out questions in discussion.[81]

Not only is the accuracy of this observation dubious – Haig did visit his Army commanders regularly[82] – but Gough's wartime behaviour suggests he did not practise what he preached. Clearly, Gough believed that an Army commander was more than a mere co-ordinator of the activities of subordinate formations: he should actually command. On 6 July, writing of preparations for the battle for Ovillers, Malcolm noted that at Corps level there was a propensity to regard Gough's interventions as meddling. Gough firmly believed that his job was to command, and Malcolm had no doubt that the Army commander would win the battle of wills.[83] In August 1916 Malcolm again noted that commanders serving under Reserve Army chafed at Gough's hands-on style of command.[84]

Gough believed that commanders should 'grip' their formations. Unfortunately, his over-enthusiastic espousal of this practice at Army level made it difficult for his subordinates to command troops in the field. Sir Alymer Hunter-Weston, commander of VIII Corps, although initially admiring of Gough, was glad to leave Reserve Army after a month of being under its command. In letters to his wife, Hunter-Weston hinted of his dislike of Gough's micro-management. Hunter-Weston also criticised Gough's 'impetuosity' and 'optimism' in a conversation with Brigadier General Philip Howell, chief of staff in Lieutenant General Claud Jacob's II Corps.[85]

Resentment at Gough's methods was clearly widespread. It led to a clash with Lord Cavan, XIV Corps commander, over Reserve Army's interference with a planned operation at Beaumont Hamel.[86] An argument between Gough and the commander of 48th Division, Major General R Fanshawe, brought the latter to the verge of resignation.[87]

One of the most serious clashes was with Philip Howell. II Corps replaced Morland's X Corps in the line in late July 1916. Gough had a low opinion of Morland, who had not performed particularly well on 1 July or in Gough's view, subsequently.[88] Jacob, by contrast, was a capable commander whom Gough later described as 'the soundest soldier in the British Army'.[89] Malcolm recorded on 28 August 1916 that II Corps did not understand orders had to be obeyed. He principally blamed Howell for promoting the notion that the planning of operations was a dialectical process involving Army and Corps, with discussion of options and perhaps even the eventual rejection of Army's plan. Malcolm recognised that, given that Gough's views were diametrically opposed to Howell's, a clash was inevitable.[90] Indeed, in a private letter of 23 September 1916, Gough called Howell 'a great thorn' who 'always tries to argue, he produces the most complicated schemes, he always wants to avoid fighting, and he never loyally carries out his orders'.[91]

Howell was not an impartial witness. Apart from being on opposite sides of the Curragh controversy, Howell was an intellectual, something of a Bohemian, and a political radical, while Gough was politically conservative.[92] Both men, however, enjoyed the trust of Douglas Haig. Howell conceded that Gough was 'very loveable in many ways', but at one stage he professed to doubt Gough's sanity.[93] On joining Reserve Army, Howell expressed an 'instinctive feeling of mistrust' for Malcolm as an Army chief of staff, and his feelings hardened over the coming weeks.[94] A letter written by Howell in August offers some support for Farrar-Hockley's views on the Fifth Army's malaise: '[Gough is] really quite a child & can be managed like one if treated as such & humoured. M is at the bottom of half the mischievous ideas & mischief making . . .'[95] Even allowing for his obvious biases, Howell was an astute observer, and his diary and letters give a clear picture of the problems involved with Gough's 'hands-on' style of command, as seen from Corps level.

On taking over from X Corps in July, Howell was told by the outgoing staff that 'relations with Reserve Army [are] very strained: much interference with details & questions [&] criticism'. Moreover, 'All seem rather fed up with undue interference in details from above'. This was partly a turf fight. Gough had centralised Reserve Army artillery under Brigadier General Tancred, a move which removed control of an important function from Corps level, which seems to have been especially resented by the gunners of X Corps.[96] Very early in II Corps' tour in the front line, on 25 July, Gough arrived at II Corps headquarters to 'to direct our minor enterprises'.[97]

Clearly, as time went on, Howell became less and less tolerant of Reserve Army's style of command. On 11 August Howell noted that he had drafted a plan 'in the full knowledge that Army will interfere in all the execution details'. Sure enough, later 'Army upset the barrage arrangements'. Howell recorded that in an attack by 12th Division on 2 August Reserve Army took 'direct control of 4 machine guns!'. Malcolm and Gough certainly spent the day with Major General Scott, the commander of 12th Division, and Malcolm's diary entry suggests that they had been prodding him to take action.[98] On this occasion, Howell had a disagreement with Malcolm. When Malcolm suggested 'that all previous failures [were) due to inadequate control [being] exercised by [Gough]', Howell retorted that it was 'still more due to army commander jumping to conclusions & overruling the man on the spot'.[99] Here, in a nutshell, is the clash between two different philosophies: Reserve Army's prescriptive, top-down command, versus II Corps' devolved, decentralised version.

At almost the very end of the Somme, Malcolm issued an extraordinary confidential document to Corps. Gough had noticed, it began, that

> in certain Corps there is a marked tendency to disregard, or to dispute the advisability of, order [sic] issued from Army Headquarters, and to consult their own convenience rather than the good of the Army as a whole . . . [Orders were] not issued without due consideration of their effect and constant objection to their execution adds greatly to the burden of command.

Gough recognised that a 'spirit of discipline and loyal co-operation' should not 'hamper legitimate initiative', for 'Every commander is glad to listen to useful suggestions for the common good'. Indeed, sometimes it was right for subordinates to tell commanders that orders could not be carried out, but 'The justification or condemnation of such objections lies entirely in the spirit in which they are made'.[100]

This memorandum might seem to be aimed directly at Howell, but he had been killed by shellfire in September. It perhaps reflects the fact that around this time Malcolm came to realise that Gough had created a culture in which his subordinates were unwilling to say what they really thought. Afraid of the consequences, they carried out orders even if they disagreed with them. While not blind to the drawbacks of Gough's command style, Malcolm was convinced that often the Army Commander did indeed know best.[101]

Thus it seems that Gough recognised, at least in theory, the importance of low level initiative – although it is interesting that Malcolm's memorandum is couched almost entirely in negative terms, referring to objections to Reserve Army orders. However, Gough interpreted such objections as personal criticism. Gough's prickly personality, combined with his abrasive and prescriptive style of command and the strong personalities of some of his subordinates, inevitably led to friction.

Hubert Gough's style of command was certainly different from that of his fellow Army commander Henry Rawlinson, and was clearly disliked by a number of his subordinates. What if any difference did it make to the success of operations?

In the case of 2nd Australian Division's first attack at Pozières on 29 July, Gough's 'direct control of operations' seems to have led to disaster.[102] This division relieved 1st Australian Division after the latter's assault had captured most of the village. Although there were tactical reasons for 2nd Australian Division's failure, there is little doubt that Gough pressurised Major-General J G Legge, the divisional commander, into attacking before preparations were fully complete.[103] Bean blamed Legge, not entirely fairly, for buckling under to Gough's demands, and said that Brudenell White blamed himself for not standing up to Gough. In later years White wrote of Gough's impulsive and hasty nature.[104] The truth is that Legge should have had greater support from his superiors at Corps levels. It was not a fair competition to pit a divisional commander (especially a 'colonial' from outside the charmed circle of the British Regular army) against an Army commander. A comment of Bean's seems entirely apt in the context of Pozières: Gough's 'impetuosity is hard to stem and leads him to press schemes of his own upon subordinate units'.[105]

Can Bean's comment be related more generally to Gough's conduct of operations? Can we extrapolate from events such as Blood River, where Gough's tendencies towards impetuosity and attacking without adequate preparation were demonstrated for the first time? On learning of the German retirement in February 1917, Gough happened to be visiting the headquarters of 91 Brigade. He ordered an immediate pursuit, but the brigade commander, H R Cumming, had to point out that 'such a move was impossible before daylight on account of the nature of the ground' and the exhaustion of the troops. After a little argument, Cumming got his way, but as he recalled, Gough's departure 'with many injunctions to press on as early and as fast as possible' allowed the brigade staff to get on with the 'thousand and one details essential to the morrow's operations'. It seems that on this occasion, too, Gough overlooked the importance of detailed planning.[106]

The episode later in that year when Gough ordered, over the protests of Anzac commanders, a hasty, ill-prepared, and ultimately disastrous attack at Bullecourt, must also be entered on the debit side of the ledger.[107] Still later in 1917, Gough was responsible for the early stages of the Third Battle of Ypres (or 'Passchendaele') and his handling of these operations have been criticised upon similar lines.[108] Yet the Battle of the Ancre would suggest that Gough *was* capable of conducting a carefully prepared setpiece attack. It is perhaps of relevance that this offensive was delayed by poor weather, creating time for preparations to be completed. Bonham-Carter's comments on Gough, cited above, appear apposite in this connection. Perhaps if Gough had been served by a chief of staff with a different temperament, one who was prepared to reign in his boss's enthusiasm, Gough might have emerged as a more rounded and successful commander. Haig also deserves criticism for not exercising greater grip over his subordinate.

Gough as a Tactician
Command style should not be the sole factor used in assessing command performance. In early October 1916 Reserve Army issued over the signature of Neill Malcolm a 'memorandum of attacks . . . written by the Army for the guidance of Divisional and Infantry Brigade Commanders'.[109] This document repays study, as it sheds much light on Gough's views on tactics. As early as the spring of 1915 some British commanders were beginning to experiment with the idea of bite and hold operations. This involved carrying out fairly limited attacks with strong artillery support, aimed at seizing a portion of the enemy line, the idea being to smash up enemy counter-attacks with artillery and machine guns, before repeating the process. A leading exponent of this broadly attritional method was Henry Rawlinson, commander of Fourth Army operating on Reserve Army's flank. Rawlinson's forces achieved a number of successes using this process, including the seizure of Bazentin Ridge on 14 July and Delville Wood on 27 July. As John Lee has recently noted, however, Hubert Gough was in the opposite camp, 'fear[ing] that

opportunities for exploitation would be lost if every unit was obliged to stop at a pre-determined line, dictated by the artillery plan'.[110]

As Gough's October 1916 memorandum made clear, he favoured substantial advances into enemy positions rather than a more limited approach, envisaging troops attacking up to five separate consecutive objectives. Recognising that considerable depth of attacking troops was 'often' desirable, he recommended that brigades attack with two battalions 'up' and two in the second line, making a total of eight waves, perhaps with the last four waves in 'small columns' for speed of movement. Gough advocated a sort of conveyor belt approach, in which successive waves were dispatched under a set of standard operating procedures (SOPs) each wave having been *previously* and *definitely* detailed to their objectives', along with timetables for the advance and artillery barrages. He argued that some attacks had failed because brigade and battalion commanders had held troops back as a general reserve, waiting for firm information about where and when to commit them, and opportunities had not been exploited.

Much of this tactical advice was sensible. Gough was fully apprised of the importance of the infantry following the artillery barrage,[111] and of 'mopping-up' parties behind the assault waves. Gough's thoughts on command were an intelligent attempt to cope with a major challenge. In stressing the need for precise timetables, Gough took some of the elements of the bite and hold approach. Yet his insistance on the need to keep pushing on was the antithesis of bite and hold. Gough envisaged divisions attacking with two brigades in the front line and the third in reserve. Two battalions would take the first objective, the other two 'follow as closely as possible, pass through, and take the second objective'. When this had been achieved, brigadiers 'reorganise their battalions on the first objective . . . detailing only sufficient men to consolidate and hold the position (this should not require very much)'. The third objective was to be assaulted by the third brigade; he judged to wait until the troops of the first two brigades had reorganised would be to waste time. However, such troops would be available to attack the fourth objective, although fresh troops would be needed for an attack on a fifth. Gough accurately observed that:

> The art and difficulty of command lies in maintaining communications, knowing the position of your troops and their tactical situation, and thus being in a position to control them and to form a sound plan based on the actual facts.

As well as the adoption of SOPs, Gough believed that a partial solution to the problem lay in getting brigade and divisional commanders forward when their troops advanced. He stressed the importance of 'moving forward with their wires', that is maintaining telephone contact with superiors and subordinates, although he appears to have believed that it was best for commanders to be forward even if their electronic communications failed. At the centre of Gough's tactical memorandum was the idea of exploitation of apparent opportunities to advance. In discussing command procedures, Gough made a revealing comment:

> When cut off from advanced troops, it is no use sending officers to reconnoitre and report before coming to a decision. Valuable time is lost, and by hesitation the decision is left to the enemy. Only the immediate energetic employment . . . [of troops] in large force [could rectify the situation].

It is easy to be critical of such a comment, which seems to underline Gough's reputation for impetuosity and hasty attacks. Yet it is undoubtedly true that fleeting opportunities did go begging because of commanders' hesitation, such as after the capture of Bazentin Ridge on 14 July 1916.

However, it is difficult to avoid the conclusion that, given the state of training and experience of both infantry and artillery in 1916, Gough was asking too much of his men. Gough implicitly underplayed the importance of artillery, relying instead on infantry. But as successful operations on the Somme, at Arras and at Third Ypres was to demonstrate, under the trench warfare conditions of 1915–17, successful use of artillery was the key to success on the battlefield.

Gough's principles of attack were over-ambitious. Even successful attacks left assaulting formations weakened; quite apart from casualties sustained, men had to be used to consolidate positions, mop up pockets of resistance and the like. Those who were theoretically available to renew the assault would have been tired. Gough's assumption that sufficient troops could be organised from the two assaulting brigades to attack a fourth objective seems over-optimistic. It paid too little attention to the realities of Clausewitzian friction on the battlefield. The important tactical manual SS144, 'The Normal Formation for the Attack', promulgated in February 1917, incorporated the experience of the Somme. As Lee comments, SS144 is a compromise that reflects both a modified version of Gough's way of thinking and the opposite, which asserted that each wave should take and consolidate only one objective, with other units leap-frogging through the wave in front to advance on the next objective. The events of 31 July 1917 cast doubt on the wisdom of Gough's approach. On this, the opening day of the Third Battle of Ypres, units of Gough's Fifth Army, having obtained 'early success' took advantage of their liberty to 'push ahead' – with, as Lee comments, 'less than happy results'.[112] It is worth noting that by this time the lessons of the Somme had been absorbed, codified and disseminated; artillery and infantry tactics were considerably more advanced than a year earlier; and troops were more experienced and better trained.

Gough's finest moment might have come with the re-emergence of mobility in the Hundred Days campaign of 1918, when the BEF took the offensive under conditions of open warfare. By then, however, Gough had been removed from his command, although as many historians acknowledge, he had demonstrated a good deal of skill in his conduct of the March retreat. Gough's military vices outweighed his virtues. Whatever his talents for mobile warfare, he was not the right man to command an Army during the battle of the Somme.

NOTES

1   C E W Bean, *Two Men I Knew* (Sydney, 1957) p.134. For a more detailed discussion of this episode, see G D Sheffield, 'The Australians at Pozières: Command on the Somme', in D French and B Holden Reid, *The British General Staff: Reform and Innovation* (London, 2002).

2   A[ustralian] W[ar] M[emorial], AWM 45, [35/1, 35112], X Corps to Reserve Army, 18 July 1916.

3   Walker's Chief of Staff, who played a role in devising 1st Australian Division's plan, was Lieutenant Colonel (later Field Marshal Sir) Thomas Blamey. D Homer, *Blarney: The Commander-in-Chief* (St Leonards, 1998) pp.43–5

4   *Ibid*, 134; AWM, Bean Papers, 3 DRL, 7953, item 34, Walker to Bean, 13 Aug.1928; P A Pedersen, 'The AIF on the western front: the role of training and command' in M McKernan and M Browne, *Australia Two Centuries of War & Peace* (Canberra, 1988) p.173.

5   AWM, Bean Papers, 3 DRL 7953, item 34, Edmonds to Bean, 16 Nov.1927, enclosing 'General Sir Hubert Gough's remarks'.

6   Sir Hubert Gough, *The Fifth Army* (London, 1931) p.133.

7   *Ibid*, pp.129, 143.

8   E Beddington, *My Life* (privately published, 1960) p.103. Quotations are from a copy in the author's possession; there is another in the L[iddell] H[art] C[entre) for M[ilitary] A[rchives], King's College London.

9   B H Liddell Hart, *Memoirs*, Vol. I, p.364. The former prime minister used his new found friend as an additional stick with which to beat Douglas Haig, claiming, for instance, that Haig used Gough as a scapegoat to divert attention from his (Haig's) own failings in March 1918. David Lloyd George, *War Memoirs*, Vol.11 (London, c. 1938) pp.1741–2, 2019.

10 LHCMA, L[iddell] H[art] P[apers), LH 1/323/16, Liddell Hart to Arthur Barker, 19 Sept.1954.

11 LHCMA, LHP, 11/1935/114, 'Talk with Gen. Sir Charles Bonham-Carter'.

12 For a cautiously favourable assessment of Gough set in the wider context of the British Army, see I F W Beckett, 'Hubert Gough, Neill Malcolm and Command on the Western Front' in B Bond *et al, 'Look To Your Front: Studies in the First World War'* (Staplehurst, 1999) pp.1–12.

13 G de S Barrow, *The Fire of Life* (London, nd) 19.

14 The Marquis of Anglesey, *A History of the British Cavalry* Vol. IV, *1899–1913* (London, 1986), 122, 186, 264.

15 A Farrar-Hockley, *Goughie* (London, 1975), 65–8; H Gough, *Soldiering On* (London, 1954), 83–9.

16 Anglesey, *British Cavalry* IV, 264.

17 For some interesting views on Gough in the 1914 campaign, see N Gardner, *Trial by Fire: Command and the British Expeditionary Force in 1914* (Westport, CT, 2003).

18 F Maurice, *Rawlinson of Trent* (London, 1928) 85–6.

19 LHCMA, LHP, LH 11/1935/72 'Talk with Sir Hubert Gough' 9 Apr. 1935; T Travers, *The Killing Ground* (London, 1987), 104.

20 D R Woodward (ed.), *The Military Correspondence of Field-Marshal Sir William Robertson, Chief of the Imperial General Staff, December 1915–February 1918* (London, 1989), 7.

21 Letter from Gough, 29 Jan.1916, quoted in R Holmes, *The Little Field Marshal* (London, 1981) 1. In later life, Gough was somewhat more charitable: *Soldiering On*, 127.

22 K Jeffrey, *The Military Correspondence of Field Marshal Sir Henry Wilson 1918–1922* (London, 1985), editor's introduction, 9–10.

23 LHCMA, LHP, LH 11/1935/72 'Talk with Sir Hubert Gough', 9 Apr. 1935.

24 Gough, *Soldiering On*, 171–3; LHCMA, LHP, LH 1/323/44, review of *Tonight* programme by Maurice Richardson, in *The Observer* 24 Mar. 1963. For the view that Wilson was more sinned against than sinning, see B Collier, *Brasshat: A Biography of Field-Marshal Sir Henry Wilson* (London, 1961), 214–15.

25 J Williams, *Byng of Vimy* (London, 1992), 36–7.

26 LHCMA, LHP, LH 11/1935/107 'Talk with Lloyd George and General Sir Hubert Gough (at the Athenaeum)', 28 Nov. 1935.

27 LHCMA, LHP, LH 1/323/17, Gough to Liddell Hart, 22 Sept. 1954.

28 Williams, op. cit., 139.

29 *Ibid*, 236.

30 J M Bourne, 'British Generals in the First World War' in G D Sheffield (ed.), *Leadership and Command: The Anglo-American Military Experience since 1861* (London, 1997), 109.

31 LHCMA, LHP, LH 11/1935/107, 'Talk with Lloyd George and General Sir Hubert Gough (at the Athenaeum)', 28 Nov. 1935.

32 Anglesey, *British Cavalry* IV, 75.

33 Gough, *Soldiering On*, 125.

34 C Carrington, *Soldier from the Wars Returning* (London, 1965), 104.

35 I Beckett, *Johnnie Gough, VC* (London, 1989) 206, 208; P Simkins, 'Haig and the Army Commanders' in B Bond and N Cave, *Haig: A Reappraisal 70 Years on* (Barnsley, 1999), 88.

36 K Simpson, 'The Reputation of Sir Douglas Haig' in B Bond (ed.), *The First World War and British Military History* (Oxford, 1991), 145.

37 G A B Dewar assisted by J H Boraston, *Sir Douglas Haig's Command* (London, 1922), 184–5. This chapter is initialled 'JHB'.

38 S Badsey, 'Cavalry and the Development of Breakthrough Doctrine' in P Griffith (ed.), *British Fighting Methods in the Great War* (London, 1996), 153–5.

39 Farrar-Hockley, op. cit., 152–3.

40 I owe this suggestion to Dr Stephen Badsey.

41 Lady A Gordon Lennox (ed.), *The Diary of Lord Bertie of Thame* (London, 1924), 114 (diary entry 10 Mar. 1917); D R Woodward, *Lloyd George and the Generals* (Newark, 1983), 51.

42 R Prior and T Wilson, *Command on the Western Front* (Oxford, 1992), 268.

43 D French, *The Strategy of the Lloyd George Coalition, 1916–1918* (Oxford, 1995), 232–3.

44 C E Caliwell, *Field-Marshal Sir Henry Wilson,* Vol. II (London, 1927), 78.

45 French, op. cit., 233.

46 Lennox, op. cit., 287, 289.

47 N(ational] L[ibrary of] S[cotland], Haig diary, 26 Mar., 3 Apr.1918.

48 Beddington, op. cit., 173–4.

49 NLS, Haig Papers, Haig to wife, 16 Jun. 1918 and Haig to Gough, 6 July 1918; Williams, op. cit., 236.

50 G J De Groot, *Douglas Haig 1861–1928* (London, 1988), 83.

51 AWM, AWM 45 30/1–30/11, 2 and 3 July 1916, 'Extracts from War Diary of G S Reserve Army'.

52 AWM, AWM 252 [A116], O.A.D. 36, 'Note of interview at Fourth Army Headquarters . . . at mid-day, 2 July, 1916; OA.D. 43, 'Note' by Kiggell, 4 July 1916; O.A.D. 39, 'Confirmation of telephone conversation between the C.G.S and the G.O.C. Fourth Army. 7.10pm 2/7/16.

53 W Miles (ed.), *Military Operations, France and Belgium, 1916* (London, 1932). Vol. II, 10–15. This is the British Official History, henceforth abbreviated to 'BOH'.

54 AWM, AWM 252 [A131] S.G.59/0/1, 'Proposed Scheme for the Capture of Courcelette and Formation of a Defensive Flank' 28 Aug. 1916; AWM, AWM 252 [A116], O.A.D. 44, 'Notes of arrangements made verbally with Sir. H. Gough on 2nd and 4th July, 1916'.

55 AWM 252 [A116], O.A.D. 68, Kiggell to Third Army, 15 July 1916.

56 Miles, *BOH* 1916 II, 102.

57 See Prior and Wilson, *Command.*

58 Farrar-Hockley, op. cit., 190.

59 O.A.D. 91, 2 August 1916, in Miles, *BOH* 1916 II, Maps and Appendices, 34–6

60 O.A.D.91, 'The Commander-in-Chief's Instructions to the Fourth and Reserve Armies, 2nd August' in *BOH* 1916 II, Appendices, 35.

61 AWM 252 [A116], O.A.D.137, 5 Sept. 1916, 'Note of Interview with Sir H. Gough, on 4th September, 1916'. See also O.A.D. 116, G.H.Q. Plan for a mid-September Offensive' 19 Aug. 1916, in *BOH* 1916, Appendices, 46–7.

62 AWM 45 [35/9] S.G 21/0/32, memo from Reserve Army, 5 Sept.1916.

63 Miles, *BOH* 1916 II, 301–2.

64 *Ibid*, 422. The last sentence is also implicitly critical of Haig.

65 *Ibid*, 420–1, 453–4

66 See *BOH* 1916 II, 476–524.

67 P Gibbs, *Realities of War* (London, 1920), 389; B Bond and S Robbins, (ed.), *Staff Officer: The Diaries of Lord Moyne 1914–1918* (London, 1987), 162–4; Beckett, 'Hubert Gough', 2–4.

68 Farrar-Hockley, op. cit., 226–9.

69 *Ibid*, 228–9; Beddington, op. cit., 102.

70 NLS, Haig diary, 5 Oct. 1917, 9 Dec. 1917.

71 P[ublic] R[ecord] O[ffice], CAB 45/201/3, Major General G S Clive Papers, Diary, 25 Nov. 1917.

72 Beddington. op. cit., 121–2; Neill Malcolm papers, diary (I am grateful to Captain Dugald Malcolm for giving me access to this diary).

73 LHCMA, LHP, LH 11/1936/31, 'Talk with L[loyd] G[eorge] and Hubert Gough' 27 Jan.1936; Gough, op. cit., 134.

74 LHCMA, LHP, LH 1/323/48.

75 See Andy Simpson's chapter elsewhere in this book, and A Simpson, 'The

Operational Role of British Corps Command on the Western front, 1914–18'
(PhD thesis, University of London, 2001).

76 Farrar-Hockley, op. cit., 188.

77 LHCMA, LHP, LH 1/323/48.

78 PRO, CAB 45/134, E G Wace to J E Edmonds, 30 Oct. 1936; P Simkins,
'Somme footnote: the Battle of the Ancre and the struggle for Frankfort
Trench, November 1916', *Imperial War Museum Review* No.9, 96–100.

79 PRO, WO 95/518, Memo, 5 Oct. 1916.

80 Malcolm diary, 29 June 1916.

81 HCMA, LHP, LH 11/1936/31 'Talk with L G and Hubert Gough' 27 Jan. 1936.

82 Simkins, 'Haig and his Army Commanders', 95–6.

83 Malcolm diary, 6 July 1916. He made a similar comment on 13 July 1916.

84 *Ibid*, 18 Aug. 1916.

85 British Library, Hunter-Weston Papers, no. 48365, Hunter-Weston to wife, 1,
12 July, 3 August 1916 (I owe these references to Andy Simpson); LHCMA,
P[hilip] H[owell] P[apers], 6/2/161, diary, 16 July 1916.

86 WO95/1293, XIV Corps note, 3 Aug. 1916.

87 Malcolm diary, 25 Aug. 1916; diary, LHCMA, PHP, IV/D/13, 25 Aug. 1916.

88 LHCMA, PHP, 6/2/161, diary, 22 July 1916 and, 6/1/190, Howell to wife, 22
July 1916; NLS, Haig diary 23 July 1916. For a positive view of Morland by a
junior regimental officer, see A Eden, *Another World* (London, 1976), 124.

89 Gough, *Soldiering On*, 132.

90 Malcolm diary, 28 Aug. 1916.

91 Beckett, 'Hubert Gough', 8.

92 [R Howell] *Philip Howell: a memoir by his wife* (London, 1942), 42.

93 LHCMA, PHP 6/1/198, Howell to wife, 12 Aug. 1916.

94 LHCMA, PHP 6/1/185, Howell to wife, 15 July 1916, 6/1/193, same to same,
29 July 1916; 6/1/196, same to same, 7 Aug. 1916.

95 LHCMA, PHP, IV/C/329, Howell to wife, 2 Aug. 1916

96 AWM, AWM45 30/1–30/11, Reserve Army memos G.339, 13 July 1916, and
S.G.3/1/7, 24 July 1916; LHCMA, PHP IV/D/13, diary, 23, 24 July 1916.

97 LHCMA, PHP IV/D/13, diary, 25 July 1916.

98 Malcolm diary, 3 Aug. 1916. 12th Division's history, co-authored by Scott,
perhaps unsurprisingly makes no mention of Gough's intervention, although
it does cite a complementary order issued by Reserve Army when the
Division passed out of his command later in August. A B Scott and P M
Brumwell, *History of the 12th (Eastern) Division in the Great War* (London,
1923), 63–4, 73–4.

99 LHCMA, PHP IV/D/13, diary, 2 Aug. 1916.

100 PRO, WO 95/518, Confidential memo. from Fifth Army to Corps, 16 Nov.
1916.

101 Malcolm diary, 21–22 Nov. 1916.

102 Pederson, 'The AIF', 174. For a fuller discussion of this attack see Sheffield,
The Australians at Pozières.

103 LHCMA, PHP, IV/D/13, diary, 29 July 1916, Howell Papers.

104 AWM, Bean Papers, 3 DRL 7953 item 4, White to Bean, 19 Sep. 1927.

105 AWM, Bean Papers, 3 DRL 7953 item 34, Bean to Edmonds, 28 Apr. 1928.

106 H R Cumming, *A Brigadier in France* (London, 1922) 44–5.

107 For Bullecourt, see E M Andrews, 'Bean and Bullecourt: Weaknesses and
Strengths of the Official History of Australia in the First World War', *Revue
Internationale d'Histoire Militaire*, No.72 (Canberra, 1990), 25–47; J Walker,
The Blood Tub: General Gough and the Battle of Bullecourt 1917 (Staplehurst,
1998).

108 See A Wiest, 'Haig, Gough and Passchendaele' in Sheffield, *Leadership and Command* 77–92.

109 PRO, WO95/1293, Reserve Army S.G.43/0/5.

110 J Lee, 'Some Lessons of the Somme: The British Infantry in 1917' in Bond, *Look to your Front*, 86.

111 Reserve Army issued a memorandum that consisted of a note from GHQ (OAD 256,16 July 1916) on the importance of the creeping barrage, with an endorsement by Gough: AWM, AWM252 [A133], S.G.31/3/1, 17 July 1916.

112 Lee, op. cit., 84.

CHAPTER V

British Corps Command
on the Western Front, 1914–1918

Andy Simpson

This chapter is concerned with the role of British corps command on the Western Front, which primarily consisted of the planning and execution of operations. The role of corps command is here differentiated from the role of corps commanders, because sources about them as individuals are, on the whole, scant and at times contradictory. It will argue that, in the course of the Great War, the role of British corps command expanded considerably, as corps developed from being a relatively unimportant, administrative link in the chain of command, to playing a central role in the organisation of operations and acting as the highest level of operational command.[1] In addition, the ideas which provided the doctrinal basis for this function and how they were applied in practice will be discussed. The Canadian and ANZAC corps are not included, as they were not typical of corps in the British Expeditionary Force (henceforth the BEF) as a whole, for two principal reasons. Firstly, they almost always consisted of the same divisions, while British corps had quite frequent changes in their constituent divisions, and secondly their relationship, as semi-independent national contingents, with the levels of command above (that is to say, Army and GHQ), was quite different from that of British corps.

In 1914 the corps was not a new part of the army's organisation. Between 1888 and the Haldane reforms of 1906–8, the army had been organised to put into the field three 'army corps', of which two were Regular and for use in overseas expeditions as required, and the country was divided into six corps areas.[2] These were renamed 'Commands' in 1904, and some debate as to whether Home forces were to be organised in three army corps or six self-contained divisions then took place. In the end, the latter won the day, as they were both 'more suitable to the size and requirements of our army' and 'more flexible than an army-corps organisation'. It was accepted that if corps were formed, they would have a permanent staff, but the view was taken that a corps could be more easily improvised than separate divisions.[3] However, from 1904 onwards, corps had moved into a kind of limbo, where their status as 'real' formations was even questioned. When the system of Commands was set up, the Director of Military Training raised at an Army Council meeting 'the question whether the Aldershot force should not still be called an "army-corps"'. The Chief of the General Staff agreed, saying that 'the objection commonly entertained to the use of the term, viz., that the corps does not really exist, does not apply in this case'.[4] This was because only the Aldershot Command, which in wartime corresponded to I Corps, had a peacetime corps staff. At a Staff College conference in 1908, Brigadier General William Robertson (later Chief of the Imperial General Staff, 1915–18) observed 'that there was no headquarters organisation laid down in war establishments between that for a division and that for an army'. The Director of Staff Duties, Major General Douglas Haig, replied that the matter 'had been thrashed out, but had not yet been published . . . It was very important, for if we went to war, it would seem impossible for one man to command efficiently six divisions.'[5] Consequently, the Expeditionary Force Tables of 1912 and 1914 showed two 'armies' below GHQ; it should be noted that corps were referred to variously as 'corps', 'army' or 'army corps'.[6] The clearest statement of corps' function, though, was made in 1913, when the Deputy Director of Military Operations, Colonel G M Harper (later a corps commander himself), stated that corps was to act simply as a conduit or post-box, through which orders would pass on their way from GHQ to the divisions.[7]

So, what was a corps, at the start of the First World War? A formation subordinate to GHQ, and from 1915 to an Army, it was usually commanded by a lieutenant general and composed of a variable number of infantry or cavalry divisions or occasionally both.[8] The infantry division, consisting of three brigades of four battalions apiece, was considered to be the basic tactical unit of all arms. In British corps, the only permanent members were the staff (i.e. those officers responsible for the administration and operations of the corps) and the corps troops, comprising at the start of the war only a cable section. The BEF in August 1914 was commanded by Field-Marshal Sir John French, whose corps commanders were Lieutenant Generals Sir Douglas Haig and Sir Horace Smith-Dorrien (I and II Corps, respectively; II Corps was initially commanded by Sir James Grierson, but he died on 17 August). Each corps consisted of two infantry divisions, and in addition, the BEF had five brigades of cavalry. Although skeleton divisional staffs had been maintained in peacetime, only the Aldershot Command, as noted above, had a peacetime corps staff.[9]

Before going on to consider how corps operated on the Western Front, it is important to clarify the theoretical basis for the BEF's operations. This was embodied in *Field Service Regulations (1909) Part I (Operations)*, henceforth referred to as *FSR*. This volume set out the principles under which the army should operate, these being amplified in the appropriate training manuals. In other words, *FSR* was a set of general principles for application by trained and experienced officers, which specifically avoided going into too much detail, assuming that those applying them should, through experience and training, know what actions to perform within their framework. This modus operandi reflected the general reluctance within the British army to accept a formal doctrine – defined as 'a set of beliefs about the nature of war and the keys to success on the battlefield.'[10] – at the time.[11] In fact, it has recently been suggested that, regarding a standardised doctrine as inapplicable, the British army adopted instead an ethos (defined as 'the characteristic spirit and the prevalent sentiment, taste, or opinion of a people, institution or system'). This worked better than a standardised doctrine, because it enabled the adoption of a flexible approach, required by the varied nature of the challenges the army might have faced before the war.[12] As a result, the BEF could absorb a huge increase in numbers and tremendous changes in technology and tactics without undergoing the sort of wholesale re-organisation which the Germans undertook, and which led to the stormtroop tactics which played such an important part in Germany's defeat, notwithstanding their tactical utility. The flexibility of *FSR* was such that it remained applicable despite the enormous changes in the way in which the army waged war. This was most crucial in the volume of artillery employed and the techniques used to make it more effective, though new weapons were also introduced and worked into the conceptual framework of the army. So long as the associated manuals were updated to take account of new developments, *FSR* provided a sound basis for action.

It is important to emphasise that *FSR* reflected Douglas Haig's views on warfare, having being drawn up under his sponsorship, sometime between 1907 and 1909, when he was Director of Staff Duties. Haig believed that warfare was structured, with battles falling into four stages, and *FSR* expounded the principles for action in each. The stages were, firstly, the preparatory, or 'wearing out' fight, designed to (secondly) pull in the enemy reserves and leading to (thirdly) the decisive assault on the weakened enemy, which would lead in its turn to (fourthly) the phase of exploitation.[13] The other important strand in Haig's thinking, and one he had in common with many of his contemporaries, was a belief in the importance of moral factors on the modern battlefield, and the consequent cult of the offensive. Given the firepower available, heavy casualties were inevitable, but the side with the greater moral force would prevail, and this would be the attackers; the defensive was held to be inherently morally inferior.[14] These views have been used as examples of Haig's traditionalist mindset, a belief in psychological factors being held (by Tim

Travers, for example) to be inconsistent with a twentieth-century technological battlefield. However, psychology is important on the battlefield; good generals usually pay attention to morale and attempt to nurture it (Field Marshal Montgomery is a good example). Furthermore, given the interest Haig displayed in tanks, gas and even, at one point, a death ray, it seems unfair to say that his belief in the psychological battlefield led him to ignore new weapons.[15] Travers is right to say that new weapons were integrated with existing ideas to some extent, but this is not unreasonable; tanks and the like were 'incapable of effective independent action,' as Haig asserted.[16] A striking (if unsuccessful) example of new and old technologies being merged is the use of gas at Loos, intended by Haig to make up for the BEF's lack of artillery power, and so help the artillery attain the superiority of fire required by *FSR* for the decisive assault.[17]

In addition to the structured battle on the psychological battlefield, *FSR* contained two other, less commonly, emphasised aspects of Haig's thought. The first was that orders should not enter into too much detail, instead leaving the man on the spot to use his own initiative.[18] This concept of 'the man on the spot' was important in *FSR* in determining how orders were to work in practice, but it was not clearly defined. However, it would seem to have approximated to 'the nearest responsible subordinate to the site of the action of the officer issuing orders'. The second relates to operational tempo. Tempo in this context is defined as 'the rate or rhythm of activity relative to the enemy'.[19] *FSR* did not explicitly mention the concept, but it is evident that Haig was aware of the need to seize the initiative in operations. The battle would be fought by pinning the enemy down through superiority of fire and a series of preliminary assaults, designed to pull in his reserves, and then victory would be won by launching the decisive assault at a preselected point.[20] Higher tempo would be attained by pinning the enemy down and using up his reserves.

The next question is to what extent the precepts of *FSR* were applied in practice. As GOC I Corps in 1914, Haig applied *FSR* whenever possible. His use of a rearguard composed of all arms during the Retreat from Mons was entirely proper. The Battle of the Aisne was a conventional assault, and the inability of the BEF to break through the German position could reasonably be ascribed to a failure to attain the superiority of fire *FSR* deemed necessary for the assault.[21] The First Battle of Ypres, the BEF's only experience of an encounter battle, rapidly became a defensive action, in which the deployment of reserves was vital, much as prescribed by *FSR*; even corps troops were used.[22] Whenever possible, counter-attacks were made, which also conformed to *FSR* for the defensive battle. However, while *FSR* saw these as the prelude to a resumption of the offensive, the manpower was not available to do this. As regards operational tempo in 1914, the BEF was perfectly capable of mounting an attack at only a day's notice, as was demonstrated by I Corps on the Aisne and II Corps between 11 and 20 October.[23] Since corps had little to do in organising the attack apart from passing on GHQ's orders to divisions, and there was no requirement for any level of command to draw up and co-ordinate the sort of complex fireplan for the artillery that became routine by the end of 1916, this swiftness is not surprising.

I Corps continued to work within the framework of *FSR* in 1915 (when Haig had become its Army commander), though the status of corps rose sharply as they increased their control of artillery in attacks. It is difficult to see how *FSR* could be applied at all, as trench warfare rendered redundant most of its assumptions about an attack; reconnaissance by a cavalry screen or the manoeuvring of troops into an advantageous position (for example) were now impossible. However, it appears that for Neuve Chapelle, the deployment of troops and other preliminary stages of the battle were now carried out the night before, and the assault, which had been in the manuals the last stage of the attack, now became its first.[24] By this reasoning, all the offensives of 1915 were to some extent in accordance with *FSR*. In a I Corps conference, just before the battle, it was stressed that the key to breaking the German line was 'offensive action'. Consequently, commanders were 'to carefully consider the employment of their reserves' to maintain momentum, though 'at the same time, the principle of securing ground already gained must not be overlooked'.[25] The stress on the offensive, the building up of the firing line and the principle of consolidation all belonged in *FSR*'s offensive battle. However, I Corps' part in Neuve Chapelle was a failure and a post-mortem took place in order to discover the lessons of the battle. Training notes issued soon afterwards contained ideas drawn both from *FSR* and from experience.[26] Importantly, they also stressed the need for corps and divisional commanders to be guided by the advice of their artillery and RE advisers. However, it is also apparent that corps were still acting only as a medium of communication between GHQ, Army and divisions, rather than taking a more active role in operations. This also applied to the next attacks, at Aubers and Festubert. However, at Festubert artillery control had proved problematic, when command of the artillery of three divisions was given to one divisional artillery commander, with no extra staff. Therefore, in August the I Corps artillery adviser, the Brigadier General, Royal Artillery (or BGRA) was given a staff of four officers and told to control all the artillery within the corps during the forthcoming attack at Loos. This represented a major increase in the importance of corps.

At about the same time, I Corps began to be less strict in its application of *FSR*. It adopted a more assertive attitude than hitherto towards its subordinate divisions, moving towards a more centralised style of command. The commander of 28th Division (Major General E S Bulfin) was sent a stinging rebuke in early October for the way in which he had framed orders to his brigades.[27] That it was deemed necessary to rebuke the commander of a Regular division so sharply may reflect corps' view of the shortcomings of a staff improvised on the unit's formation. *FSR* generally recommended a decentralised style of command, but it was intended to be used by properly trained officers, and corps was compelled to centralise authority if subordinate formations lacked these, particularly on the staff.

Indeed, one of the most significant problems faced by the BEF in 1915–16 was that its rapid expansion led to a shortage of staff officers. In the period from the outbreak of war to the end of 1914, the BEF expanded from two to four British infantry corps. By the end of 1915 the number had gone up to thirteen, and all their staffs had to be improvised apart from that of I Corps. This expansion was accompanied by an increase in the number of staff officers at corps HQ from eighteen at mobilisation to twenty-four by June 1916. At the same time, the administrative responsibilities of corps increased, as they took over a number of divisional functions. The greater responsibilities of corps were demonstrated by the rise in number of Corps Troops. From consisting of only a cable section in 1914, by early 1916 they were composed of a corps cavalry regiment, a cyclist battalion, a motor machine-gun battery, the corps signal company and associated troops, the corps ammunition park, three supply columns, an Army Service Corps company, mobile ordnance workshops, several Heavy Artillery Groups, and engineer and RFC detachments.[28] Corps took over from divisions responsibility for traffic control and road maintenance, and controlled the movement of supplies from railheads to the divisional loading points. One reason for corps taking over such functions from division was that though divisions were rotated through corps relatively frequently, corps were far less mobile. It was decided early in the war that it was too difficult to move entire corps around the front and that divisional reliefs were easier.[29] This also had the effect that corps staffs had time to become thoroughly familiar with their sectors, as did the heavy artillery under their command (which also tended towards immobility, as those batteries were very time-consuming to move – a 9.2-inch howitzer, for example, took thirty-six hours to prepare for transit).

Given its expansion, the BEF had perforce to learn from experience, and in late 1915 corps' role began to change. This stemmed from the formalisation of the artillery arrangements made before Loos, providing a good example of the ability of the BEF to learn from experience. After the battle, the Chief of the General Staff at GHQ (Sir William Robertson) stated that the recent fighting had demonstrated the need for a carefully worked-out artillery plan, which required effective artillery command for its execution.[30] Consequently, the BGRA became the 'General Officer Commanding Royal Artillery' (or GOCRA) of the corps. The memorandum went on to say that he 'will be charged with the co-ordination of the action of the artillery of the Corps, and the executive command of such portions of it as the Corps Commander may direct . . .' Although this did not extend to the heavy artillery, divisional artillery could now be withdrawn from the command of the divisional GOC if the corps commander wished it, representing a significant transfer of power to corps, and by the following May the GOCRA commanded the heavy artillery of the corps (in practice, at least) as well. In addition, a corps wing RFC was allotted, to work with the artillery.

Before discussing the BEF's operations in 1916–18, it is necessary to comment on its decision-making process. There are two diametrically opposed views on this matter. The first is that of the Official Historian, who asserted that 'Before any offensive took place there were . . . not only conferences between the Commanders-in-Chief, but between the Commander-in-Chief and his Army Commanders, between the Army Commanders, their staff, and their corps commanders, etc., etc.'[31] The second is exemplified by the work of Travers, who argues that discussion, especially of GHQ's plans, was by no means encouraged, and that a similar tendency applied at Army and corps commanders' conferences.[32] However, this seems not to be borne out by the evidence at corps and Army level, at least. Nevertheless, from late 1915 through to late 1916 corps' greater control over artillery led them to breach *FSR*, in that they tended to leave their subordinates less and less scope for the exercise of initiative, despite the view of *FSR* that the man on the spot knew best. But to some extent he did not, if he was a divisional commander on the Western Front. Once an attack had been launched, he quickly lost touch with events, whereas, because of the information supplied by the corps wing RFC, a corps commander could be in a better position to understand the situation in the front line than his divisional commanders, and the duty of passing information forward as well as back fell to corps.

Corps' most important role, in 1916 as it was later, was in the planning of operations. In discussing this point, this chapter will go into rather more detail for the planning for 1 July 1916 than for the other offensives the BEF undertook in the second half of the war because it is an important turning point as the prototype of the later operations, which built upon the command structures in place in mid-1916. For some commanders, planning was all. The optimistic Sir Aylmer Hunter-Weston, GOC VIII Corps, wrote to his wife, the night before the Somme offensive began, that 'I have, with my excellent staff, done all possible to ensure success . . . I have nothing more to do now but to rest till well after the attack has taken place.'[33] During the planning for the Somme, Army and GHQ decided on the frontage of attack for each corps, and once this had been settled, it was up to the corps to take the necessary steps to ensure they could do their jobs.[34] Firstly, from March 1916, artillery resources had to be gathered and positions prepared. Dugouts for gunners, magazines, observation posts, telephone lines and exchanges, roads, light railways and tramways (these last three for the carriage of ammunition) all had to be constructed.[35] The Administrative Staff had to arrange traffic control and ammunition supply, and signalling arrangements were made.[36] As well as artillery, each corps was told how many divisions it had been allotted, what RFC support it could expect and what labour was available for its preparations.[37] In addition, liaison with neighbouring corps was undertaken, owing to the necessity of siting some batteries in their areas to provide enfilade fire.[38]

While the infrastructure for the attack was being created, the details of the advance required had to be settled and communicated down the chain of command. Objectives were generally agreed between Army and corps (within the framework of the plan agreed by Army and GHQ) and Army would assign corps the resources which it was hoped would be adequate for the task. Although Fourth Army (to which the main attack was entrusted) was not prescriptive in its attitude to tactics (contrary to popular belief it did not order that everyone advance across no-man's-land at a slow walk), it was necessary for the MGRA (Major General, Royal Artillery – the Army artillery adviser) to co-ordinate all corps' artillery, so the first ever Army Artillery Operation Order was produced. This was not unduly detailed, but, crucially, the timetable was very much Army's, though corps could make their own arrangements within it.[39] Next divisions were informed of their objectives and the artillery plan and expected to come up with the detailed plans of attack, with corps co-ordinating these between their various divisions. But there was discussion and consultation at all stages during this process, the GOCRA, for example, being careful to include locations in his plan which divisions felt needed special attention. So, in general, divisions operated within the parameters set them by corps, but were not merely dictated to. However, VIII Corps was something of an exception to this. At Hunter-Weston's conferences, on 21 and 23 June, the specific object of which was 'to give Brigadiers an opportunity of discussing their plans with each other', he did all the talking.[40] This included a rueful acknowledgement that the dead would be too numerous to allow their cremation, and so they should be buried in pits. It is fortunate that the section headed 'All Units Must Push On Resolutely' preceded, rather than followed, this encouraging advice. The sheer volume of the corps scheme – over seventy pages under twenty-eight headings – perhaps explains Hunter-Weston's feeling that he could do nothing more once the attack had started. It went into great detail, and seems to have been constructed on the basis that nothing could or would go wrong.[41] It is unfortunate that VIII Corps suffered the highest casualties for the smallest gain of ground of all the corps involved.[42]

But a degree of inflexibility was built into the overall plan, as for the first time, corps retained overall control of their artillery after zero, whereas in previous attacks control had reverted to division at that time.[43] Consequently, GOsC of divisions and brigades were unable to change the fireplan if things did not go as expected. However, the significance of this can be overstated, given the paucity of information available to divisional commanders after zero. In any case, all a corps GOC could do once the attack had begun, was to distribute his reserves and to alter the artillery plans to take account of the situation as it appeared at corps HQ. Hunter-Weston, notwithstanding his belief that he would have nothing to do on the day, actively directed the operations of his divisions to prevent further losses after the first assault and to make what gains they could.[44] In contrast, Lieutenant General W N Congreve, of XIII Corps (whose divisions took all their objectives and had only lightly defended positions in front of them afterwards), actively directed his divisions only twice during the day.[45] The reason would seem to be that the more things went to plan, the less the corps commander had to do; under those circumstances, divisions could look after themselves. And once XIII Corps had taken its objectives, there was no more to be done on its front, as no reserves were available for quick exploitation.[46] The inflexibility of Fourth Army's plan robbed its subordinates of the chance to use their initiative unless it broke down. This was one of a number of factors which denied both Fourth and Fifth Armies the chance to attain higher tempo than their opponents during the whole campaign. The others were lack of strategic surprise and the sheer slowness of the advances made, combined with the lack of enough artillery both to support them and simultaneously to advance to assist the next attack. The Germans always had sufficient time to react and the BEF lacked the men and material to launch a major attack elsewhere in order to unbalance them.

On 4 July the Reserve Army came into the line. Its GOC was General Hubert Gough, whose command style was far more prescriptive than that of Sir Henry Rawlinson of Fourth Army. At the same time, corps continued to work as far as possible in the spirit of *FSR*. The two left flank corps (VIII and X) of Fourth Army came under the command of the Reserve Army, and VIII Corps was sent to the Ypres sector at the end of July and replaced by XIV Corps, under the Earl of Cavan, one of the outstanding corps commanders of the war. Cavan and Gough had very different command styles. Cavan, for example, began his service on the Somme with a rather apologetic assertion of authority. On 3 August he issued a document which clearly indicated a command style consonant with *FSR* and a willingness to learn within its framework.

> Without wishing in any way to curb the initiative of Divisional Commanders, I should like to impress the following short memoranda on the minds of all, which are based on the experiences of this battle, backed by the teaching of our text books.[47]

Cavan's relationship with Reserve Army was less diffident than that with his subordinates. In correspondence with Army over a plan to capture Beaumont Hamel, he began by stating that 'After further discussion with Divisional Commanders, I would prefer to adhere to the original plan submitted . . .', and went on to dissect Army's memorandum, paragraph by paragraph, to explain why.[48] His parting shot was to observe that VIII Corps had made the same attack on 1 July with far more support from neighbouring corps. All this argues against the one way, top-down communication and climate of fear described by Travers, although Cavan was less likely to fear the termination of his military career than most, having retired from the army once (in 1913) already.[49]

However, Gough left his corps commanders in no doubt of his views on how they should do their job, feeling the need to exercise close control over the planning of operations because he had far less capacity to control events after zero hour. For example, one memorandum (16 July) read:

> The Army Commander considers that in any bombardment scheme the exact points to be attacked by Heavy Howitzers should be selected by the G. Branch of the Corps in conjunction with the Corps Artillery Commander.[50]

Others in a similar vein followed, constituting what has been described in a different context as a 'boys'-own-guide' to drafting orders and commanding a corps. It is not surprising, therefore, that Reserve Army attack orders reflected this style.[51] Those for 24 August 1916, for example, went into far more detail than anything from Fourth Army. The objectives of the attacking divisions were given – not as lines to be seized by corps, but explicitly by division. Each division was told what it should do in the way of flank protection, pushing forward patrols in the event of a success, and maintaining a reserve. Corps were only mentioned when their boundaries were outlined and the need to cut wire along the whole of their fronts was brought up. In effect, Army used them as postboxes. This approach is explained by Gough's realisation that higher commanders were almost powerless to influence events once the attack had started. Therefore, close control of planning gave the Army commander the best chance he had of controlling how the attack went, and this led to the development of increasingly structured attack plans.

This less flexible approach to command reflected a degree of confusion regarding how best to proceed in the army as a whole. Gough's style may have been a quite reasonable reaction to the completely different nature of warfare in late 1916, compared to anything contemplated earlier. In July the CIGS (Sir William Robertson) had written to Haig, in a somewhat bewildered tone, that 'no war was ever so peculiar as the present one, and Field Service Regulations will require a tremendous amount of revising when we have finished . . .'[52] This exemplifies the difficult and novel situation to which the High Command struggled to adapt in 1916. At this time solutions were tried which were later discarded in favour of more traditional approaches and Gough was doing this in his command style, which was a departure from *FSR*. The methods he advocated were implicitly inflexible, and relied upon having enough troops attacking in depth to cater for any eventuality because communications were bound to break down and so deprive anyone but the man on the spot (if he had enough troops to hand) of the ability to influence matters. By the end of the battle, Fourth Army seems to have taken the same view about the need for a strictly structured attack, under the close control of corps. It is a measure of the problems involved in adapting to the new warfare that commanders moved – temporarily – away from *FSR* in this way. Nevertheless, the pattern of discussion at all levels within Fourth Army continued throughout the battle, and though in August Rawlinson was criticised by Haig for not supervising his subordinates sufficiently closely, this was only intended to apply to the planning and not the execution of the fighting. In any case, it seems to have made no difference to the generally hands-off way in which corps handled their divisions.

By the end of the Battle of the Somme, corps were in a position of far greater importance than at the start of the war. Crucially, it had been realised how important it was for them not only to pass information back to Army, but forward to division, as a consequence of their access to contact aeroplanes. From being a postbox in 1914, the corps was becoming a vital clearing house for information by late 1916. It should also be noted that the importance of counter-battery fire had been recognised during the Somme, and there was considerable growth in counter-battery techniques for suppressing or neutralising the German artillery. Consequently, a Counter-Battery Staff Officer with his own subordinate staff was established at the corps level, further increasing its importance. In addition, a corps Machine-Gun Officer was added, reflecting the increasing use of machine-gun barrages in attacks.

The plan for the Battle of Arras drew heavily upon the lessons of the Somme, though after a promising start, the battle degenerated into a slogging match. For corps and divisions, the ideas derived from the Somme were encapsulated in the pamphlet *SS135, Instructions for the Training of Divisions for Offensive Action*, first issued in December 1916. This supplement to *FSR* clearly laid out the respective duties of Army, corps and divisions in the preparation of an attack, and that the attack itself should be well-organised and structured. Army devised the principles of the artillery plan, but the GOCRA was to produce the detailed scheme for the attack, in consultation with divisions; corps now was the highest operational level of command. However, the infantry plans were still the province of division, and as on the Somme, were to be coordinated by corps; divisions were to attend to local and specific matters and corps to the overall principles of the attack. And traditional ideas were still employed, in that SS135 stated that the man on the spot still knew best when to employ his reserves. SS135 introduced an important degree of standardisation into the planning of operations, with other pamphlets produced between the Somme and Arras dealing with numerous aspects of the BEF's activities from communications to the use of machine-guns. The scheme followed for the start of the Battle of Arras conformed to the pattern set by the new pamphlets, and as in 1916, corps and divisions discussed the plans freely. However, Arras fell into the pattern so common amongst attacks on the Western Front. An initial success was followed by a day or so of limited successes, followed by the decline of the battle into a series of smaller operations attended by high casualties, as the carefully prepared attack of the first day was succeeded by increasingly improvised ones.

Turning to the question of whether the BEF was able to achieve higher tempo than the Germans, it must be said that the situation was little better than in 1916. Staffs were now experienced and a formula for launching a successful limited attack had been devised, but artillery techniques were still at a stage of development where observed fire was essential to achieve accuracy, and such fire necessarily took time and advertised the location of the forthcoming attack to the defenders. Even when a success such as that of 9 April 1917 was achieved (errors on the part of the German commander leading to it being to some degree a strategic surprise), the tempo of the attack was not high enough for the advance to be pressed before the Germans brought up reserves. Had the BEF had the artillery, a feint bombardment could perhaps have been launched elsewhere on the front, but this was not possible in early 1917.[53] And communications were still not yet good enough to assist in raising the tempo of operations; once attacking troops left HQs with telephones behind, they were still effectively lost to view.

Planning for the Battle of Messines followed much the same pattern as for Arras, though Second Army had a uniquely hands-off style of command, and corps took more care over liaison with their divisions. Care was taken to disseminate the lessons of Arras, notably in the pamphlet SS158, Notes on Recent Operations on the front of First, Third, Fourth and Fifth Armies. A notable difference, however, was that Second Army's managerial style of command led to it only outlining the overall objectives and principles for the artillery plan, and providing corps with the schedule for the attack. Corps now set the detailed objectives and actually planned the operation. In addition, the GOCRA and especially the CHA (Commander, Heavy Artillery, also at corps level), liaised more closely with divisions than at Arras and sufficient artillery was available for divisions to take some out of the barrage if it was required for other tasks. In order to ensure that principles were applied correctly by divisions and brigades, Army and corps sent staff officers to all subordinate formations so that they could act as their eyes and ears and report any problems, or opportunities for the higher formations to help. However, during the battle itself communications still proved a major problem; once attacking troops had gone beyond the telephone network, the position in the front line of an attack was still obscure to higher commanders. Nevertheless, Messines demonstrated that the BEF possessed the techniques to break into any German defensive system at the beginning of an attack. How to maintain the momentum after the first day was a greater problem, however.

Third Ypres was planned in much the same way as Messines, based on the application of experience to the SS pamphlets, and Second Army dealt with its corps in much the same way as it had at Messines. However, Fifth Army's approach differed from before, in that Hubert Gough adopted a much more consultative and hands-off style of command than in 1916, actively soliciting his corps commanders' advice at times, especially Sir Ivor Maxse's, who seems to have been rather a favourite. He may well have had more confidence in them than in his corps commanders in 1916 (who included two of the same officers!), as by 1917 all were of proven ability, if only sometimes at the divisional level. Sir Ivor Maxse of XVIII Corps had been a highly successful divisional commander in Gough's Army on the Somme. Sir Claud Jacob of II Corps had established a high reputation as a corps commander, also in Fifth Army, on the Somme, as had the Earl of Cavan (though principally in Fourth Army). The exception was H E Watts of XIX Corps. Like Maxse, he had not commanded his corps in a major offensive before, and it seems that he did not always enjoy the confidence of Fifth Army.[54] Nevertheless, he had a reputation as a safe pair of hands; Haig commented in 1916 that Watts was 'a distinctly stupid man and lacks imagination. But a hard fighter, leader of men and inspires confidence in all both above and below.'[55]

Gough also seems to have been rather more cautious than is usually supposed; his cavalry background is alleged to have led him into the error of attempting a breakthrough on the first day of the attack, but this was not the case. Maxse actually wanted more ambitious objectives for the first day than Gough originally intended, and examination of the Fifth Army and corps papers for the period do not reveal Gough to have been in favour of the sort of wild and uncontrolled thrust forward as has often been alleged. One of the more significant events in the planning process was the production of a memorandum by the Brigadier-General (Operations) at GHQ, John Davidson. It put forward his views on the need to conduct the new offensive as a series of careful, step-by-step, limited attacks, with plenty of time between each in order to bring artillery forward, restore communications and minimise casualties.[56] None of this really differed too much from Gough's own views, and his reply was that he fully acknowledged the need for a careful, step-by-step approach.[57] The real difference lay in the fact that Davidson would limit the advance no matter what the state of the defenders on its front, whereas Gough's view was that if they were in poor condition and ground was there for the taking, it should be taken. Maxse and Gough believed that the first day of the Arras offensive had been a lost opportunity and did not intend to make the same mistake.[58] But at no time did either Gough or Maxse advocate a 'rush-through,' as has been said elsewhere.[59] That Sir Henry Rawlinson (often quoted as saying that Gough wanted to charge through with a 'hurroosh') believed that this was Gough's plan may reflect his opinion of the Fifth Army commander's temperament rather than his having been included in these discussions.[60]

Though corps command at Third Ypres was not substantially different from corps command at Messines, a number of changes of emphasis took place, not least that corps became responsible for all the detailed planning of operations while devolving more to divisions than in 1916. In relationships with Army, it is noticeable that Fifth Army was much less assertive and prescriptive than in 1916; Second Army continued to be the paragon already observed at Messines. This, it is safe to assume, reflected the growing experience of staff officers at all levels of command, so that Army and corps could devolve responsibility more to divisions, as prescribed by *FSR*. Army again set rough objectives, based as much on a schedule as on points of geography, and the MGRA devised artillery policy around these. Corps had the task of implementing these plans and principles on the ground, and as such the corps was the level in the BEF which organised the details of operations at Third Ypres. This was a tendency which increased as the battle went on, as the style of offensive became so stereotyped, Army issuing corps with instructions less than a page long and with a map attached showing the objectives to be taken, and leaving the rest for corps to decide.[61] This standardised approach permitted operations to increase in tempo as the battle went on, with shorter and shorter pauses between attacks. Though this was not enough to ensure a breakthrough (tempo after all being relative, and the Germans were well aware in which sector they were going to be attacked), it did give the Germans cause for concern. Divisions continued to act as the man on the spot, and even regained some of the independence they had lost in 1915 and 1916. Indeed, corps devolved control of some of the field artillery and of machine-guns to division, and the latter passed control of tanks to brigade, all of which argues for the locus of control moving forwards. The tactical flexibility of the infantry improved considerably during Third Ypres but it could not compensate for the need to overcome poor battlefield communications by trying to make sure all eventualities were met in a comprehensive artillery plan, and this was produced by corps.

And as long as five different barrages were necessary to secure the (relatively) safe passage of the attacking troops into the German positions, corps would still dominate the planning and organisation of offensives.

The Battle of Cambrai was notable as the first major surprise attack the BEF had attempted since Neuve Chapelle in 1915. However, it was considerably less revolutionary from the corps perspective than might be supposed. Because there was no preliminary bombardment, tanks were necessary to crush the wire in front of the German defences and suppress strongpoints, enabling the infantry to get forward. However, they were not the primary feature of the attack but an auxiliary (albeit an important one) to the infantry and artillery. Indeed, from the point of view of corps, Cambrai was the product of previous experience more than of revolutionary innovation – of continuity as much as change. The preparation of the offensive was routine, apart from the need for careful camouflage of what was being done and that the attacking divisions were only brought into the line at the last moment.

The plan for moving artillery forward once the advance had started – one of corps' main preoccupations before the attack – was based on the lessons of the advance to the Hindenburg Line the previous March.[62] And once the offensive started, it quickly fell into the familiar pattern, where initial success proved impossible to follow up adequately and the offensive bogged down. As ever, a major reason for this was that communications were impossible to maintain, in this case partly because the tanks themselves repeatedly cut the telephone lines relied upon by HQs.[63] However, problems of command did arise at Cambrai. IV Corps (under Lieutenant General Sir Charles Woollcombe) displayed a notable lack of grip once the original attack had started, and IV and VII Corps handled their defensive preparations incorrectly. However, this does not constitute a 'paralysis of command', as Travers terms it, so much as simple ineptitude.[64] The report on the debacle of the German counter-attack is usually cited as unfairly criticising the ordinary soldiers while ignoring their superiors' shortcomings.[65] However, though the enquiry was critical of the troops on the ground, it also referred to the poor dispositions of corps, the paucity of their defensive preparations and the need for a defensive doctrine.[66] One criticism made by later commentators was that no reserve of tanks was left for use on the second day. It appears that this was a corps decision, the reasoning being to maximise the impact of the first assault.[67] Tank Corps were not in a position to overrule it, because the corps tank advisers viewed themselves as subordinate to the wishes of the formations to which they were attached.[68] Another problem was that the delegation of training by corps to divisions meant that infantry–tank co-operation did not follow a standard pattern, and some divisions worked more successfully than others with the tanks. In any case, the potential to attain a higher tempo than the Germans slipped away after the initial assault. Had the resources been available to launch another attack – not necessarily with a large tank element – soon after, the Germans might have been caught off-balance and more achieved. As it was, the inept handling of the cavalry and some infantry divisions, combined with the stubborn German resistance, meant that the opportunity was lost, and the Germans themselves achieved higher tempo than Third Army in their counterattack on 30 November. Nevertheless, the Cambrai offensive, rather than being the revolutionary idea almost strangled at birth by red-tabbed reactionaries which some historians have described, was an excellent example of the BEF's ability to learn from its experiences and to bring old and new ideas to work successfully together within the existing command structure.

Moving on to the March Retreat, it is apparent that the novel position of being on the defensive, combined with lack of manpower, led the Fifth and Third Armies into grave difficulties, but not a state of collapse. A new defensive system for the BEF was developed in late 1917, based on the German system of defence in depth.[69] Corps played a familiar role in the development of plans for defences and their construction, discussing them with Army. However, the Armies were more assertive than usual at this point, presumably because of the unfamiliarity of the defensive role, so that corps had not yet proved their competence to work almost unsupervised, as they had in attack.[70] Notwithstanding this, corps did co-ordinate the divisions in their sectors. Unfortunately, it appears that the German defensive system had not been fully understood at GHQ, and so was misapplied in the British version. This is given by Martin Samuels as an important reason for the problems of the Fifth and, to a lesser extent, the Third Armies in March 1918.[71] Travers argues that the command structure of the BEF was too rigid to permit the defences to be constructed properly and that once the retreat began, it failed to cope with the situation – indeed, it collapsed.[72]

However, whether the German system was misapplied or not, the main problem the British faced on and after 21 March 1918 was that they were short of manpower. When a very high proportion of the troops in the forward defensive zones was wiped out or captured after facing a devastatingly intense German bombardment, followed by an infantry assault in overwhelming numbers, this manpower shortage was exacerbated. All corps could do was fall back and tell their divisions where to retreat; it has been said that the March Retreat was a corps commanders' battle. As they fell back, short of manpower and in the absence of prepared fortifications, their weakness became all the more apparent. Gaps opened up between formations as much because they were thinly spread as because of a 'collapse' of command structure. The initiative was completely with the Germans until sufficient reserves could be organised for counter-attacks to be mounted. Contrary to Travers' assertions, the command structure continued to function, albeit rather

1. The winning command team: Haig (centre), flanked by Plumer (left) and Rawlinson (right), accompanied by other Army commanders and senior officers, at Cambrai, 11 November 1918.

2. Field Marshal Sir John French, C-in-C BEF 1914-15. Although brave, French's command style was inappropriate for the conditions of the Western Front.

3. Haig as commander of I Corps with his Chief of Staff Johnnie Gough (second from right). Haig and Gough made a formidable team in 1914. Gough's death in 1915 deprived the army of an excellent staff officer and possible future high commander.

4. Many senior officers had experience of the trenches. Here, Brigadier General H.E. Watts stoops to avoid sniper fire during the winter of 1914-15. Watts later commanded XIX Corps.

5. General Sir Hubert Gough, commander of Reserve (later Fifth) Army 1916-18. A 'thruster' and protégé of Haig's, Gough was the model of a 'hands-on' high commander.

6. Lieutenant General Sir Walter Congreve with King George V on the Somme, August 1916. The Corps level was a vital, but hitherto neglected, link in the BEF's command chain.

7. Not all generals were standoffish figures: here Major General Walter Braithwaite wins third place at the New Zealand division horse show in 1917. Braithwaite went on to command IX Corps.

8. A German prisoner, Ypres, 1917. Plumer's attacks at Third Ypres were designed to inflict casualties on the enemy rather than gain ground.

9. The battle of Menin Road in which the Australians took a prominent part.

10. Observation balloons played an important role in identifying targets for the artillery. This officer's parachute became entangled in a tree after he jumped from his balloon; battle of Menin Road, 20 September 1917.

11. Brigadier General J.V. Campbell VC addresses 137 Brigade at Riqueval bridge after their storming of the Hindenburg Line. This action graphically demonstrated the importance of the brigade as the 'building block' of the BEF.

12. Brigadier General H.E. 'Pompey' Elliot of 15 Australian Brigade. Dynamic and independently minded, Elliot was a highly effective leader but his often pugnacious command style may have contributed to thwarting his ambitions for promotion.

13. The Somme, August 1916. This picture suggests both the relative sophistication of the BEF's communications by this period, but also their vulnerability.

14. Infantry section in 1918: note the Lewis Gunner on the right. By the end of the war, firepower and command had devolved to the lowest level, to great effect.

15. An 18-pounder field gun in action. The development of advanced tactics and command techniques in the field of gunnery played the key role in the combined arms solution to trench deadlock.

16. A 12-inch howitzer on the Somme, September 1916. The need to integrate heavy weapons into increasingly sophisticated fire plans placed heavy demands on artillery commanders.

17. A Forward Observation Officer of the RFA, with a linesman with a field telephone. Such FOO parties formed the vital link between the infantry and the guns.

shakily at times, particularly once staff officers overcame their depen-
dency on the telephone as the principal means of communication. Nor
was it true that corps and divisional staffs lost touch altogether and sat in
their HQs. The commander of V Corps, Lieutenant-General E A
Fanshawe, wrote that because 'it was difficult to grasp the situation,
unless one went to see', his BGGS went up to the front on 24 March and
Fanshawe himself on the 25, and they 'motored' round his divisions on 26
March.[73] This is not to say that communication problems did not arise;
they were bound to, under the circumstances.[74] As had been discovered at
Cambrai, in open warfare (and without adequate wireless communications), mounted despatch riders worked best. It should also be noted that
when the Germans attacked at Arras on 28 March, the defenders, situated
in a conventional trench system of defence, and far less thinly stretched
than Fifth Army had been on 21 March, were able to repel them.[75] This
demonstrates that manpower was the key to the problems faced by Fifth
Army and also that the German model was not the only defensive system
that could work in 1918.

When the next blow fell, on the Lys in April, much the same problems
arose as in March. But at the same time, information regarding the lessons
to be learnt was digested and disseminated. The troops worst hit in the
German attack were divisions which had already taken severe punish-
ment in March and had been moved north for a rest. However, the retreat
in April was far slower, and down the lines of communication, which
made command and control far easier.[76] Once the situation had been
stabilised, strenuous efforts were made to learn the lessons of March and
April (the disaster to IX Corps on the Aisne in May was the result of these
not being applied), and the pamphlet *SS210, The Division in Defence*, was
issued. Armies and corps developed new defence schemes, based on this
and their own experiences. In addition, lessons in techniques of open
warfare were disseminated (especially regarding communications) and
artillery was reorganised in order to make it more mobile. The need to
train troops in open fighting techniques was recognised and efforts made
to improve training in general. Not the least of these was the appointment
of an Inspector-General of Training in July; part of his remit was to ensure
that training was carried out in accordance with *FSR* and the instructional
pamphlets.[77] This, even at this late stage in the war, indicated the
continuing validity of its principles if properly applied.

The BEF's offensives of the Hundred Days were based around the
principles enunciated in a new version of *SS135, The Training and
Employment of Divisions, 1918*. Like its predecessors, it was expected to be
used in conjunction with *FSR*, but it also encapsulated the lessons of 1917,
and was written with the transition from trench warfare to the open
variety in mind. The relationship between corps and division was left as
before, the artillery plan being central. The GOCRA was to plan overall

operations, with divisions supplying input regarding their specific requirements; the man on the spot was still important. Some decentralisation to divisions was to occur, with them taking control of their own heavy artillery whenever possible and now divisional Commanders, Royal Artillery were to plan their own barrages, the GOCRA co-ordinating different divisions' plans.[78] The overriding principle was that if control of operations could be passed down to divisions it would be.[79] This was what was done during the Hundred Days. When set-piece operations (such as the Battles of Epéhy, the St Quentin Canal or the Sambre) were envisaged, corps laid down the plan (in consultation with divisions and the CHA) and co-ordinated divisions' activities. But when the Germans were retreating more swiftly, corps left divisions to organise their own artillery plans and advances. Even in planning set-piece operations, corps were more likely than before to solicit divisions' views on how best to proceed, especially if unfamiliar terrain – such as the heavily wooded Forest of Mormal – lay ahead.[80] In the field of communications, the Corps Squadrons RAF were ordered to report to divisions as well as to corps, so that their information could be disseminated more quickly. This flexible mode of command was arrived at by applying the combination of SS135 and other pamphlets with FSR and was done at a higher tempo than at any other time in the war.

The question arises of how the increased tempo was attained. Perhaps the most important factor was that by the middle of 1918, the BEF finally had enough artillery and ammunition for it to conduct large-scale operations at more than one point on its front.[81] By comparison, it should be noted that for the bombardment before the Battle of Pilckem Ridge (31 July 1917), Fifth Army had to borrow more than half of Second Army's artillery and significant quantities from First and Third Armies too.[82] There was obviously a substantial logistical overhead in moving over 1,500 artillery pieces from other sectors to Fifth Army, and it also took time. Furthermore, only Fifth Army could undertake a major operation if other sectors were denuded of artillery. Another factor in 1918 was that the sustained bombardments before the attacks in 1916 and 1917 were not generally required (though three days were spent on the preliminary bombardment in front of the Hindenburg Main Position). Intense, hurricane bombardments were more commonly employed. A second factor, which ties in with the availability of artillery and ammunition, was that the BEF had the logistic base necessary to support the material-based offensives which characterised the Hundred Days, though it should also be noted that the planning times before the Battles of the Selle and Sambre (beginning on 17 October and 4 November, respectively) were extended by the need to wait for heavy artillery and ammunition to come up.[83] Nevertheless, Ian Brown pointed out that in this respect – the tying of operational aspirations to logistic necessity – the British showed a better grasp of the reality of fighting on the Western Front than the Germans had in the spring. Surprise played a greater part in the conduct of operations than at any other period in the war, and this too helped maintain the tempo. And the role of corps staffs in preparing for the set-piece operations in very short times was vitally important, given their share in organising the artillery.

In conclusion, corps began the war essentially as an administrative level of command, in place so that GHQ would not be overstretched in dealing with six divisions. However, as the need for artillery and the co-ordination of its action grew during 1915, the importance of corps grew. This trend continued into the Battle of the Somme, which saw the period of greatest conceptual confusion in the BEF, when it became apparent that the assumption before the battle, that a hole could simply be blasted through the German defences, was incorrect. Corps had a more centralising role than before or after, though operations were usually discussed with divisions and not simply imposed upon them. Once the lessons of the Somme had been digested, and confusion diminished, command became less centralised, as the new system of attack, most notably expressed in the pamphlet *SS135*, was worked into the procedures followed by the BEF.

By September 1917 the style of attack was such that army merely passed to corps the outline of what it had to do, and corps organised the whole operation, delegating to divisions as necessary. By the time of the Hundred Days, the command structure was sufficiently flexible for corps to leave divisions to get on with attacks with minimal supervision, unless a co-ordinated approach was especially required. At the same time, a sufficiency of artillery and improved staff work led to the tempo of the BEF's operations reaching a higher level than at any other time in the war. The Hundred Days also contains one of the most striking examples, in the whole war, of corps influencing the outcome of a major operation. This was the suggestion by the commander of IX Corps, Sir Walter Braithwaite, that he be permitted to attack across the St Quentin Canal on 29 September 1918, leading to 46th Division's brilliant success in the storming of the main Hindenburg Position. This has been described as 'perhaps the most extraordinary achievement of any BEF division on a single day.';[84] without it, the operation as a whole would have failed. The importance of the operational role of corps needs no more forceful demonstration.

NOTES

1   It should be noted that the term 'operational command' is not used in its modern sense (the level of command concerned with the direction of military resources to achieve military strategic objectives' – *British Defence Doctrine. Joint Warfare Publication (JWP) 0–01* (London, MOD, 1996). 1.9.). It is used in the way in which it was employed during the Great War, where it connoted

operations involving any formation from a brigade upwards. Usually it will refer to corps- or Army-level operations, depending upon the context.

2 *Parliamentary Papers 1904.* Volume 40, 364. *Royal Commission on the South African War.* Evidence given by Wolseley on 27 November 1902. Regarding corps areas, *Minutes of proceedings and Précis Prepared for the Army Council for the Year 1904*, 93. Précis No. 22, PRO, WO 163/9.

3 *Minutes of Proceedings and Précis Prepared for the Army Council for the Year 1906*, 58, Précis No. 278. PRO, WO 163/1.

4 *Minutes of Proceedings and Précis Prepared for the Army Council for the Year 1904*, 412–13 Précis No. 154. PRO, WO 163/9.

5 *Report on a Conference of General Staff Officers at the Staff College. 7th to 10th January, 1908*, 21 and 25. PRO, WO 279/18.

6 PRO, WO 33/606 and WO 33/660, respectively.

7 Minute (1 October 1913) from G M Harper to DMO, in Staff Manual, War, 1912. PRO, WO 32/4731.

8 This could be none when the corps was in reserve, or as many as five or six.

9 J Edmonds and others, *History of the Great War: Military Operations, France and Belgium 1914–18.* 14 volumes plus appendices and maps (London, 1922–48). Henceforth 'OH' with volume and page numbers. OH, 1914 Volume 1, 7. See *Mobilization Appointments. Part I. Expeditional Force. 1st April, 1914.* PRO, WO 33/611.

10 J Gooch, 'Military Doctrine and Military History' in J Gooch (ed.), *The Origins of Contemporary Doctrine.* (The Strategic and Combat Studies Institute. The Occasional, No. 30. September 1997), 5.

11 The argument regarding the dislike of doctrine in the Edwardian army is made in 37–41 of T Travers, *The Killing Ground: The British Army, the Western Front and the Emergence of Modern Warfare 1900–1918* (London, 1987).

12 A Palazzo, *Seeking Victory on the Western Front. The British Army and Chemical Warfare in World War I* (Lincoln, NE and London, 2000), 8–7.

13 *FSR*, 133–45.

14 This view was also expounded in J Boraston (ed.), *Sir Douglas Haig's Despatches (December 1915–April 1919)* (London, 1919), 325.

15 For the death ray see Haig diary entry for 28 September 1916. PRO, WO 256/13.

16 Travers, op. cit., 75–7. Boraston, op. cit., 329–30. For the limitations of tanks see D J Childs. 'British Tanks 1915–18. Manufacture and Employment' (PhD thesis, Glasgow University, 1996), 155, 183.

17 R Blake (ed.), *The Private Papers of Douglas Haig, 1914–1919* (London, 1952), 100, 103. R Prior and T Wilson, *Command on the Western front,* (Oxford, 1992). 113.

18 *FSR*, 27–8.

19 J Kiszely, 'The British Army and Approaches to Warfare since 1945' in B Holden Reid (ed.), *Military Power. Land Warfare in Theory and Practice* (London and Portland, OR, 1997), 180. The definition is expanded in the same author's 'Achieving High Tempo – New Challenges' in *Journal of the Royal United Services Institute for Defence Studies*, December 1999, 47–53.

20 *FSR*, 133, 136.

21 *Operations of the 1st Corps on the River Aisne, 13th to 30th September, 1914*, PRO, WO 95/588.

22 I Corps War Diary for 3 November 1914. PRO, WO 95/588. *FSR*, 150.

23 OH, 1914 Volume 2, 76–86.

24 OH, 1915 Volume 1, 81–2.

25 *Notes at Conference on 5/3/15*, PRO, WO 95/590.

26 *2nd London Division, T.F. Scheme of Training for the Present when in Reserve,* quoting *1st Corps No: 236 (G),* which quoted *GHQ O.A.* 042,14th March 1915. PRO, WO 95/590.
27 *No. 520 (G),* 6 October 1915, PRO, WO 95/592.
28 OH, 1916 Volume 1, 58.
29 OH, 1916 Volume 1, 186. fn. 3.
30 *O.B./446,* 23 October 1915, PRO, WO 95/757.
31 OH, 1916 Volume 1, 25, fn. 2.
32 Travers. op. cit., 105–7.
33 Letter dated 30 June 1916. Hunter-Weston Papers. British Library, no. 48365.
34 For planning in X Corps see *Part Played By Artillery Illustrate* [sic] *From Somme Battle,* 2nd January 1917. PRO, WO 95/863. Hereafter *'Part Played by Artillery'.*
35 *Part Played by Artillery,* 4.
36 Ibid., 11.
37 Ibid., 7.
38 Ibid., 12–16.
39 M Farndale, *History of the Royal Regiment of Artillery, Western Front 1914–18* (London, 1986), p.142.
40 *Notes of two Conferences held at Corps Headquarters – 21 & 23-6-16.* PRO. WO 95/820.
41 *VIII Corps Scheme for Offensive.* Undated. PRO, WO 95/820.
42 OH, 1916 Volume 1, 431. Prior and Wilson. op. cit., 165.
43 OH, 1915 Volume 2, 176. *Part Played by Artillery,* 21–2.
44 *Narrative of operations of 1st July 1916, Showing the Situation as it Appeared to General Staff, VIII Corps, From Information Received During The Day.* Undated. PRO, WO 95/820.
45 OH, 1916 Volume 1, 337 and 340.
46 Prior and Wilson. op. cit., 184.
47 *XIV Corps S. 72,* 3 August, 1916. PRO, WO 95/910.
48 *XIV Corps S. 72,* 4 August, 1916. PRO, WO 95/910.
49 Travers, op. cit., 168–9.
50 *Reserve Army G.A. 3/1/1,* 16 July 1916. PRO. WO 95/518.
51 *Reserve Army Operation Order No.22,* 24 August 1916. PRO, WO 95/518.
52 D R Woodward (ed.), *The Military Correspondence of Field-Marshal Sir William Robertson, Chief of the Imperial General Staff, December 1915–February 1918* (London, 1989), 73.
53 OH, 1917 Volume 1, 542.
54 Malcolm Diaries, cited in personal communication from Professor Ian Beckett, based on his chapter in P H Liddle (ed.), *Passchendaele in Perspective* (London, 1997).
55 Haig diary entry for 9 May 1916. PRO, WO 256/10.
56 Like Prior and Wilson, I have referred to Maxse's copy of this memo, 25/6/17. Maxse Papers, Department of Documents, Imperial War Museum, London (hereafter IWM), 69/53/10, 35/2. See R Prior and T Wilson, *Passchendaele: The Untold Story* (New Haven, CT and London, 1996), 76.
57 Memo by Gough, 26/6/17. Maxse Papers, IWM. 69/53/10, 35/2.
58 Memo by Gough, 26 June 1917. Maxse's marginalia, 4. Maxse Papers, IWM. 69/53/10, 35/2. Prior and Wilson, *Passchendaele,* 76.
59 T Travers, *How the War Was Won. Command and Technology in the British Army on the Western Front 1917–1918* (London and New York, 1992), 14.
60 Prior and Wilson, *Command,* 270.
61 See *Fifth Army Order No. 22,* 23 September 1917. PRO, WO 95/520. See also Nos. 23–30 in PRO. WO 158/250.

62   *Third Army Artillery Instructions No. 19,* 10 November 1917, 2. PRO, WO 95/368.
63   *Lessons From Recent Operations. Communications.* Undated. PRO, WO 158/316.
64   Travers, *How the War Was Won . . .* , 28–30.
65   Travers, *How the War Was Won . . .* , 30.
66   Report of the Court of Enquiry in the Maxse Papers, IWM, 69153/11, 40.
67   *IV Corps, Havrincourt–Bourlon Operations November 20th to December 1st . . .* , undated but obviously retrospective. PRO, WO 158/318.
68   *Notes on Tank Operations April–October 1917.* Undated, but presumably just predating the Cambrai attack. PRO, WO 95/92.
69   OH, 1918 Appendix 6.
70   See, for example, *Policy on the Army Front for 1918, 20th January 1918, Section II – Defensive Measures,* paras 4 and 5. PRO, WO 95/434.
71   M Samuels, *Command or Control: Command, Training and Tactics in the British and German Armies, 1888–1918* (London, 1995), 203–10.
72   Travers, *How the War Was Won,* 58–9.
73   Undated letter from Sir E A Fanshawe to Edmonds. PRO, Cab 45/185.
74   See extract from General J A L Haldane's Diary. PRO, Cab 45/185.
75   OH, 1918 Volume 1, 62–3.
76   *Report on Operations Undertaken by IX Corps Between 9th and 21st April 1918, 20th May 1918.* PRO, WO 95/836.
77   *O.B./2255,* 20 June 1918. Maxse Papers, IWM, 69/53/13, and its *Appendix A.*
78   *The Training and Employment of Divisions, 1918* (hereafter *SS135, 1918) passim.*
79   See for example, *XVII Corps Artillery Instructions No.2,* 25 August 1918. PRO, WO 95/943.
80   *V Corps G.S.518,* 28 October 1918. PRO, WO 95/751.
81   OH, 1918 Volume 5, 595–6. P Griffith, *Battle Tactics of the Western Front* (New Haven CT and London, 1994), 147.
82   OH, 1917 Volume 2, 108.
83   I M Brown, *British Logistics on the Western Front 1914–1919* (Westport CT and London, 1998), 198–204.
84   J P Harris with N Barr, *Amiens to the Armistice. The BEF in the Hundred Days' Campaign, 8 August–11 November 1918* (London and Washington, 1998), 224.

CHAPTER VI

Command and Control in Battle: British Divisions on the Menin Road Ridge, 20 September 1917

John Lee

Basing his observations on his years of practical experience of the performance of men in battle, General Sir Ian Hamilton once declared that a rifleman might as soon try to control the bullet once it had left the muzzle, as a general try to control his troops once they had launched an attack. This encapsulates to a nicety the problem of command and control in battle in the First World War. We have to put aside all our modern expectations of rapid and efficient electronic communications, which in the computer age will before long see every unit, or every man and piece of equipment, identified on a screen by the use of satellite-based global positioning systems.

After two years of bitter experience the British army was perfectly aware that modern battle was a truly chaotic environment. It had learnt to cope with this chaos in two complementary ways.

First, the whole attack was subordinated to the artillery plan and the capabilities of the available artillery for the attack. It was obvious that an inadequate artillery preparation invariably led to failure. But equally important was the dismal fate of the attacking infantry once they had outstripped their artillery support. The solution was the gradual adoption of the limited objective attack, also known as the 'bite and hold' method of attack. Each infantry formation was given a precise and achievable objective, to be reached by closely following a 'creeping barrage'. At various predefined points for reorganisation and along the final line to be prepared for defence the attackers would be protected by 'standing barrages'.

Second, and this is an enormous step forward often neglected by military writers, was the transformation in the handling of the infantry itself. This can be dated from February 1917, based on the lessons of the 1916 fighting on the Somme and Ancre. The infantry was organised and

119

trained in a totally standardised way, so that all infantrymen were thoroughly familiar with a battle drill that would serve them in all the unpredictable circumstances they might encounter on the battlefield. This new 'Standard Operational Procedure' would enable them to carry out their clearly assigned mission, formulated to conform to the artillery plan, but which would see them repeatedly succeeding despite the loss of officers and senior NCOs, and sometimes even after they had lost the creeping barrage. If the generals accepted that they had little chance to 'control' the battle once it had started, their solution was to do everything in their power to create the conditions for success before it began. This included the careful training of the infantry so that all ranks understood the task ahead and the battle drill that would see them achieve success.

The basis of this drill was the training pamphlet issued throughout the army in February 1917 known as SS143 *Instructions for the Training of Platoons for Offensive Operations.* This important document has been fully discussed by this author elsewhere[1] and by other authors in this collection. Put simply it organised the platoon into four specialised sections – two to provide firepower and two to provide a manoeuvre element. The Lewis gun and rifle grenade sections provided local fire support; the rifle and bomber sections were to close with the enemy as rapidly as possible. Great emphasis was placed on seeking out and turning the enemy's flank in any circumstance and the use of the initiative of the platoon commander was favoured. But the principal aim of the document was the standard organisation and training of the whole body of the infantry so that all generals from brigade up knew that they were operating to a well-known system.

At the divisional level a different 'Standard Operating Procedure' had been in effect for somewhat longer. Since December 1916 all divisions were meant to organise their major training exercises, which preceded all set piece offensive battles, around the pamphlet SS135 *Instructions for the Training of Divisions for Offensive Action.* This covered the virtual siege warfare techniques required for attacking prepared positions (known as trench-to-trench attacks in their day); the semi-open warfare of subsequent attacks on an enemy turned out of his main positions; and the longed for return to open warfare when the enemy was finally 'on the run'. Incorporating, as it did, the *Preliminary Notes of the Tactical Lessons of Recent Operations* (SS119 of July 1916) it was intended to get all British divisions working to a similar pattern based on the experience of the Somme fighting.

With its thirty-three section headings and two appendices, it is a useful reminder of just how complex an organisation was an infantry division of the period 1916–18 and how much work had to go into the planning of an attack by its many component parts. Every section of the pamphlet is, in its own way, a means of addressing the problem of command and control

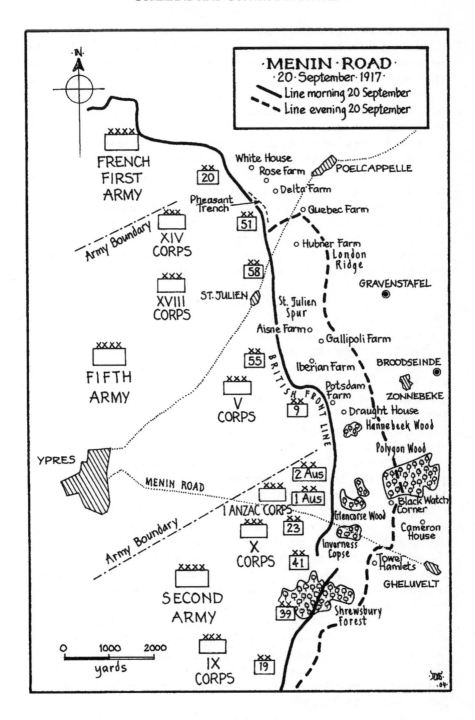

in battle. If we think about it, command and control is all about the flow of information in both directions. The intentions of the commander must be made clear and properly communicated to all components of the attacking force. Once the attack had begun then all attacking units should make a high priority of passing accurate and timely information back to designated command centres to keep the commanders fully in the picture as the battle unfolded.

Before the issue of the final Operation Orders there were a series of preliminary 'instructions' to be issued, covering seventeen categories of work, from the artillery plan and the action of massed machine-guns, tanks and co-operation with contact aeroplanes to the organisation of stragglers' posts and the collection and escort of prisoners. The care and attention lavished on the preparation of the trenches before the attack, the consolidation work of the Royal Engineers and the pioneers, the forming and forward movement of supply dumps and medical arrangements were all conditioned by the knowledge that once battle was joined there would be little enough that higher commanders could do to influence events; everyone involved would have to know what was expected of them and largely be left to get on with it.

Great attention was paid to the constant need for information to be gathered and transmitted from the fighting front to the command posts in the rear. The primacy of the infantry/artillery co-operation was recognised and it was realised that it was a particularly difficult problem. In the initial chaos of the assault, and before the signallers could set up more permanent communications, reliance was on signal rockets, coloured flags and the contact flights made by the Royal Flying Corps. The careful rehearsal of the infantry in co-operating with the artillery, and in the timing of the lifts of the creeping barrage and the consolidation of the positions won behind standing barrages, were all part of the solution to the problem of command and control during the attack itself.

One of the largest sections of SS135 is devoted to Signal Communications. 'The rapid establishment of good signal communications, immediately after the assault, is one of the most important, though one of the most difficult things to be dealt with.'[2] Signals linesmen would follow immediately behind the last wave of the attacking infantry and the establishment of cable links for telephone and telegraph, preferably buried (to a depth of six feet) and utilising the 'ladder system' of several lines all linked together laterally (making it harder for enemy fire to break the link completely), was still the most reliable means of keeping contact between commanders and attacking units. Before the cables could be properly buried and made secure use was to be made of any 'Russian saps' leading out from the British lines and any enemy communication trenches to give some protection to the precious cables.

During and immediately after the attack there was often heavy reliance on visual means of signalling, all of which required the allocation of specialist parties going forward to signal back to pre-arranged back stations. The humble carrier-pigeon often gave excellent service and was selected for particularly important messages. The use of wireless sets, allocated by Corps Headquarters to a Division, was restricted in the attack and they were rarely deployed forward of Brigade. More useful was the Earth Induction set, or Power Buzzer, which could be got forward to be operated by battalion signallers sending back safe and secure messages to back stations operated by Corps specialists. More often than not the final instrument of communication, 'the one means . . . which can be relied on when all others fail', was the runner. They were to be pre-selected and trained, with particular attention to their knowledge of the terrain and trench systems of the battlefield.

The sending back of clear and precise Situation Reports to superiors and across to neighbours was a prime duty. Special reconnaissance by staff officers, the exchange of liaison officers (between infantry formations, and between infantry and artillery) and the use of specially selected observers to watch the overall development of the attack were all designed to supplement the information coming back from the attacking units. There were frequent reminders that communicating with units on each flank was every bit as important as feeding information to the rear. The document repeatedly stressed that the use of initiative by officers of all ranks in the attacking formations was to be commended. It was widely accepted that the man on the spot was to be encouraged to make the most of the situation in which he found himself, whether it be reacting defensively to fierce enemy counter-attack or even pushing on beyond the final objective line to exploit 'fleeting opportunities' of further success. While saying this in a training document does not mean that the British army suddenly became a wonderfully fluid and adaptive organisation, it does at least give the lie to the idea that only the Germans were thinking along these lines for ways to cope with the chaos of modern battle.

The question of the movement of headquarters was discussed sensibly. The divisional HQ should not be moved during the battle. If the divisional commander and elements of his staff felt the need to go forward to investigate developments personally, they should only do so after making quite clear their intentions to senior and responsible officers who remained at HQ with executive powers to act in the absence of the commanding general. No assault brigade should move its HQ but an Advanced Report Centre could usefully be set up in the vicinity of the enemy front line once the first two objective lines had been successfully stormed. This would reduce the pressure on runners conveying news to the rear. Brigades designated to push on to further objectives would need to set up headquarters closer to their attacking units. A Brigade Orderly Officer, with scouts and signallers in hand, would go forward and select a suitable location somewhere in the newly-captured enemy first line for a brigade HQ and this would be communicated to all parties who were required to know it.

Of increasing importance throughout the war was the co-operation with the Royal Flying Corps in matters of command and control. The 'contact patrol' provided by aeroplanes of the RFC helped commanders keep track of the progress of attacking formations, watched the reactions of the enemy (especially signs of incipient major counter-attacks) and relayed specific messages from the leading troops. There were separate aircraft working with the artillery; the infantry were to be familiar with the markings of the aeroplanes assigned to them and an elaborate system of signalling by coloured flare was put in place. The infantry was to signal their position on the ground at designated times so that an overall impression of their progress could be obtained. This practice led to considerable discussion when first instituted as it was held by the RFC that the infantry were reluctant to signal their whereabouts lest it bring down German retaliatory fire. It had to be impressed upon the infantry, by instruction and by experience, that it was far better to let their superiors, and their own artillery, know their exact positions than to worry about some notional advantage to the enemy. Messages could be communicated from ground to air by flare, lamp or signal sheets laid out in pre-determined fashion. Air to ground signals could be made by klaxon horn or flare. The Morse code was widely used and a number of standard messages were known to all; i.e. a succession of Ns signified a shortage of ammunition, a succession of Xs, 'held up by machine-gun fire'. These coded messages covered the following other eventualities – enemy retiring at . . . , enemy offering stiff resistance at . . . , further bombardment required, to lengthen, raise or lower a barrage, to call for reinforcements, to declare a shortage of water or grenades, or to say if held up by uncut wire. The fact that more than eight pages of SS135 (ten percent of the document) are given over to this aspect of communication signifies the importance attached to co-operation with the RFC.

A major difference between SS135 and the documents relating to battle in 1917 was that in 1916 the tactical unit to which all references are made was the rifle company. There were separate instructions for all the detached specialists – the bombers, the Lewis gunners, the snipers and scouts. By 1917 these had been absorbed back into the primary unit of the infantry – the platoon in its new four-section organisation described above.

Now let us look at the division in battle from the point of view of command and control. The British offensive that opened on 31 July 1917 was the start of a projected series of battles that was intended to push the Germans off the northern ridges before Ypres and break through into the Flanders plain, seize the important railheads of Roulers and Thourout and drive for the Belgian coast and the German naval bases of Ostend and Zeebrugge. The fact that this was strategically vital ground (which was more than could be said of the Somme battlefield the previous year) made it certain that the enemy would contest the area vigorously, providing the British army with many opportunities to inflict heavy casualties on them as the campaign developed.

Despite the elaborate preparations for the attack of 31 July, including very thorough training, and the most powerful British artillery bombardment to date, the results were mixed. The day ended with the gain of the enemy's outpost zone and the capture of many thousands of prisoners, but also with the loss of ground taken in the initial assault to stupendous counter-attacks. Moreover, the day marked the start of the worst weather in this part of Europe for seventy-five years. The main assault was being conducted by Sir Hubert Gough's Fifth Army, supported on his left by the French First Army and on the right by Sir Herbert Plumer's Second Army. Despite the atrocious rainfall Gough persisted in attacking through August in conditions that led to inevitable defeat and a severe loss of morale amongst the usually steady and reliable British infantry.

On 25 August, the day after German counter-attacks had recaptured Inverness Copse, Sir Douglas Haig informed Plumer that his Second Army was to become the principal instrument of the attack with effect from the 26th, and that Gough's Fifth Army would conform to his plans. There are many, of course, who thought that Plumer should have been allowed to develop the campaign after his success on the Messines Ridge in June 1917 and some three months had been lost before this most meticulous of planners could get on with the battle he had always intended to fight.

General Headquarters had been thinking deeply about the problems posed for the attack by the new, very deep German defensive positions with their reliance on strong points and 'pill boxes' to break up attacking formations and the use of counter-attacks to regain lost ground. Early in August they had sent questionnaires to all subordinate armies seeking their views on the tactical problem and the reply sent in by Plumer on 12 August on behalf of Second Army was the perfect statement of the case for the use of the limited objective ('bite and hold') attack, firstly to seize important tactical features from the enemy; secondly, and every bit as importantly, to destroy the inevitable enemy counter-attacks in the most calculated way.[3] In effect Plumer was going to fight these battles by turning the predictable German tactics against them.

The defence in depth was to be overcome by an attack itself organised in great depth, with fresh formations leap-frogging forward to take each successive objective line, always covered by massive creeping and standing barrages, and with each subsequent advance to an objective being shorter than the one before it. Every consideration was given to the physical capability of the infantry to carry out the task set. The guiding principle for Plumer was flexibility. 'The enemy has deliberately substituted flexibility for rigidity in his defence, and I think the response should be a corresponding flexibility in our attack.'[4] Gaps in the line held no terrors for Plumer. The old linear tactics were thoroughly redundant by the autumn of 1917.

On 31 August 1917 Second Army issued its own *Notes on Training and Preparation for Offensive Operations* effectively updating SS135 to the new German defensive methods and the need for more depth and flexibility in the attack, with particular emphasis on the need for every commander down to company level to keep a reserve in hand to meet and defeat the inevitable counter-attacks. The usual stress was laid upon the need for a steady stream of information being passed back to command centres, and it is indicative of the overall importance of the circulation of the standardised training pamphlets throughout the armies in France and Flanders that Plumer's excellent Chief of Staff, 'Tim' Harington could simply state that 'the system of inter-communication is laid down in SS148' before going on to highlight a few points that drew lessons from recent fighting.[5]

Having secured a breathing-space of some three weeks before the renewal of the general offensive, Plumer and his staff began that meticulous and humane planning for which Second Army was famous. On 1 September the preliminary operation order was issued, specifying the area from Broodseinde southwards as the first objective, to be followed by a series of attacks to secure the Passchendaele–Staden Ridge. A total of four corps (fourteen divisions) were assigned to the attacks. Birdwood's I Anzac would commit 1st and 2nd Australian Divisions to the first attack, with 4th and 5th Australian Divisions to follow through. Morland's X Corps would use 23rd, 39th and 41st Divisions first, with 21st and 33rd Divisions subsequently. Hamilton Gordon's IX Corps would just commit 19th Division to complete the attack up to the line of the Ypres–Comines canal. In reserve was Godley's II Anzac, with the New Zealand, 3rd Australian and 7th and 49th British Divisions. Fifth Army would conform with all these attacks, committing a total of thirteen divisions in all; five on 20 September extending the attack up to the line of the Ypres–Staden railway.

The central 'battering ram' for Plumer to seize the Menin Road Ridge end of the Gheluvelt plateau, the first of four steps to clear the plateau to its eastern edge, was to be the 1st and 2nd Australian, and the 23rd and 41st British Divisions. We shall look at the preparations of two of them in some detail and survey the others to see how the set-piece attack had become a well-practised routine by the autumn of 1917. After a corps commanders' conference on 27 August, Plumer submitted his scheme to GHQ two days later and on 31 August was able to give his generals the outline of the attack plan.

The 1st Australian Division (Major-General H B Walker) had not been heavily engaged since the fighting at Bullecourt in May and had spent the whole of August on the training grounds of Vieux Berquin. It was expecting to go into the line in the Armentières sector and was in very good condition – well-rested and, with 646 officers and 14,175 other ranks, the strongest of the Australian divisions. It was on 7 September that a conference was called at divisional headquarters and the attack was introduced to the assembled combat and staff officers. A reconnaissance of the forward areas was held for officers of all arms the next day and on 10 September Divisional Order No. 31 (dated 9 September and timed at 7.30 pm) was issued to all component parts of the division. It opened with the 'Intention': 'The Division in co-operation with other troops will attack the enemy on a day to be notified'.[6] It was explained that 23rd Division would go in on their right; 2nd Australian Division on the left. The Division would attack with 2nd Brigade on the right and 3rd Brigade on the left, with 1st Brigade in reserve. Each brigade would attack on a one-battalion frontage, feeding a second battalion through to the second objective and two battalions on to the third objective, for a total advance in three stages of some 1,500 yards. A map was provided at this stage showing the boundaries and the Red, Blue and Green objectives. The artillery support for the division's 'creeping barrage' (five brigades of Australian field artillery) was detailed and the barrage itself, obviously an early component of the plan, was described. The brigades were given careful details of the flanking units involved and were called upon to work up detailed plans for the attack paying special attention to the 'mopping up' of ground captured, the assigning of definite units to take each known strong point, and the construction and garrisoning of new strong points to defend the captured territory. Colonel T A Blamey of the Division's General Staff signed off with the proviso that detailed instructions would follow.

On 11 September an Advanced Divisional Headquarters was opened near Reninghelst, Divisional Order No. 32 gave the march orders for assembly south-west of Ypres, and General Plumer watched a dress rehearsal attack by 3rd Australian Brigade at Vieux Berquin. 2nd Brigade were put through their paces next day and on the 13th the divisional HQ opened at the Scottish Lines, Reninghelst as the troops began their two-day approach march to the Salient. On 14 September Instruction No. 2 to Divisional Order No. 31 was issued, giving more details of the artillery barrage and of the approach march routes. On 15 September further reconnaisances were made of the front lines and work began on communications, supply dumps and dug-outs for the division's use. That night and every night after the signallers were at work burying cables to the requisite six feet. A small flood of further 'instructions' to Order No. 31 were issued on the 15th. Instruction No. 3 began to fill in a lot more detail of a general nature – details of the size and locations of the strong points to be built, five in 2nd Brigade sector, three in 3rd Brigade, each to hold a platoon of infantry; dress and equipment were to be as in Section 31 of SS135, with slight alterations in the number of rounds of rifle ammunition carried (more for the battalions on the final objective); distinguishing patches would be worn on the helmets of the attacking infantry, red, blue and green according to which objective line they were assigned to; on the question of reserves: 'It is the intention of the Divisional Commander to hold the 1st Australian Infantry Brigade in readiness to support either of the leading brigades, or to deal with the inevitable counter-attack, should either such course be necessary'. Special care was to be taken to avoid the loss of direction, both by issuing compass bearings to officers and by the extensive use of white tape to mark approach routes, jumping-off points and unit boundaries. The infantry were requested to lie down along the jumping-off tapes and keep quiet. To reduce the possibility of detection an amendment to this instruction was issued the next day requiring the infantry not to fix their bayonets until after the commencement of the barrage.

Instruction No. 4 dealt with 'Intelligence Instructions for the Examination of Prisoners, and the rapid procuring and dissemination of information concerning the enemy'. Besides detailing the Corps prisoner-of-war 'cages', it was stressed that prisoners had to be got back to a divisional collecting station as quickly as possible. There two named officers would interrogate them, assisted by German-speaking and reading NCOs and men. Two further officers would interview the wounded men as they returned through the lines. All captured documents and maps were to be put in properly labelled sacks and sent back to the divisional collecting point. Specially selected men from each battalion's intelligence section, wearing special armbands to identify them, were to scour the battlefield for such material. These men would be provided with special maps showing all known enemy headquarters, signals offices and dug outs.

The whole of Instruction No. 5 was taken up with the importance of liaison between units. The principal liaison officers were appointed between the brigades and divisional headquarters and their duty was to obtain first hand information, by reconnaissance, and report back to the divisional commander. Each brigade liaised with its neighbouring brigade, as well as with the flank brigades and the neighbouring divisions. Every battalion was to liaise with its neighbours and, of necessity, every headquarters location was to be made quite clear to all concerned. Artillery liaison officers were appointed down to brigade level and the infantry were reminded that the 'utmost use must be made of the services of these officers'. Battalion and company officers were especially enjoined to keep in close touch with the artillery's Forward Observation Officers.

Instruction No. 6 concerned the work of the engineers and pioneers and was largely taken up with details of the strong points to be built by the field companies in the captured territory. One engineer field company was attached to each attacking brigade and one was kept in reserve; all were to move under the orders of divisional headquarters. The vital role of the pioneers was delineated: 'The 1st Pioneer Battalion will be responsible for the maintenance and extension of all communications, including tramways, mule and duckboard tracks and communication trenches'. The two main supply routes to the front were laid down. An amendment to this instruction issued next day added engineer officers to those needing to liaise with brigade headquarters.

The blizzard of paperwork continued unabated on 16 September. Instruction No. 7 was of particular importance: 'Signals Communications within the Division'. Seven categories of communication system were discussed:

a) Telegraph and telephone, with deep buried cables in place from divisional to brigade headquarters.
b) Visual means, with six visual reporting stations in place.
c) Wireless, with two wireless stations connected to an Advanced Corps Directing Station, which would then pass messages to Division HQ by telegraph.
d) Two power buzzers were provided, with a spare apparatus kept in reserve.
e) Motor cycle despatch riders were available for use between division and brigade headquarters; runners would liaise forward of brigade.
f) Five runners' posts were set up and their location made clear. Runners were to be deployed in pairs with not more than fifty yards between each pair.
g) Pigeons were kept at Brigade HQ, and a further ten pairs were made available for the use of the artillery FOOs.

Two separate communication lines were available for the exclusive use of the artillery. Liaison between ground forces and the contact aeroplanes was to be as per SS148 and all infantry battalions would be provided with panels of material to make signals to the aircraft.

Instruction No. 8 gave details of the medical arrangements from the rear area Casualty Clearing Stations to the forward Regimental Aid Posts (each with a Medical Officer and four stretcher bearer squads). Evacuation routes were delineated. Instruction No. 9 dealt with the role of the machine-guns in the attack. Under divisional control were seventy-two guns firing as part of the 'creeping barrage' and each attacking brigade had a machine-gun company under its command. The Divisional Machine-gun Officer was enjoined to keep close contact with brigade headquarters, ready to respond to SOS calls from the infantry. Instruction No. 10, just to emphasise the importance of the topic, was a 'Summary of Arrangements for Co-operation between Infantry and Artillery on Forthcoming Operations'. Artillery liaison officers were to be provided down to infantry battalion level. A complete brigade of field artillery (three batteries of 18 pounder field guns and one of 4.5-inch howitzers) was 'superimposed' on the barrage plan to be available to respond to any request from an artillery liaison officer at an infantry brigade head-quarters to call down fire on a 'target of opportunity' as the need arose. Similarly two 6-inch howitzer batteries (of four guns each) were available to Divisional HQ to be used as required. Instruction No. 11 covered the arrangements for the Military Police. Besides their function in collecting and relaying back prisoners of war, and directing traffic (where they were a vital source of information to runners looking for reporting centres), they also provided five Battle Straggler Posts to be equipped with spare gas helmets, steel helmets, field dressings and rations – nothing called a soldier of the BEF back to his duty like a hot, sweet mug of tea.

On 17 September only one Instruction was issued: No. 12 covered various matters of detail concerning equipment to be carried forward (wire cutters, etc.) or not to be carried forward (telescopic sighted rifles). Concerning command and control matters it was announced that a troop of Light Horse would be made available to the Divisional GOC to communicate his orders and that the number of telephones in the front line was to be restricted to reduce the chance of the enemy 'listening in'.

The last flurry of Instructions on 18 September were all concerned with command and control in their own way. No. 13 drew attention to the confusion that could arise if all and sundry had access to the telephone system during an attack. It gave an approved list of those who could use the Divisional Exchange (all the principal general and administrative staff officers); at Brigade it was just the GOC and his Brigade Major; at battalion and company level only the commanding officer could use the 'phone. No. 14 dealt with a few minor, last-minute changes and made available pairs of pigeons to the parties in liaison with flank divisions. No. 15 made a useful addition to the wireless net. 'A wireless tank section is being provided for the purpose of working back during the forthcoming operation from the captured area to a receiving station in the rear . . .' It was to set be up at the south-east corner of Glencorse Wood by Zero plus 2½ hours and was available to the infantry battalions in the area to send back messages and could also serve as an emergency forward wireless station for both the Australian divisions involved in the battle.

All these Instructions were detailed amendments to the original Divisional Order No.31 of 9 September 1917.

On the right of this Australian division was one of those unglamorous but thoroughly reliable British divisions, the 23rd. It should come as no surprise that their planning for the battle follows exactly the same pattern as 23rd Division's staff officers worked to the same Standard Operating Procedure.[7] A warning order of 3 September assigned the division to X Corps for the forthcoming offensive operations and by 6th September the divisional staff issued its Plan of Operations (SG 180/6/10) giving preliminary details of the artillery, machine-gun and trench mortar barrages, the method of attack (infantry units 'leap-frogging' to take three objective lines) and an early stress on the importance of flank liaison and the consolidation of captured positions with strong-points. It announced that eight appendices would follow covering artillery, signals communications, the machine-gun barrage, the work of the Royal Engineers and pioneers, fighting kit, contact aeroplanes, the examination of prisoners and intelligence and the Concentration March. These were all issued between 9 and 15 September, with a few amendments two days later. The brigade commanders were instructed to prepare their detailed plans as their brigades went into a period of intensive training and rehearsal.

On 8 September a X Corps instruction was passed to the division showing how the problem of communications was in the forefront of everyone's mind:

> In order to get Divisional Commanders on to their offensive fronts early for the adjustment of signal communications and in order to enable them to supervise during the preliminary bombardment, Commanders of Divisions will take over command of their divisional fronts as follows:-
>
> 13th September 23rd Division will go into Headquarters at Burgomasters Farm and take over command of their offensive front under arrangements made with 24th Division. GOC 23rd Division may either direct a brigadier to represent him at Burgomasters Farm or detail one to march the Division from the training area.
>
> Brigades of 23rd and 41st Divisions will take over their brigade headquarters for the offensive by September 16th and place a detachment of the Brigade Signals Company in them to ensure the working of the communications.

The intensive gathering of intelligence relevant to the battlefield and the enemy was fed into the planning process and necessary changes made. Thus the War Diary noted on 15 September:

> Aeroplane photographs taken yesterday reveal the Dumbarton Lakes district south of Inverness Copse is much more marshy than was at first thought, due to heavy shelling damming the stream and smashing the banks. In consequence the Divisional plans for attack have to be modified.

This entailed some quite tricky manoeuvring by the infantry, as battalions had to side step and follow each other around the inundations, and caused some problems on the day of battle. As late as 18 September the 23rd Division was agreeing slight alterations to the jumping off line of 1st Australian Division and the subsequent adjustment of the barrage plans of both.

An exchange between Major General Babington (23rd Division) and Lieutenant General Morland (X Corps) shows that the British generals were far more tactically aware than their critics give them credit for, and that it was not only the Germans who thought about reverse slopes and timely counter-attacks. On 11 September Babington replied to a Corps memo that he was aware of the need to meet enemy counter-attacks and that he intended leaving the details to his brigade commanders, but did point out that the area suggested by Corps for the deployment was actually a forward slope. He said he would use the area in rear of the Blue Line to keep his reserves 'less shaky' and fresh. Morland replied next day that Corps had no wish to interfere but wanted only to stress that counter-attack troops must be able to counter-attack immediately while the enemy was trying to reorganise. It was the Brigade in Divisional Reserve that would make any prepared counter-attacks as necessary.

A Final Order was issued on 17 September summarising all arrangements made to date, without yet giving the actual attack date. It gave information about the enemy opposite them (the Bavarian Ersatz Division – not, it has to be said, one of Germany's finest) and of possible counter-attack routes. With this in mind it stressed that in selecting the final consolidation line care should be taken to have good observation over the Reutelbeek and Kronnebeek valleys. It also requested that Situation Reports must be sent in by brigades on reaching their objectives and also regularly every two hours after Zero hour.

Both divisions achieved all their objectives in the battle entirely up to the timetable. In accordance with best practice both also wrote extensive after action reports, drawing out tactical and organisational lessons from the fighting to be incorporated in future training and combat. The Australians did make use of their Light Horse squadron to assist the Divisional Commander in keeping a grip on the battle. At 9.20 am on 20 September the War Diary recorded that

> no information had been received as to the situation of the right of the 2nd Australian Infantry Brigade. A patrol of Light Horse was therefore given the following order: The situation of the Right Brigade ... is not clear. Move by the south of Glencorse Wood and Black Watch Corner and report if the latter place has been taken by us.[8]

At 1.30 pm the patrol reported in, sending its message by one of the wireless tanks:

> 8th Battalion occupying Black Watch Corner. 7th and portions of 8th Battalions have reached third objective in front of Black Watch Corner. Enemy massing in vicinity of Cameron House.

This information about a potential counter-attack would have been passed straight to the heavy artillery who would have liberally shelled the area immediately.

At 1.30 pm another mounted patrol was sent forward as the Divisional Commander wanted confirmation of the report from a contact aeroplane that British infantry had been seen firing flares from a very forward trench. At 4 pm the patrol reported back by telephone that the trench in question was not occupied by Australian or any other troops.

In the very extensive reports written by 23rd Division there was a great deal of comment on the various aspects of command and control through signals communication. The message maps, based on the 1/10,000 maps in widespread use, were cluttered with too much detail (especially after most trenches had been rendered unidentifiable by the Royal Artillery). The response to calls for flares from contact aeroplanes was not good, partly because the flares themselves had become damp during the overnight rain but also because, after high casualties amongst officers and senior NCOs, the men were still reluctant to light them on their own initiative. The new SOS rifle grenade was praised as 'the best thing of its kind that has been issued', whereas the SOS Daylight Mortar Signal had been not used at all as it was not helpful when the men were scattered about in semi-open warfare. A daylight rifle grenade signal would be far better. Old-fashioned visual communication had been very good (more Lucas Lamps were needed per battalion) and pigeons were praised yet again for their reliability. When the division issued another 'Comment on Operations'[9] a few days later, with an extended discussion about the problem of communication between infantry and aircraft, it was printed up as a Second Army document and issued under Harington's signature. When Second Army summarised the fighting of 20 and 26 September there was much comment on the value of deep buried cables, power buzzers, runners and pigeons, and on the need for more training in the use of the prismatic compass, and on the excellence of models and replicas used on the training grounds.

Of the six divisions committed to the attack by Second Army, five (1st and 2nd Australian, 19th, 23rd and 39th British) achieved all their objectives on time. Only the 41st Division ran into trouble and achieved 'only' about seventy-five per cent of what was required of it. There is nothing in the way the division prepared for the battle, or in the record of its commander, Major General Sidney Lawford, to explain this inability to match the divisions either side of it. We must look for an explanation in the cruel realities of the battle itself. The overnight rain, which had caused such alarm before the attack began, left the going slippery for all infantry but it seems to have been particularly bad on the 41st Division's front. The barrage moved away at its pre-determined rate and the infantry began to fall behind. The German retaliation added immediately to the mounting difficulties. The infantry went in at 05.43 hours and the first message received at Division was at 06.10 from their 124th Brigade saying that all forward communications had been cut by enemy shell fire and only one of its four battalions had reported in. While messages were received from 23rd and 39th Divisions to say things were going well, it was 07.00 before 117th Brigade (39th Division) gave the news that 10th Queens were held up by an enemy strong point, had lost the barrage and were taking heavy casualties. They (117th Brigade) were going to order their neighbouring unit to assist but had themselves lost contact with 124th Brigade, asking 41st Division to relay the message forward.

As messages flowed in from various sources – flanking units, corps headquarters, Divisional Observation Officers, artillery Forward Observation Officers – the picture was of 122nd Brigade struggling forward with difficulty and 124th Brigade being badly held up. 10th Queens on the right were in such a bad way that the follow-on battalion, 32nd Royal Fusiliers, sent a message in by pigeon that they had made almost no progress and were more or less still on their old front line. The contact aeroplanes reported that their calls for flares from the ground had met with no response. By midday, with 23rd and 39th Divisions consolidating on their final objectives, 124th Brigade was still struggling forward between its first and second objectives.

Lawford ordered his reserve (123rd) brigade up and by 08.30 two of its battalions were being fed into the battle. The day ended with 122nd Brigade on most of its final (third) objective and 124th Brigade just beyond its second objective, held up by the formidable defences of the German 'Tower Hamlets' position, but able to join in the defeat of all German counter-attacks during the day. The commanding officers of the attacking battalions had done everything in their power to get their men forward – more than one of them became engaged in close small arms fire with the enemy – two were killed and three wounded during the battle.

If the imponderable human factor could offer inspiration and lead men to achievement in the face of terrible danger, it could also expose weakness and frailty. It is clear that large parts of the two leading battalions of 124th Brigade broke and fled at one stage, before being rallied and returned to duty. One commander of an artillery brigade spoke very frankly that his Forward Observation Officers and battalion liaison officers had been 'very bad' and had 'let me down badly' on the day.[10] The true history of any battle is made up in equal parts of such human endeavours and failings.

Gough's Fifth Army supported the attack with five divisions, two of which achieved all their objectives (9th Scottish and 58th London Divisions) and three of which did not (20th Light, 51st Highland and 55th West Lancashire). Again it is the case that these divisions are doing nothing to outward appearance differently from each other or other divisions in the BEF (with one interesting exception which we shall come to presently). It is significant that the two successful divisions were wholly fresh to the battle; the other three had all been engaged in serious fighting since 31 July. In a general sense Fifth Army seems to have been more willing to place higher demands in terms of trench duty and labouring on those divisions soon to be involved in major assaults than is the case in Second Army. This is a phenomenon that requires further research but the anecdotal evidence of soldiers preferring service in Second, or any other, Army rather than the Fifth is hard to ignore.

The 58th (2nd/1st London) Division was a second line Territorial formation which had come out to France in January/February 1917 and had seen some fairly stiff fighting at Bullecourt in May. It was in the front line from 1 September and actively patrolled and raided to dominate No Man's Land. The attack orders went out on 9 September and by 13 September 173rd Brigade had relieved the assault and reserve brigades (174th and 175th) so that they could get on with training and rehearsal. The various 'Instructions' described above were issued between 14 and 18 September.[11] There were some extra provisions in that Instruction No. 3 (15 September) covered the work of one of the 'special companies' of the Royal Engineers, who were to deploy 350 Livens projectors for a possible gas attack. The details of signals communications included the use of messenger dogs, and Instruction No. 9 (17 September) covered the question of infantry co-operation with tanks. These instruments of war were, relatively speaking, still in their infancy and were a long way from being the certain salvation of any infantry they were sent to support. The problem of battlefield communication was heightened by these behemoths lumbering about with very limited vision. It is with deep compassion for these difficulties that we might read the instruction: 'Infantry requiring the help of tanks will wave their steel helmets on top of their rifle', and understand the imperative order:

> Infantry are on no account to wait for the arrival of tanks. On the other hand, if a tank has pushed ahead of the Infantry and seized an enemy strong point, it must be immediately supported by the nearest infantry.

As it happened the overnight rain before the battle made the going very difficult for the tanks and they were not able to keep up with the attack.

58th Division was wholly successful in its attack. 173rd Brigade made a feint to distract the Germans from a powerful blow by 174th Brigade, which penetrated the enemy lines to a great depth and then turned and rolled up their defences. To give some idea of what a Divisional Commander and his General Staff coped with during a battle we shall survey the 120 messages that came into his command post during the day.

The earliest messages were delivered verbally by artillery Forward Observation Officers down their telephone lines saying things were going well, and from individual tanks reporting that they were unable to get forward at all. Then the leading battalion (2nd/8th Londons, Post Office Rifles) reported good progress and flank and brigades and divisions began reporting in. Brigade Headquarters sent in progress reports, including the rapidly growing prisoner count. They soon after corrected an over-optimistic report about the early fall of Schuler Farm on 55th Division's front. Corps HQ sent a message summarising the early reports of the contact planes, giving an approximate front line reached. At 10.28 the 51st (Highland) Division sent in a message by a wounded London Regiment officer saying all was going well and that the enemy had been seen running away in considerable numbers. The interrogation of German prisoners yielded useful information, including the warning of a counter-attack approach route and the assessment that their morale was 'rotten', with many 18-year-olds in the line. At 11.47 a messenger pigeon, wounded but still 'at duty', arrived with news sent by an FOO of a counter-attack forming. This sort of information was passed immediately to the Royal Artillery who destroyed most counter-attacks on the day in their earliest stages. At midday Fifth Army sent round a general summary of the news, including cheery bits of foreign news! The early afternoon saw a flurry of messages from 51st Division about their difficulty in meeting German counter-attacks, casualty returns from attacking units and a 55th Division report about the continuing problems at Schuler Farm, revealed by an RFC contact patrol failing to get any response from the infantry in the vicinity. Fifth Army circulated detailed weather reports and forecasts at 15.40 and 20.04 hours. Towards the end of the day the news was of general progress (from Army HQ) and the successful defeat of all enemy counter-attacks (from brigade HQs).

Thus the divisional commander was able to watch his own portion of the battle unfold to plan; his reserves were not called on at all. On his right the 55th (West Lancashire) Division was having a more torrid time. They knew the power of the German defences before them, which had defeated two attacks already. The division attacked with ten of its twelve infantry battalions to try to overwhelm the position. Interestingly, all three brigade headquarters and both Artillery Group commanders were grouped together in the tunnelled dug-outs near Wieltje for the maximum possible co-operation. The after action report detailed the ferocious fighting on this sector; despite the steady capture of the first objectives, 'meanwhile the creeping barrage had gone right on so the whole of this fighting and also the subsequent fighting was done without the immediate support of Artillery.'[12] The small 'hills' in this sector were vital as observation posts for the Germans and, as well as being immensely strong points in their own right, were defended by tremendous and continuous counter-attacks.

The problem of command and control was exacerbated, as in any battle, by twists of fate. 164th Brigade reported:

> At this stage in the battle news had been reaching HQ very slowly owing to all the wires between the Forward Station and Cable head being cut immediately after Zero, casualties to runners and the distance to be traversed by them, and smoke obscuring visual communication.

Reconnaissance officers were sent out from the HQ complex at 10.00 hours to clear up the situation and they reported back that the support battalions had all been drawn into the fighting and all forward impetus had been lost. Through the Forward Signals Station it was arranged that the colonel of 1st/5th King's Own would gather all those of his men 'that he still controlled' and hold them as a counter-attack force should the enemy make any progress against the division. Actually the German counter-attacks were being as comprehensively destroyed by British artillery and machine-gun fire here as elsewhere on the battlefield. The slaughter amongst the German infantry was tremendous.

This after action report by the division contained a six-page document entitled 'Action Taken at Advanced Divisional HQ' which was a complete record of all messages received and transmitted during the day. It conveys very well the chaotic environment generated by modern battle, the problem of contradictory and erroneous messages and the desperate quest for up-to-date information on how the battle was developing at the front.

Thus an early message from 58th Division, via one of their FOOs, that British troops were seen in Schuler Farm was soon replaced with news from the same source that it was under attack by units of 58th and 55th Divisions from north and south respectively. At 09.15 division cabled to 164th and 165th Brigades that they must inform them immediately any reserve units of 166th Brigade were used. 166th Brigade was told to be ready to move at fifteen minutes' notice by order of the Divisional GOC, but if communication was lost they were to respond to requests for assistance from Brigade commanders.

At noon an order went from Divisional HQ to 165th Brigade both verbally by telephone link and by cable:

The capture and retention of Hill 37 is of supreme importance. To this end you will use all troops at your disposal who are not engaged elsewhere. You will call upon Division for any extra troops you may require and these will be placed at your disposal. You will send an officer forward to clear up the situation as regards Hill 37 and as to touch with the Brigades on your flanks.

Corps HQ told Division soon after that they were sending a special contact plane to try to ascertain the situation in the Hill 37–Kansas Cross area.

A wounded officer, returning as part of an escort of 150 German prisoners, reported that Schuler Farm had fallen, which seemed to confirm another message from 58th Division to that effect. It was not until 14.50 hours that this was proven not to be the case by other officers returning from the front. The real difficulty for the Divisional Commander and his artillery officers was illustrated by the request for 165th Brigade to confirm that none of their troops were forward of Hill 37 so that the artillery barrage could be brought back to work over the ground again.

By 16.10 hours the GOC, the thoroughly competent Major General Jeudwine, sent out the general order:

Ensure that all ground gained is thoroughly consolidated and posts established in depth as ordered. Ground is to be gained up to the Green Line wherever possible and similarly treated. All troops not required for this or for carrying will be reorganised under hand of their commanders so as to be available as Reserve, in case of counter-attack or to gain ground. Report dispositions, line held and what posts are held in depth stating garrisons as early as possible.

At about this time the Corps Commander (Lieutenant General Sir Ivor Maxse) released 176th Brigade (59th Division) from his reserve to assist 55th Division as the whole of 166th Brigade had been fed into the battle by then.

The total number of messages passing through the Divisional HQ Signals Office at Canal Bank was logged at 1,145.

It is interesting briefly to compare the approach to battle of the 55th Division, where its entire infantry was drawn into desperate fighting, and that of Major-General Harper's 51st (Highland) Division. Harper had clearly and logically thought through his own idea of battle and decided that attacking with large numbers of infantry merely invited heavy casualties. He assigned just one brigade, reinforced to six battalions, to carry out the attack where most other divisions were going in 'two up'. While the Highlanders did achieve all their objectives at one stage in the battle, they found themselves too depleted and disorganised successfully to resist the massive organised counter-attacks that hit them later in the afternoon. While not every division achieved all its objectives, only on this sector did the British actually lose ground once gained to the Germans, causing great difficulty for the neighbouring formations.

This last example shows that the executive conduct of the battle was firmly in the hands of the Divisional Commander. We have spent a good deal of time showing how they all conformed to a standard operational Procedure in the planning and preparation of their battles and how the central problem was one of command and control. Once the battle had commenced there was little enough the individual general could do to influence its course and conduct. The friction of war and the fragility of most available means of communication made the overall situation complex and difficult and it was only by inculcating these standard procedures and battle drills that the British generals could commit their troops to battle with confidence.

NOTES

1 J Lee, 'Some Lessons of the Somme: The British Infantry in 1917' in B Bond *et al, Look to Your Front: Studies in the First World War* (Staplehurst, 1999).
2 SS135, December 1916, 39
3 J Edmonds, *Military Operations: France and Belgium 1917 Vol. 2* (London 1948), Appendix XXIV, 456–9.
4 ibid, 458.
5 SS148 *Forward Inter-Communication in Battle* was issued in March 1917.
6 1st Australian Division's General Staff plans. Public Record Office (PRO), Kew, WO 95/3/58.
7 PRO, WO 95/2169, 23rd Division General Staff.
8 PRO, WO95/3158. All divisions produced a Narrative of Operations after major actions and many specifically studied the lessons to be learned. The quality and thoroughness of these reports are a valuable source of study when assessing the performance of individual divisions and of the evolution of the BEF in general.
9 PRO, WO95/2169.
10 PRO, WO95/2617, 41st Division General Staff.
11 PRO, WO95/2987, 58th Division General Staff.
12 PRO, WO95/2903, 55th Division General Staff.

CHAPTER VII

'Building Blocks': Aspects of Command and Control at Brigade level in the BEF's Offensive Operations, 1916–1918

Peter Simkins

The infantry brigade can be described as the 'building block' of the BEF's offensive operations on the Western Front during the First World War. From the advent of the trench warfare deadlock in late 1914, on through the great battles of attrition of 1916 and 1917, and even in the mixture of set-piece assaults and semi-open warfare that characterised the 'Hundred Days' offensive of August–November 1918, the most common attack formation employed by British and Dominion infantry divisions involved the deployment of two brigades on the divisional attack frontage with a third in support or reserve. Until the reorganisation of the BEF in early 1918, the standard British and Dominion division contained three infantry brigades, each of which, in turn, was composed of four battalions. In the spring of 1915, when the first of Kitchener's New Army divisions were preparing to embark for active service, the war establishment of a British infantry brigade in the field, including headquarters personnel, was 4,116, of whom 125 were officers and 3,991 were other ranks.[1] Between late November 1915 and July 1917, a machine-gun company and a light trench mortar battery were added to each brigade, increasing its personnel by another 200 officers and men.[2] In most big attacks, a proportion of each battalion would normally be left out of action in order to form the nucleus of a reorganised unit in the event of heavy casualties. For example, at Serre on 1 July 1916, the 12th York and Lancaster Regiment (Sheffield City Battalion) – part of the 94th Brigade in the 31st Division – sent between 740 and 750 officers and men into action out of a total strength of 980. In the same brigade, the 11th East Lancashire Regiment (Accrington Pals) went over the top some 720 strong while the 13th and 14th York and Lancaster Regiment (1st and 2nd Barnsley Pals), in support, attacked with a combined total of 1,442.[3] Thus, even allowing for those left out of battle for various reasons, a brigade on the Somme might still go into action with a fighting strength of around 3,000 – a number substantial enough to test the mettle of any officer charged with the command and control of the formation in question.

The cumulative effect of casualties and continuing manpower problems caused the reduction of the majority of the BEF's infantry divisions from twelve battalions to nine at the beginning of 1918 and, at the same time, most brigades were reduced from four battalions to three. Even among the British divisions there was an exception, the Regular 5th Division, which came back to the Western Front from Italy in April 1918 and retained its full complement of twelve battalions – with four battalions in each brigade – until as late as October that year. A second measure that affected the strength of brigades from March 1918 onwards was the removal of their machine-gun companies, which were thenceforth grouped together to form divisional machine-gun battalions.[4] In contrast to British units, the four Canadian divisions on the Western Front kept their twelve-battalion organisation (four per brigade) throughout the war, thanks largely to the commander of the Canadian Corps, Lieutenant-General Sir Arthur Currie, who, early in 1918, stuck to his belief that the twelve-battalion division possessed far more offensive power than the smaller formation then being generally adopted. Having first won the support of the Canadian Overseas Minister, Sir Edward Kemp, Currie persuaded all the relevant authorities to break up the 5th Canadian Division, then in England, and to post its men to under-strength units in France. By this means, battalions could be brought up to a strength of 100 men over and above war establishment without any alteration to the existing infantry structure or any increase in staffs.[5]

The New Zealand Division, which, for a few months from mid-1917 actually contained as many as *four* brigades, each of four battalions, reverted to the three-brigade system in February 1918 but thereafter maintained a four-battalion organisation in each of these brigades by breaking up its 4th Brigade to furnish reinforcements and to form three 'entrenching battalions' as a reserve.[6] The five Australian divisions – which, unlike the British, Canadian and New Zealand elements of the BEF, still relied in 1918 upon voluntary enlistments rather than con-scription to provide their manpower – similarly managed to keep their three-brigade, twelve-battalion organisation relatively intact until the late autumn, although three battalions of the Australian Imperial Force (AIF) were disbanded in April and May 1918 and eight more were advised in September that they would soon follow suit. In the wake of strong protests and 'mutinies' against the proposed disbandments and amalgamations by men of the battalions concerned, the process was deferred – with the consent of Rawlinson, the Fourth Army commander – until after the assault on the Hindenburg Line. The disbandments duly took place, though not without further incidents, in October 1918.[7] By then the Australian Corps had fought its last battle, at Montbréhain, so the belated

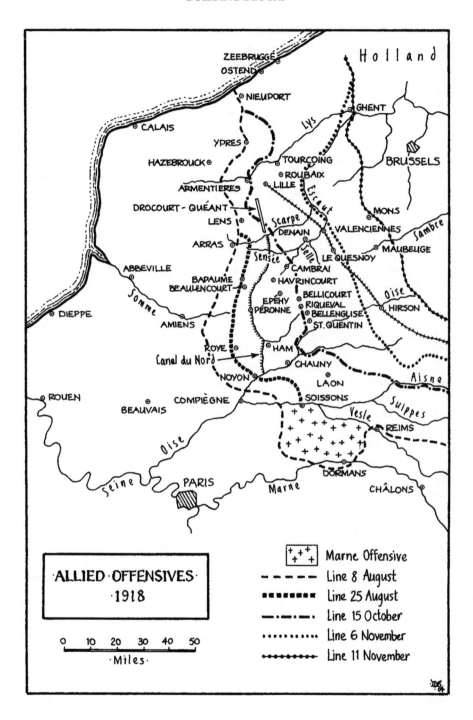

ALLIED·OFFENSIVES·
·1918

Marne Offensive	
Line 8 August	
Line 25 August	
Line 15 October	
Line 6 November	
Line 11 November	

0 10 20 30 40 50
·Miles·

reduction of Australian brigades from four battalions to three did not, by itself, have such a serious impact on the Fourth Army's operations in the final month of the war as it would have done two months earlier.

There was, of course, no escaping the stark facts of the overall decline in the combat strength of the BEF, even if this was offset, to some extent, by the greater firepower available to the front-line infantry, particularly in the form of Lewis guns and rifle grenades. For instance, on 31 August 1918, in the 174th Brigade of the 58th (London) Division, the 6th London could muster only nine officers and 344 other ranks for the attack on Marrières Wood, near Péronne, and three of these officers had been lent by the 7th London while fifty-three of the men were from battalion headquarters. The other two battalions in the brigade were no better off.[8] The same day, in the savage struggle for Mont St Quentin, the 5th Australian Brigade was down to only seventy officers and 1,250 other ranks, its attack being delivered by 550 men with 200 in support.[9] In the 5th Australian Division on 29 September 1918, the trench strength of the 8th Australian Brigade was 1,926, that of the 15th Australian Brigade was 1,584, and the 14th Australian Brigade had just 1,131 all ranks. Similarly, at the end of that month, the 43rd Brigade of the British 14th (Light) Division had a fighting strength of sixty-three officers and 1,667 men.[10] Nevertheless, despite all such reductions in numbers through re-organisation, battle losses and general manpower shortages, the brigade continued to be a key component in the chain of operational planning and command and, to the end of the war, it remained the principal 'building block' of divisional attacks, representing an indispensable link between corps and divisional headquarters on the one hand and the front-line infantry on the other. It is therefore perhaps somewhat surprising that, in the historiography of the First World War, comparatively little attention has been paid to the infantry brigade as a command element or battlefield formation.[11]

It cannot be denied that the disparities in size and organisation between British divisions and brigades and their Dominion counterparts in 1918 did cause increased difficulties in the planning and conduct of offensive operations in the BEF during the 'Hundred Days'. The retention of the four-battalion organisation unquestionably gave Australian, Canadian and New Zealand brigades more 'punching power' in attack than British brigades now possessed, and the smaller British formations simul-taneously saw their capacity to undertake *sustained* offensive operations downgraded.[12] Even during periods of routine trench warfare, a brigade with four battalions could place two of them in the front line, leaving one in support and one in reserve. With only three battalions per brigade, the problems of inter-battalion reliefs were compounded, for only one battalion was available to relieve those in the front line, making it imperative to keep one of the front-line battalions in the fire trenches for a longer spell. Hanway Cumming, who, in 1918, commanded the British 110th Brigade (21st Division), commented that this was also, incidentally, 'a great waste of Staff' as 'it was just as easy to administer and command four or even five battalions as three'.[13] In major offensive operations, the difficulties arising from the smaller brigade organisation were correspondingly exacerbated, for both the weight and impetus of British divisional attacks were thereby reduced; the ability of a British brigade commander, in an assault, to 'leap-frog' fresh battalions through each other to take successive objectives was inevitably more limited; there were fewer troops available to mop up and consolidate objectives or deal with German counter-attacks; and the commander and staff had fewer options open to them when trying to adapt their plans to respond to fleeting opportunities or cope with unforeseen crises. However, the adverse effects of these very real problems on the actual operational *performance* of British formations should not be exaggerated. As I have argued elsewhere, during the 'Hundred Days' ten British divisions achieved a success rate in attacks at least equal to – and in a few cases better than – the leading six or seven Dominion divisions.[14] Clearly, then, factors other than size and organisation also helped to determine success or failure in performance and command and control and brigade level.

Historians and soldiers alike have generally tended to emphasise the limitations of the brigade commander's role and influence on planning in the Great War. John Gellibrand, one of the most successful of all Australian brigade and divisional commanders of the war, succinctly summarised the constraints rather than the opportunities of brigade command when he wrote, a decade after the Armistice: 'The Brigadier had little scope beyond oiling the works and using his eyes'.[15] Others point out that the main strategic and tactical objectives of operations were usually predetermined at higher command levels, as were the broader aspects of the allocation of resources, including artillery support, for any given attack. The primary responsibilities of the brigade commander, it has been suggested, were training and administration, while, in battle, he was expected to get his troops to the right place at the right time to fulfil the plans of those above him. Before an assault he would decide how many of his battalions should be assigned to the task in hand and how they might best be deployed in action. Once the attack was under way, the brigade commander was often called upon to make detailed adjustments to the original plan as the operations unfolded, and to seize the initiative, if a chance to do so presented itself, by committing his own reserves at the critical juncture. He could therefore exert *some* influence on the course and outcome of the battle, provided that he had sited his headquarters or command post wisely, was able to keep in touch with his subordinates and could consequently judge what was happening in the front line. In practice, however, the uncertain nature and vulnerability of battlefield communications forward of brigade headquarters restricted his freedom of action and influence even in these areas of command.[16] In a defensive battle, his chief tactical decisions were concerned with the positions of his various battalions and the commitment of the brigade reserve.[17] On taking over the 110th Brigade (21st Division) on 18 March 1918, Hanway Cumming spent the afternoon checking the defensive scheme he had inherited as well as methods of supply, reliefs, communications, artillery support 'and the thousand and one other details which it behoves a Brigadier to have at his finger-ends . . . if he wishes to keep his finger on the pulse of his command'.[18]

When out of the line, the brigade commander was supposed to ensure that his men were trained to the desired standards in addition to being properly clothed, equipped and fed. Man-management and the maintenance of the morale of the officers and men under his command constituted a vital part of his activities. In Dr John Bourne's words, a brigade commander's relationships with his subordinates were 'essentially face-to-face and day-to-day. They were often in the trenches and sometimes beyond them'.[19] The brigade commander had to be satisfied that his own staff and subordinate officers were efficient and also well briefed on the content and nuances of orders and battle plans so that they could direct operations in his place should he become a casualty or lose contact through a failure of communications.[20] In the demanding conditions and circumstances of the Western Front, even the most dedicated, experienced or gifted of commanders were rarely able to meet all of these criteria at the same time and the unremitting pressure inevitably undermined the physical or mental resilience of many. When Colonel H Pope, the British-born commander of the 14th Australian Brigade, was sent home shortly after the Battle of Fromelles in July 1916, Lieutenant-General Sir Alexander Godley of II Anzac Corps remarked to Senator Pearce, the Australian Minister for Defence: 'I think few people realise what a terrific strain is put upon a man in high command in these desperate actions of modern warfare . . .'[21]

As Roger Lee reminds us, the brigade was the smallest formation to have a *formal* staff structure. To assist him in the execution of his duties, the brigade commander had two principal officers – the brigade major (or BM) and a staff captain. The brigade major – normally a major or senior captain in rank – fulfilled the 'G' functions for the brigade, his central task being to plan the brigade's operations within the larger context of the divisional or corps scheme. Much of his time was spent interpreting commands from higher headquarters and converting them into precise orders and detailed objectives for each of the brigade's subordinate formations. He was also called upon to keep his own commander abreast of all matters concerning the efficiency or strength of the brigade, to advise the brigadier-general as to which local objectives could and should be reached, and to co-ordinate whatever actions might be necessary by smaller units in order to secure those objectives. His responsibilities would therefore embrace liaison with neighbouring formations and the co-ordination of the relevant artillery and trench mortar support on the brigade front. In short, it was at his level 'that the minor tactical planning for the battle was undertaken' and the brigade major's ability was a crucial factor in shaping a brigade's battle performance.[22]

Whereas the brigade major carried out the 'G' functions of his brigade, the 'A' and 'Q' aspects were the responsibility of the staff captain. It was he who had to make sure that the brigade had all the equipment and supplies it needed, that its administration was sound and that, as far as possible, it was up to strength. When attacks were being proposed or in progress, it was the staff captain's job to supervise arrangements for the co-ordination of all support services in the brigade's area, including re-supply, the collection of stragglers and prisoners and the provision of evacuation routes for battle casualties. Others who worked at headquarters included the Brigade Intelligence Officer, Signal Officer and Veterinary Officer. Specialists such as the Brigade Bombing Officer, Trench Mortar Officer, Gas Officer, Musketry Officer and Transport Officer were similarly attached to the brigade staff, advised the brigadier-general and were responsible for training in their own individual spheres of expertise. The latter were not, however, officially part of the brigade headquarters and usually accepted these tasks in addition to other duties.[23]

The rapid expansion of the BEF in 1915–16 created an unprecedented demand for such staff officers and it is small wonder that the fiery furnace of the Somme quickly exposed the inexperience of a large number of them. Walter Guinness noted in his diary on 23 August 1916 that 'many of our young staff officers seem quite unfit for their jobs and are hopelessly careless about details such as giving map references, places and times of rendezvous accurately'.[24] Contrary to popular perception, the life of a staff officer at brigade level was both dangerous and exacting, even under a comparatively benign officer such as John Ponsonby, who commanded the 2nd Guards Brigade from July 1915 to November 1916 and again from March to August 1917, before taking over the 40th Division. Oliver Lyttelton, who was a staff captain under him in 1917, has portrayed him as an officer who was genuinely loved by his men and who had 'a highly developed sense of humour and of the ridiculous', but added that Ponsonby was a 'rather old-fashioned' soldier and 'relied much upon his staff in planning and drafting orders'.[25] Anthony Eden, the future Prime Minister, was serving with the 198th Brigade of the 66th (East Lancashire) Division in late September 1918 and, at the age of 20, was then the youngest brigade major in the British Army. He later recalled how, during the final Allied offensive, the work was particularly strenuous. Even by the standards of trench warfare, he wrote, 'there was little chance of sleep; by day attack, by night preparing and issuing orders for the next advance.[26] The dynamic yet foul-tempered Keppel Bethell – who, in 1917, commanded the 74th Brigade (25th Division) at the age of 34 and, the following year, went on to command the 66th Division – was one officer who frequently drove his exasperated staff almost to breaking-point with his demands. His brigade major, Walter Guinness, recorded on 6 April 1917 that Bethell 'becomes frightfully impatient and unreasonable when things don't go right' and on 2 August, during the early stages of Third Ypres, his temper 'became absolutely impossible'. Guinness noted that Bethell was 'asking everybody to do about six things at once and hardly gave us time to sit down and start on one of them before he called them back and asked them to do something else'.[27] All the same, Guinness felt that 'a Brigade Major's job is the most attractive to my taste' and Eden too coveted the post. 'The brigade and its staff,' Eden declared, 'seemed of exactly the right size and scope for individual effort to be rewarding, while the contacts with units were close enough to have a human interest. This applied particularly to the last months of the war when the brigade could be expanded to include cavalry and artillery.'[28]

It is now widely accepted by those who have taken the trouble to mine the rich vein of after-battle reports in the unit war diaries of Haig's forces that, certainly from early 1916 onwards, a continuous process of tactical evaluation, operational analysis and often robust criticism was taking place at all levels of command in the BEF. This process of rigorous, and sometimes brutal, self-examination not only fertilised but also nourished and propagated the shoots of tactical and technical improvement which subsequently enabled the BEF to win a succession of impressive victories in the second half of 1918. Brigade operations, like everything else, became the subject of intense scrutiny and discussion. In the ongoing debate about such operations, the siting of brigade headquarters and the need for personal observation were two of the themes most frequently aired. The pamphlet *Preliminary Notes on the Tactical Lessons of the Recent Operations* (SS119), issued by GHQ in July 1916, laid down that brigade headquarters should move as seldom as possible – a stricture more honoured in the breach than the observance two years later – and stipulated that they should not be situated 'so close to the fight that brigadiers and their Headquarters become involved in the firing line. As a general rule they should be at the most forward place that can be reached in comparative security from rifle fire'. The pamphlet acknowledged that direct observation by the brigade staff 'was of great value and must always be obtained if possible' and decreed that, when two brigades attacked side by side, their respective headquarters should be near to each other. It also advised that brigade commanders and brigade majors should not be away from their headquarters at the same time.[29]

Opinions appear to have varied as to just how close to the front line a brigade headquarters should actually be sited, although the local terrain and tactical conditions plainly helped to shape such decisions. At Serre on 1 July 1916, Brigadier-General H C Rees – by taking advantage of the contours of the ground – placed his command post about 600 yards behind the front line and had 'a perfect view' of the ill-fated attack of his 94th Brigade.[30] For an assault on the Falfemont Farm–Guillemont line in August 1916, however, XIII Corps instructed its divisions that brigade battle headquarters should be 'within about 1,500 yards of our front line'.[31] A characteristically prescriptive memorandum circulated by Gough from Reserve (Fifth) Army Headquarters on 5 October 1916 contained strict guidelines on the handling and reorganisation of a brigade's assaulting and supporting battalions for the capture of second and, possibly, third objectives. To do this, Gough insisted, a brigadier must move forward, 'taking his wires with him', up to or close to the troops who had gained the first objective: 'It is a very serious error, almost an unpardonable one,' Gough states, 'when Brigadiers do not go forward as their command advances.'[32] At a conference at V Corps Headquarters on 16 November 1916, after the opening phase of Gough's attack astride the Ancre, the Corps commander, Lieutenant-General E A Fanshawe, stressed that brigade commanders and staffs must not simply wait for information to come in: 'Brigadiers must know where their flanks rest, and whether there are any gaps in their line; unless these measures are taken, further attacks will not be successful'.[33]

The close connection between personal observation and the timely use of reserves was another related topic that was frequently aired. 'Commanders must control the fight,' GHQ instructed the five Armies on 13 August 1916, in a document that made a series of points specifically directed at brigade and battalion commanders. Isolated advances by detachments beyond reach of support should be avoided, GHQ warned, but the advance must not be delayed by large bodies of men hanging back for those on their flanks. Instead, the note affirmed – in a distinct echo of the stormtroop tactics being developed simultaneously by the German Army – every effort should be made to turn the flanks of centres of resistance and surround them. Reserves should not be wasted in frontal assaults against 'strong places' but 'should rather be thrown in *between* these strong places to confirm success where our advance is progressing favourably and to overcome the enemy's centres of resistance ... by attacking them in flank and rear'.[34] A little over a year later, when assessing the causes of success and failure of Canadian Corps operations during the Third Battle of Ypres, Arthur Currie highlighted the importance of the correct use of reserves in dealing with pillboxes and the German system of defence in depth. In this type of fighting, Currie claimed, there were almost sure to be gaps in the advance and only the prompt deployment of reserves could then remedy the situation. Though conceding that it was not always possible to achieve the ideal, Currie argued that the brigade commander should aim 'to be in a position where he can see for himself the course of the action and in such close proximity to his reserve that he can at once direct them to the right point on the necessity arising'.[35] In the changed tactical conditions of the spring of 1918, GHQ continued to underline the value of personal observation yet now also asserted the need for formations to operate with more streamlined headquarters – working, if necessary, with only a message book. 'In warfare of movement it is neither possible nor desirable for Commands and Staffs, especially those of Divisions and Brigades, to carry out their functions with the facilities and deliberation which have come to be looked on as normal in trench warfare'.[36]

The more sedate pace of issuing orders during the period of relatively static warfare is evident in the advice on 'Staff Work' which is included in the pamphlet SS119, dating from July 1916. Corps and divisional orders, GHQ indicated, should be issued in sufficient time for battalion and company commanders to reconnoitre the ground, make all the necessary preparations and give their own orders. It was estimated that six hours was the minimum time that should be allowed for orders to pass from the corps down to front-line company commanders.[37] Major-General W G Walker, then commanding the British 2nd Division, was convinced in August 1916 that this time allowance had been considerably under-estimated. In presenting his case to Walter Congreve, the commander of XIII Corps, Walker summarised the steps that he thought were necessary in preparing a brigade attack. On receipt of orders from divisional headquarters, Walker maintained, the brigade commander had to study them and go over the ground on which he would be called upon to operate. He should then confer with his battalion commanders before the brigade orders were typed, copied and issued through the Signal Service. The staff captain, meanwhile, would be making arrangements for the supply of ammunition, food and water; the brigade signals officer similarly had to supervise the laying of new lines and the repair of existing ones; and medical arrangements also had to be put in hand, with appropriate instructions circulated to aid posts and dressing stations. Unless due time was given for all such tasks to be 'worked out carefully and deliberately', failure was likely to ensue, Walker predicted, adding: 'It must also be remembered that the late issue of orders to Brigades means sleepless nights for the Staff who probably enter the fight with two sleepless nights behind them'. Brigade and battalion commanders, he contended, should be facing 'critical times in the best mental condition'.[38] One might perhaps note, in passing, that, for the attack on Frankfort Trench on 15 November 1916 – an attack made under very trying conditions – 99th Brigade, one of Walker's own subordinate formations, allowed four hours and twenty minutes between the issue of orders and Zero hour for its assault battalions.[39]

Because it is shared by a number of highly distinguished scholars and soldiers, the view that the parameters of brigade command were comparatively narrow during the Great War obviously merits respect. It is my contention, however, that if this assessment was largely true of brigade command in 1916, and slightly less so in 1917, it certainly did not universally apply to the BEF in the defensive and offensive battles of 1918. Early in April 1918, GHQ itself emphasised the fundamental importance of the brigadier-general's role in the more open warfare that now prevailed, pronouncing that the present battle should be conducted by 'the Commander on the spot (that is, in the majority of cases, the Infantry Brigade Commander) ... according to the actual events'.[40] Even on the Somme, or at Arras and Passchendaele, once the set-piece phase of an assault was over, or had broken down – possibly as a result of German counter-attacks – brigade commanders had opportunities to exercise initiative and *real* local command. In the semi-open warfare of the 'Hundred Days', tactical challenges and objectives were changing daily, sometimes hourly, and, because there was no longer any single tactical formula that could be employed in the majority of operations, a much greater degree of flexibility was required of, and allowed to, divisional and brigade commanders and their staffs. By late August 1918, as Robin Prior and Trevor Wilson have perceived, operations were more or less continuous and smaller in individual scale: 'Plans were improvised by divisional generals or brigadiers as the situation demanded. Often there was no time to refer these plans to corps commanders, let alone to the Army commander'.[41]

Much, of course, depended on the calibre of the man 'on the spot'. Who were the officers who held brigade command? Until recently – with a few exceptions – they have remained individually and collectively almost entirely unknown to the general public. Some – like Lord Cavan (4th Guards Brigade), Arthur Currie (2nd Canadian Brigade), Cyril Deverell (20th Brigade), Bernard Freyberg VC (88th Brigade), William Glasgow (13th Australian Brigade), Edmund Ironside (99th Brigade) and John Monash (4th Australian Brigade) – went on to hold high rank or office or became prominent national figures. Others left published memoirs, have been the subject of biographies or are remembered simply for their courage, leadership or tendency to attract controversy. This group includes Arthur Asquith (189th Brigade), Adrian Carton de Wiart VC (12th Brigade), Frank Crozier (119th Brigade), H E 'Pompey' Elliott (15th Australian Brigade), John Gellibrand (6th Australian Brigade), James Jack (28th Brigade) and Frank Maxwell VC (27th Brigade).[42] At the time of writing, Dr John Bourne's massive multi-biography of British generals of the First World War is eagerly awaited but the impressive work carried out to date by Dr Bourne and the Abbots Way Research Group has already illuminated many previously dark corners of our knowledge of the key level of brigade command in the BEF.

According to Dr Bourne, the fifty-one infantry brigade commanders whose formations were part of the order of battle on the Somme on 1 July 1916 were principally Regular officers and almost all infantrymen by background. Two of them – H Bruce-Williams (137th Brigade, 46th Division) and G C Kemp (138th Brigade, 46th Division) – were sappers while only J B Jardine (97th Brigade, 32nd Division) was a cavalryman. Four of the fifty-one had begun the war as infantry battalion commanders, twenty-two more had been infantry battalion officers – all but four of them majors – and sixteen had been staff officers, though only eleven had passed staff college. Five brigades on 1 July were commanded by 'dugouts', officers who had been brought back from retirement. Two of these five (W J T Glasgow of 50th Brigade and R B Fell of 51st Brigade) were in the 17th (Northern) Division. The most remarkable of the five 'dugouts' was J D Crosbie, who had retired as long ago as 1893 and, having rejoined in 1914, was appointed to the command of 12th Brigade (4th Division) just twenty-seven days before the Somme offensive started. Eight other brigade commanders – including O de L Williams (92nd Brigade) and H C Rees (94th Brigade), both in the 31st Division – had been in post under a month and four had been in command less than two months. R B Fell was the oldest at the age of 55 and the youngest, at 35, was Frank Burnell-Nugent (167th Brigade, 56th Division).

In the light of the disaster of 1 July 1916 it is small wonder that, on the whole, the careers of this particular group of brigade commanders did not blossom. Only five (or just under ten per cent) subsequently rose to divisional command. Two of the five, H W Higginson (53rd Brigade) and T H Shoubridge (54th Brigade), came from Ivor Maxse's outstanding 18th (Eastern) Division. The others were H Bruce-Williams, Cyril Deverell and W de L Williams (86th Brigade). Not counting those who were killed or wounded, eighteen lost their commands before the end of 1916 and five of these had been relieved by the end of July. Four of the overall group of fifty-one were, however, still commanding brigades at the Armistice. The one who deserves special mention is E S D'E Coke of the 169th Brigade in the 56th (London) Division, who was the only officer to command his particular brigade. As Bourne notes, this was the sole brigade in the BEF 'which did not experience a change of command during the course of the war'.[43]

Another eighty-one brigade commanders were to become involved in the Somme offensive after 1 July. Again primarily Regular officers, fifty-three of these had been to Sandhurst or Woolwich but only twenty (or just under 25 per cent) had passed staff college. Like those who commanded brigades on the first day of the Somme battle, they were predominantly infantrymen (91.4 per cent) and, of the five cavalrymen in this second sample group, Arthur Solly-Flood (35th Brigade, 12th Division) had started out in the infantry. The highest rank any of the eighty-one had held by August 1914 was colonel and thirty-seven (45.7 per cent) had been majors. One, B R Mitford (72nd Brigade, 24th Division), had commanded his brigade since September 1914 and thirteen had been in post for more than a year but thirty-five (or 43.2 per cent) had led their brigades for less than six months and twenty-five (or 30.9 per cent) for three months or less.[44] Nine of the group were 'dugouts' – a proportion (11.1 per cent) roughly similar to the brigadiers of 1 July. A number of these 'dugouts' acquitted themselves sufficiently well on the Somme to retain their brigade commands until well into 1918 or even until the end of the war. They included W H L Ailgood (45th Brigade), R C Browne-Clayton (59th Brigade), L F Green-Wilkinson (166th and 148th Brigades), M L Hornby (116th and 137th Brigades), R O Kellett (99th Brigade) and George Pereira (47th and 43rd Brigades). The oldest of the post-1 July group of brigadiers was H J Evans (115th Brigade), who was nearly 56 and was removed from his command in the 38th (Welsh) Division, apparently on age grounds, at the end of August 1916. The youngest was H P Burn (152nd Brigade), who was 34. Only two of the British brigade commanders on the Somme were Territorial officers – Arthur Hubback (2nd Brigade), who was an architect, and Henry Page-Croft (68th Brigade), a maltster. Neither, however, commanded Territorial brigades. As many as twenty-six (or 32.1 per cent) of the brigade commanders who joined the Somme offensive *after* 1 July were subsequently given divisional commands but others fell by the wayside, brigade commanders being convenient scapegoats when things went wrong. Of twenty-seven divisions that entered the Somme battle after 1 July, only five had no changes of command at brigade level during, or just after the end of, the offensive.[45] The rate of turnover is rightly attributed by John Bourne to the widespread 'de-skilling' which was the inevitable result of the vast and rapid expansion of the British Army from 1914 to 1916. The huge growth in the size of the BEF, and in the demand for officers, diluted the amount of relevant experience available at all command levels. During the Somme campaign, Bourne writes, 'the BEF was compelled to undergo a particularly brutal form of on the job training. Some commanders rose to the challenge. Some did not'.[46]

By 29 September 1918, when the BEF finally broke through the Hindenburg Line and crossed the St Quentin Canal, its 189 brigade commanders on that date were still predominantly men who had been Regular officers in August 1914. Only two – H E ap Rhys Price (113th Brigade) and E A Fagan (12th Brigade) – had an Indian Army background and only six were Territorial officers, including G D Goodman (21st Brigade), Viscount Hampden (185th Brigade), Arthur Maxwell (174th Brigade), W F Mildren (141st Brigade), J B Pollok-M'Call (25th Brigade) and R E Sugden (151st Brigade). Of these, Maxwell was a banker by profession while Mildren was a company director. A few (some of whom possessed pre-war military experience) had been civilians on 4 August 1914. Amongst these were Bernard Freyberg VC, George Gater of the 62nd Brigade (an educational administrator), George Rollo of the 150th Brigade (an engineer) and E A Wood of the 55th Brigade. A fair proportion of the Dominion brigade commanders came from similar backgrounds to the latter group. Australian brigade commanders, for example, included H G Bennett, an accountant; J H Cannan, who worked in insurance; J C Robertson and Edwin Tivey, who were stockbrokers; H A Goddard and R L Leane, who were businessmen – Leane having left school at the age of 12; J C Stewart, who worked in a bank; S C E Herring, who was an estate agent; W R McNicoll, a headmaster; and 'Pompey' Elliott, who was a solicitor. Several of the Australian brigade commanders, however, had also seen some pre-1914 military service, either in the South African War (Elliott, Goddard and Tivey) or at home in the militia.[47] Most of these officers from civilian backgrounds proved at least competent as brigade commanders, and some were outstandingly successful, clearly demonstrating that they were more than capable of transferring their own professional talents into a military context. In this sense, the brigade commanders of late September 1918 – like officers at other command levels in the BEF – collectively constituted much more of a true meritocracy than hitherto.

A notable feature of the September 1918 brigade commanders was their relative youth. One hundred and twenty of them (63.5 per cent) were under 45 and forty-nine of them (25.9 per cent) were under 40 years of age, the average age of *British* brigadiers then being just over 42 and that of Australian brigade commanders being just under 41. In all twenty-eight officers under the age of 35 – five of whom were Australians – had been promoted to brigade command during the war.[48] H G Bennett, one of the Australians, had been the youngest, at 28, when he was appointed to the 3rd Australian Brigade in December 1916, but even he had to give pride of place to Roland Boys Bradford VC, who, on 10 November 1917, was promoted to command the 186th Brigade when he was only 25. Bradford was killed twenty days later during the Battle of Cambrai.[49] One of the most remarkable of the younger brigade commanders was George Gater who was Assistant Director of Education for Nottinghamshire at the outbreak of war and, having then gained a commission, rose to the rank of brigadier-general by 1 November 1917, the date on which he was given command of the 62nd Brigade. At that time he was still only 30.[50] Hanway Cumming, a fellow brigade commander in David Campbell's 21st Division, observed that Gater had 'never seen or thought of soldiering before the war' but had become a 'very able and quick' brigade commander. Cumming described him as a 'delightful companion and a good comrade' who was 'universally liked throughout the Division'.[51]

Brigade commanders generally exhibited the leadership qualities – and weaknesses – of regimental and battalion officers. This was only to be expected as most of them still had the *substantive* rank of regimental officers and had commanded a battalion only a short time before. A large proportion of them had seen active service as younger officers, on the North-West Frontier, in the Sudan and South Africa or in one of the numerous smaller colonial campaigns fought by the British Army in the late 19th and early 20th centuries. They unquestionably possessed more collective and individual experience of combat than their German counterparts had accrued prior to 1914. Indeed, they were schooled to accept discomfort and personal danger and to display bravery, devotion to duty and a paternalistic concern for the welfare of their men.

They were certainly not lacking in courage. Those who already held, or were to win, the Victoria Cross (some of them posthumously) included R B Bradford, J V Campbell (137th Brigade), Adrian Carton de Wiart, Charles FitzClarence (1st Guards Brigade), J Forbes-Robertson (155th Brigade), Bernard Freyberg, Frederick Lumsden (14th Brigade) and Frank Maxwell. The Regular 8th Division had two brigade commanders, Clifford Coffin and George Grogan, who won the VC as brigadier-generals – surely a unique distinction for any division. By the end of the war, in all formations, many other brigade commanders, brigade majors and staff captains had earned decorations for gallantry. For example, by 11 November 1918, Coffin's successor in command of the 25th Brigade, Brigadier-General The Hon. R Brand, held the DSO while the brigade major and the staff captain had both won the MC.[52] W D Croft (27th Brigade), yet another in the series of notable brigade commanders in the 9th (Scottish) Division, had four DSOs, as did E A Wood (55th Brigade). Wood was also Mentioned in Despatches nine times, wounded on five occasions, gassed twice and buried once. This extraordinary officer won the respect of the neighbouring Australians at First Villers Bretonneux on 4 April 1918, and at Ronssoy on 18 September he once more displayed amazing coolness. That day he first entered a German dugout alone, bringing out seven fully-armed prisoners and, later, again single-handed and unarmed, he captured twenty-two more by pelting them in their dugout with old boots and lumps of chalk. The divisional historian pays tribute to the 'smooth readiness of his decisions' and paints a vivid picture of Wood 'stalking along monumentally, a big cigar between his teeth, the familiar lance used as an alpenstock in his grasp'.[53]

The popular misconception that most British generals of the First World War were elderly cavalrymen has been shown above to be false, even if the image is still firmly fixed in the public mind. An equally pervasive and persistent myth is that generals spent all their days and nights safe in luxurious headquarters miles behind the lines, while their men lived and died in mud and squalor. As early as 1922, David Campbell, in his introduction to Hanway Cumming's *A Brigadier in France,* was already finding it necessary to try to dispel the 'absurd idea that the lot of generals and such like was cast in fine *châteaux* and motor-cars'.[54] That Campbell was correct will quickly be appreciated by anyone reading the recent work *Bloody Red Tabs,* by Frank Davies and Graham Maddocks. Thirty-eight British and Dominion brigadier-generals from infantry formations were killed or died of wounds on the Western Front, all but six of them after the start of 1916. Ninety-five (of whom four were later killed) suffered wounds, were gassed or were taken prisoner. Six of these officers were wounded twice. It should also be noted that, on at least thirty-three occasions, their brigade major or staff captain – or, indeed, both – became a casualty at the same time as the brigade commander.[55] Not everyone, however, approved of generals appearing in or near the firing line. Lieutenant-Colonel H M Davson, who commanded an artillery brigade in the 32nd Division, criticised Brigadier-General Frederick Lumsden VC of the division's 14th Brigade for 'dancing about in No Man's Land'.[56]

Some personalities stand out from the mass of brigade commanders for reasons other than, or beyond, battlefield gallantry. This group would include gifted tactical thinkers such as Arthur Solly-Flood, who, having commanded the 35th Brigade in the 12th (Eastern) Division in 1915–16, was made head of the GHQ Training Directorate early in 1917 and succeeded to the command of the 42nd (East Lancashire) Division the following October. Solly-Flood has recently been identified by historians as one of the major influences behind the publication of the seminal *Instructions for the Training of Platoons for Offensive Action* (SS143), the manual that helped to transform the BEF's platoon organisation and tactics in 1917.[57] Others, such as Harold Higginson, who commanded the 53rd Brigade from 1916 to 1918, displayed a consistently high level of tactical grip on the battlefield. The 53rd Brigade's part in the capture of Irles, north-east of Miraumont, on 10 March 1917 was a model attack in both planning and execution, the village being taken after a converging, rather than a frontal, assault. To ensure that the troops kept as close as possible to the barrage, 53rd Brigade even issued diagrams illustrating the bursting patterns of shrapnel. The divisional history called it a 'pretty little victory'.[58] On 22 October 1917, during the Third Battle of Ypres, the brigade took Poelcappelle Brewery, Meunier House and Tracas Farm in another exemplary attack in which Higginson bluffed the enemy with a dummy attack south of the village and then outmanoeuvred the Germans with a thrust to the north.[59] Tactically innovative formations such as the 9th (Scottish) and 18th (Eastern) Divisions seem to have produced an impressive proportion of brigadiers who subsequently rose to divisional command, suggesting, perhaps, that those divisions may have been successful partly because they permitted their brigade commanders to exercise initiative and encouraged them to show tactical flair. The three brigade commanders in the 9th (Scottish) Division on 1 July 1916, for instance – H T Lukin (South African Brigade), A B Ritchie (26th Brigade) and S W Scrase-Dickins (27th Brigade) – were all given divisional commands within six months.[60] Higginson's case, moreover, appears to indicate that, in the best divisions, the devolution of *real* tactical command downwards had begun, and had reached brigade level at least, by the spring of 1917.

Standards of brigade command and control were not necessarily uniform even within the same division, as illustrated by the sharp contrast in the respective performances of the 5th and 6th Australian Brigades (2nd Australian Division) at the Second Battle of Bullecourt on 3 May 1917. Brigadier-General R Smith, the commander of the 5th Brigade, was 'careful, but conventional and unimaginative', according to Eric Andrews.[61] John Gellibrand, commanding the 6th Brigade, was, on the other hand, judged by Bean to be the best 'inspirer of brigade staffs and battalion commanders in the AIF'.[62] While Smith's headquarters for the battle were placed at Noreuil, 2,300 yards from the front, Gellibrand sited his headquarters very close to the start line. When the attack began, Gellibrand's brigade fought its way into the Hindenburg Line but the 5th Brigade on its right – under heavy flanking fire from German positions near Quéant – stopped at the German wire and then fell back in some confusion to its own line, with survivors relating that an unnamed officer had ordered the retreat. Too far back, Smith was unable to respond quickly enough to the crisis and therefore lost control of events, the outcome being 'perhaps the most serious rout of Australian troops in the war'.[63]

Personality and temperament also played a part in determining command performance at brigade level. Some of the most noteworthy 'fighting' brigadier-generals were far from ideal team members. The youthful H Gordon Bennett (3rd Australian Brigade) was undeniably a brave and resourceful front-line commander, being Mentioned in Despatches eight times during the course of the war and winning several decorations. However, his superiors found him prickly and argumentative. As his divisional commander from mid-1918, William Glasgow – himself said by Bean to have the characteristics of the 'best type of English country gentleman' – called Bennett 'a pest'.[64] When Gellibrand succeeded Monash in command of the 3rd Australian Division, he had a number of clashes with W R McNicoll of the 10th Australian Brigade, who proved obstructive, insubordinate and disloyal and seems to have retained his own command thanks to Monash's misguided patronage.[65]

Possibly the most difficult subordinate of all at times was the pugnacious Harold 'Pompey' Elliott, an officer who defies easy categorisation. Historians are generally agreed that Elliott was one of the truly outstanding brigade commanders of the war, combining an aggressive spirit and great self-confidence with a genuine flair and a capacity for tactical flexibility even at the height of battle. Bean singles out his qualities of 'staunchness and vehemence' that helped to turn his formation, the 15th Australian Brigade, into a 'magnificently effective instrument'.[66] Whereas Gellibrand was admired and respected by the majority of his officers, Elliott was worshipped by his men. Nevertheless, like Keppel Bethell, Elliott also had an explosive temper and 'a habit of plain speaking and writing that did not always endear him to his superiors'.[67] Partly as a consequence of his unhappy experiences when attacking alongside British formations at Fromelles in 1916 and Polygon Wood in 1917, he became savage in his criticisms of the performance of British officers and troops. In the Polygon Wood attack on 26 September 1917, the 15th Australian Brigade successfully executed a tricky manoeuvre whereby it side-stepped into the British zone of operations and took an objective originally assigned to the British. Unfortunately, Elliott's detailed after-battle report was considered so unfair in its condemnation of the failings of the British 33rd Division and 98th Brigade on his right that Birdwood, the I Anzac Corps commander, refused to accept it or include it in the official records, though a copy survived.[68] In April 1918, at Villers Bretonneux, Elliott threatened that any British stragglers who refused to rally and re-form would be summarily shot. His divisional commander, Hobbs, who shared some of Elliott's disenchantment with British performance, was obliged to intervene and, at the end of the month, Birdwood – now commanding the recently-created and homogeneous Australian Corps – circulated a letter urging 'the restriction of comparison between Dominion and English troops'. Such incidents, and what Bean sees as 'a hot-headed tendency to use his brigade as if it were independent of the rest of the BEF' explain why Elliott, despite his undoubted powers of leadership, was never promoted to divisional command.[69]

On the Somme in 1916, at a time when the vastly expanded BEF was struggling to adjust to the widespread effects of 'de-skilling' and was simultaneously seeking to reshape and improve its operational methods and tactical doctrine, rigidity and over-centralisation were still all too prevalent in the planning and conduct of attacks, often stifling the initiative of brigade commanders. Fear of failure or dismissal inhibited many commanders and the majority do not appear to have yet possessed sufficient experience and self-confidence to question their superiors with any hopes of success. Shortly before 1 July 1916, J B Jardine (97th Brigade, 32nd Division) received only a patronising and discouraging reply when he advised Rawlinson of the advantages of infantry following closely behind the artillery barrage – a tactic which Jardine had observed during the Russo–Japanese War.[70] As the raw 31st Division prepared to attack at Serre, Hubert Rees (94th Brigade) was appalled to find that the scheme for the offensive – a 'terrible document' in his words – comprised seventy-six pages, to which 31st Division alone added 365 supplementary instructions. Rees spent three days condensing this mass of detail to eight pages and five maps.[71] Those with the moral courage to stand their ground could occasionally make *some* difference at a *local* level. Rees, for example, had a 'severe argument' with his corps commander, Hunter-Weston, before persuading the latter to allow the 94th Brigade an extra ten minutes to secure an orchard 300 yards beyond Serre.[72] At Thiepval on 1 July, Jardine – employing another tactic learned from the Japanese – ordered the assault companies of the 17th Highland Light Infantry to move out into No Man's Land seven minutes before zero hour and to creep to within thirty yards of the German front line.[73] R C Gore, the commander of the 101st Brigade (34th Division), ordered the headquarters of each of his four battalions to stay out of the initial assault when their units advanced at La Boisselle, thereby preserving them more or less intact and available to reorganise their shattered battalions that night.[74] Similarly, at Thiepval on 26 September, Harold Higginson avoided potential early losses among the support battalions of the 53rd Brigade (18th Division) by the simple expedient of keeping them out of the assembly trenches vacated by the assault waves when the attack began, a measure which enabled the follow-up troops to escape the inevitable German counter-barrage on those assembly trenches.[75] However, the often confused state of command and control arrangements on the Somme and the continuing limitations of the brigade commander's influence were clearly shown by the failure to exploit the opportunities offered on 14 July, after Brigadier-General H C Potter (9th Brigade, 3rd Division) had discovered that High Wood was apparently unoccupied by the Germans.[76]

Tim Travers recounts how Haig once told Edmonds that he had 'degummed' more than 100 brigadiers.[77] The strong possibility that one might be relieved of command if one carried protests too far bred caution and frequently outweighed common sense. When the 53rd Brigade was attached to the 9th (Scottish) Division for an attack at Delville Wood on 19 July, Higginson protested to Furse, the GOC 9th Division, about the lack of time for reconnaissance and the absence of a proper fire plan. Furse – who was himself unhappy about the attack – could only reply 'Corps has ordered it', blaming XIII Corps and, ultimately, the pressure being applied from above by GHQ and Fourth Army.[78] Examples of sackings of brigade commanders litter the Somme offensive. R S Oxley of the 24th Brigade (8th Division) was removed because of his brigade's failure to hold on to Contalmaison on 7 July.[79] Frederick Carleton of the 98th Brigade (33rd Division) was replaced as a result of the disappointing performance of his brigade at Wood Lane Trench on 27–28 August. In his damning report to XV Corps, his divisional commander, Major-General H J S Landon, stated that the qualities required of a brigade commander – 'quick, practical methods of command, and a cheerful outlook which will communicate itself to the troops' – were 'not possessed' by Carleton. Although Carleton subsequently appealed against his dismissal and was given another brigade, his next posting was to Salonika, where his health was fatally undermined.[80]

The position of brigade commanders could be tenuous even in the most successful divisions. After the capture of Thiepval by the 18th Division on 26–27 September 1916, Ivor Maxse was singularly unimpressed by the progress of the 55th Brigade in its attempts to clear the Schwaben Redoubt over the next few days. Maxse swiftly 'degummed' Brigadier-General Sir Thomas Jackson, recording that the brigade had not been handled properly and the attacks had been 'too partial'. The situation, wrote Maxse, 'should have been grasped more firmly by the brigade commander concerned and he was so informed'. The dismissal caused some bitterness in the ranks of the brigade.[81] Two more brigadiers – C W Compton of the 14th Brigade and C Yatman of the 96th Brigade – were sacked after the 32nd Division's abortive attempt to take Frankfort Trench on the Ancre in mid-November, although much of the blame for the failure can be laid at the door of Gough, the Fifth Army headquarters and V Corps.[82]

The pattern certainly continued in 1917. Despite standing up successfully to Gough on 23 February, Hanway Cumming, then commanding the 91st Brigade in the 7th Division, was twice overruled in March by his own divisional commander, Major-General G de S Barrow, when he pointed out the defects in attack plans during the pursuit of the Germans to their newly-constructed Hindenburg Line. At Bullecourt on 12 May, Cumming, not without justification, again sought to persuade his new divisional commander, Major General T H Shoubridge, to modify plans to take account of the changing local tactical situation. After the brigade's attack on 12 May had been halted in, and to the east of, Bullecourt village, Cumming argued against any further attacks that day and proposed instead to make a surprise assault, without a prolonged artillery barrage, to take place the next morning. Shoubridge refused to entertain the idea and appeared 'somewhat annoyed'. A few minutes later, Shoubridge telephoned to tell him that he (Cumming) was 'too tired to cope with the situation', that his 'judgement was therefore warped' and that he must relinquish his command.[83] Cumming was obviously too talented an officer to remain at home for long and it is indicative of the changed circumstances and more meritocratic command climate of 1918 that he was brought back to the Western Front to take over the 110th Brigade. David Campbell, his divisional commander in 1918, later described him as 'not only a magnificent leader of men, but also a soldier of the very highest class' whose advice 'was of considerable value'.[84]

Cumming's experiences notwithstanding, there is plentiful evidence that, in some divisions at least, the trend towards a more devolved command style gathered pace in 1917 as brigadier-generals were allowed, and seized, increasing opportunities to exercise a greater degree of direct tactical control of operations at a local level. The successes of Higginson's 53rd Brigade at Irles and Poelcappelle have already been noted. Another good example of a brigade commander who took advantage of such opportunities to parade his professional skills more fully may be found in the person of Berkeley Vincent, a 45-year-old gunner who had transferred to the 6th Dragoons in 1908 and had held various staff appointments before taking command of the 35th Brigade (12th Division) in January 1917. On 9 April 1917, the first day of the Battle of Arras, Vincent – whose brigade was initially in reserve – brought his troops into action, ahead of schedule, at just the right moment to help break stubborn German resistance on Observation Ridge. Two of his battalions subsequently charged down the eastern slopes of the ridge to capture more than thirty German field guns deployed in Battery Valley. The following day, Vincent again revealed his finely-tuned tactical instincts when he turned the Wancourt–Feuchy line in his area by ordering one battalion to wheel right and move down behind it while the other three battalions advanced frontally.[85] At Cambrai on 30 November, when the Germans launched their sudden and damaging counter-stroke, Vincent displayed considerable powers of personal leadership in organising and conducting a masterly fighting withdrawal from Villers Guislain to Revelon Ridge with a scratch force which included headquarters personnel, machine-gunners, Royal Engineers and a company from the divisional pioneer battalion. On 1 December his composite force was boosted by the arrival of 500 Canadian railway troops as it consolidated its position on Revelon Ridge, where it remained until relieved on the night of 3–4 December.[86] This astute and resourceful officer stayed in command of the 35th Brigade until the Armistice, except for a brief period between 7 August and 19 September 1918 when he was recovering from the effects of gas.[87]

It is not difficult to trace other similar cases of outstanding leadership, initiative and tactical grip at brigade level during the Battle of Cambrai. One could cite, for example, the recapture of Gouzeaucourt on 30 November by the 1st Guards Brigade under Brigadier-General C R Champion de Crespigny, who had ridden forward with his battalion commanders in advance of his troops and decided to attack at once – before the Germans became too firmly established – even though the Guards had to pass through retreating troops and vehicles and make the attack without artillery support.[88] The same day, Brigadier-General G R H Cheape and his staff of the 86th Brigade (29th Division) distinguished themselves in the fighting around Masnières. Captain Robert Gee, the brigade's staff captain, with a handful of signallers and orderlies and also one officer from the 1st Lancashire Fusiliers, used a Lewis gun to clear

Germans from the main street of Les Rues Vertes, a village which the Germans had entered from the south. Gee later grappled hand-to-hand with two Germans, killing one with his iron-shod stick before reinforcements from the Royal Guernsey Light Infantry came to help him erect barricades in the village. As the Germans attempted to dig in south-west of the village, Gee employed a Stokes mortar and his own revolver to account for two separate machine-gun posts before he was wounded in the knee. Gee won the Victoria Cross for his initiative and gallantry at Les Rues Vertes. Cheape, meanwhile, capably organised an all-round defence of the village. The 29th Division's reserve brigade, the 88th, under Brigadier-General H Nelson, carried out a spirited counter-attack south of Marcoing, in which platoons and companies from several battalions became mixed but were able to continue 'without any orders' and apply sound fire and movement tactics – according to the divisional historian – as the brigade major, Captain J K McConnell, rode bareback on a transport horse up and down the line. The net result of these operations was that the 29th Division held its part of the Masnières–Marcoing sector largely intact, saving the right of IV Corps from a dangerous German penetration on its right flank.[89] Such brigade actions, one ventures to suggest, went far beyond merely 'oiling the works'.

The process of devolution in tactical command in the BEF gained extra momentum during the defensive battles of the spring of 1918. As Dr Gary Sheffield has written, the 're-emergence of open warfare left the BEF no choice but to shake off some of their trench-bound habits'.[90] In the crises of March, April and May 1918, the best divisional and brigade commanders in the BEF learned that, even when major elements in the formal command and control system temporarily broke down, improvisation at a local level could still retrieve the situation. Equally important, GHQ and Army and corps commanders – having been reassured of the resilience of the BEF's command and control system – were prepared to adopt a more 'hands off' approach when the Allies began their own final offensive. By mid-1918 the BEF's higher commanders were much happier than they had been in previous years to leave basic tactical decisions to the man 'on the spot'.

The more flexible command climate was in evidence at Villers Bretonneux during the defence of Amiens on 24–25 April 1918, when William Glasgow and 'Pompey' Elliott of the 13th and 15th Australian Brigades played a crucial role in the planning, timing and execution of the decisive counter-attack. This was partly due to the willingness of Butler and Heneker – the British corps and divisional commanders involved – to accept sensible advice from below, while the fact that Haig and Rawlinson were prepared to leave the conduct of a critical battle largely to their subordinates made it easier for the latter to respond effectively to the demands of the situation.[91] The German offensives paradoxically allowed numerous British officers to underscore their ability to operate within a looser command system. Two such officers, George Gater and Andrew McCulloch, were in the British 21st Division, one of the formations unlucky enough to be caught up in the German March, April *and* May offensives. Both Gater and McCulloch commanded improvised composite forces with distinction during these operations – McCulloch near Morlancourt in March and Kemmel in April, Gater too in late March and again on the Aisne in late May and early June.[92]

Gater, it will be recalled, was already a brigadier – and, indeed, one of the youngest in the BEF – while McCulloch, then commanding the 9th King's Own Yorkshire Light Infantry, was rewarded in July when he was appointed GOC 64th Brigade. With Gater and Cumming (who also led a composite force in March), McCulloch completed a remarkable trio of brigade commanders in the 21st Division at the start of the 'Hundred Days'. That a New Army division like the 21st – which had undergone a disastrous baptism of fire at Loos three years before – could now call upon such an array of command talent further emphasises the more meritocratic make-up of the BEF in 1918. The 64th Brigade's night advance of over 3,000 yards across difficult ground on 23–24 August in order to secure an important spur south-east of Miraumont provides an excellent illustration of the high standards of enterprise and leadership which were becoming common at brigade level by this stage of the war. Before he was wounded in the thigh by fire from a German machine-gun, McCulloch adroitly modified the original attack plan at least three times over a twelve-hour period to meet changing or unforeseen circumstances.[93] Brigade commanders in the 'Hundred Days' were increasingly required to issue orders 'on the hoof'. A battalion commander in the 2nd Division later expressed his admiration for Edmund Ironside's command style on 23 August 1918 when the commander of the 99th Brigade first gave him verbal orders on the ground and then confirmed them in writing in only a few brief paragraphs.[94]

The formations adopted by divisions and brigades in offensive operations between 1916 and the Armistice offer more evidence of the increasing flexibility in the BEF's battle tactics as the war progressed. Although the most common use of the 'building blocks' by divisions was to place two brigades in the front line and the third in support or reserve – as at Messines Ridge on 7 June 1917, for example – there were many variations on this basic form of deployment. Even on 1 July 1916, several divisions – including the 18th at Carnoy-Montauban, the 21st at Fricourt, the 34th at La Boisselle and the 8th at Ovillers – deployed all three brigades (or large elements of all three) in the initial assault. At Arras on 9 April 1917, divisions such as the 9th and 34th, which attacked north of the Scarpe and had greater distances to cover than most, similarly adopted a three-brigade assault formation.[95] The method of 'leap-frogging' fresh units through the assault waves to maintain the impetus of an attack and secure second and third objectives had certainly been recognised in principle by GHQ by early May 1916.[96] The tactic was then described as 'an extremely difficult operation' but by 1917 it was fairly standard practice and had become almost instinctive throughout the BEF in the final months of the war. It was employed to particularly good effect at Amiens on 8 August 1918 when the 2nd Canadian Division, for instance, assigned its 4th Brigade to take the first objective, the 5th Brigade to seize the second and the 6th Brigade to capture the third.[97] During the 'Hundred Days', all-arms brigade groups or advanced guards were frequently formed as the BEF strove to remain in contact with retreating German forces. Near Peronne on 30 August 1918, the 58th (London) Division used its 175th Brigade as the nucleus of its divisional advanced guard, the vanguard of this group consisting of the Northumberland Hussars, cyclists, two field guns and two machine-guns.[98] The apparent ease with which a British second-line Territorial infantry division could adopt such mobile all-arms formations is again indicative of the greater degree of tactical skill and sophistication then possessed by most front-line units in the BEF. Another example, from among many, is provided by the advanced guard of the 33rd Division south-east of Cambrai on 9 October 1918. Made up of the 19th Infantry Brigade, the 156th Brigade Royal Field Artillery, the 11th Field Company Royal Engineers, a machine-gun company and a squadron of the North Irish Horse, this composite force helped the division to press forward more than seven miles that day.[99]

Similar conclusions can be drawn from the manner in which the BEF's brigades deployed their own subordinate battalions. As in the divisional deployment of brigades, the normal practice in 1916–17 was for brigades to place two battalions in the front line for an attack, either with two in support or one in support and one in reserve. Here too, however, there were numerous variations. At Arras on 9 April 1917, the 64th Brigade of the 21st Division used three battalions in line, deployed in section columns. The same day, the 26th Brigade of the 9th (Scottish) Division assaulted on a three-company front with three more in support. On 10 April the 8th Brigade of the 3rd Division attacked with all four battalions in line.[100] In the approach to the Hindenburg Line, on 18 September 1918, brigades of the 1st and 4th Australian Divisions adopted different formations to take account of the special features of their own sector. The 12th Australian Brigade, on the right, made the assault on a one-battalion front, with the other three battalions carrying on to successive objectives and the line of exploitation; the 4th Brigade advanced on a three-battalion front; and the 1st and 3rd Brigades of the 1st Australian Division each deployed on a two-battalion front with the remaining battalions 'leap-frogging' the assault battalions – the first objective.[101] Considerable adaptability was also shown by the units of the 50th (Northumbrian) Division in the Battle of the Selle on 17–18 October 1918. When the battalions of all three brigades had become intermingled in the firing line by the late afternoon of 17 October, the divisional commander, Major-General H C Jackson, divided the front into three sectors with the three brigade commanders each taking responsibility for the mixture of battalions that now happened to be in their own particular area, regardless of their original formations.[102] The fact that the division went on to complete the capture of all its objectives on 18 October testifies to the decentralised nature of command and control in the BEF in this final phase of the war. It is all a far cry from the negative picture of a rigid and over-centralised BEF as drawn by the likes of Denis Winter, Martin Samuels and Tim Travers.[103]

It would be highly misleading to claim that the 'Hundred Days' was a period of undiluted success for the BEF. When set against its losses in other offensives, its average daily casualty rate between 8 August and 11 November 1918 (3,947) was second only to the daily rate of the 1917 Arras offensive (4,076) while, numerically, the total of around 379,000 casualties in the 'Hundred Days' was only exceeded by the losses incurred on the Somme in 1916.[104] With rehearsals for attacks – once standard – becoming much rarer, the transition from methodical set-piece assaults to more open fighting revealed the shortcomings of some officers. Examples of bad staff work, inadequate co-ordination and liaison and faulty command decisions are spread throughout the operations of the BEF during its final offensive. Despite the increased availability of wireless down to divisional, brigade and battalion level, communications difficulties still abounded, particularly as the relatively static trench-warfare telephone systems of 1916–17 were left behind, and formations continued to rely heavily on runners and despatch riders. Battle losses among the latter as well as traffic congestion on the roads and the frequent movement of headquarters inevitably led to orders being delayed or going astray. Yet, on the whole, the BEF's subordinate commanders, not least its brigadiers, retained sufficient grip to make a significant contribution to the ultimate victory. In the more mobile operations of the 'Hundred Days', the BEF required, and got, effective local control of the battle by its brigade commanders, yet, to date, the importance of their role in the chain of command has undoubtedly been greatly undervalued. It is to be hoped that, as research into the history of the Great War progresses and broadens in scope, the abilities and achievements of officers such as George Gater, Harold Higginson and Berkeley Vincent will receive wider recognition.

NOTES

1 *War Establishments of New Armies* (London, 1915), 17, 101–2.
2 Army Order 414 of 1915, see *Army Orders, November 1915,* 13–16; see also A F Becke, *History of the Great War: Order of Battle of Divisions, Parts 1 to 4* (London, 1935–45), passim. The 1st, 2nd and 3rd Guards Brigade Machine-Gun Companies (Guards Division) were formed, slightly earlier than most, in September 1915.
3 R Gibson and P Oldfield, *Sheffield City Battalion: The 12th (Service) Battalion, York and Lancaster Regiment* (Barnsley, 1988), 164, 184; W Turner, *Pals: The 11th (Service) Battalion (Accrington), East Lancashire Regiment* (Barnsley, 1987), 140 and J Cooksey, *Pals: The 13th and 14th Battalions, York and Lancaster Regiment: A History of the two Battalions raised by Barnsley in World War One* (Barnsley, 1986), 226.
4 A H Hussey and D S Inman, *The Fifth Division in the Great War* (London, 1922), 208–9, 262–3; Becke, *Order of Battle of Divisions, Part 1: The Regular British Divisions* (London, 1935), 68–71.
5 Currie to Sir Edward Kemp, 7 February 1918, Currie papers, National Archives of Canada (NAC); unsigned manuscript, 'The Canadian Corps – Principal Differences between Canadian Corps and British Corps', NAC, RG9, III, D2, Vol. 4809, File 196; G W L Nicholson, *The Official History of the Canadian Army in the First World War: Canadian Expeditionary Force, 1914–1919* (Ottawa, 1962), 230–2; D G Dancocks, *Sir Arthur Currie: A Biography* (Toronto, 1985), 101–4; A J M Hyatt, *General Sir Arthur Currie: A Military Biography,* (Toronto, 1987), 72–3, 95–105; S B Schreiber, *Shock Army of the British Empire: The Canadian Corps in the Last 100 Days of the Great War* (Westport, CT, 1997), 19–21; J Edmonds (ed.), *History of the Great War: Military Operations, France and Belgium, Vol. I* (hereafter *OH*); (London, 1935), 55; S F Wise, 'The Black Day of the German Army Australians and Canadians at Amiens, August 1918', in P Dennis and J Grey (eds), *1918: Defining Victory* (Canberra, 1999), 31.
6 *OH, 1918, 1,* 55; H Stewart, *The New Zealand Division, 1916–1919: A Popular History Based on Official Records* (Auckland, 1921), 163, 182, 328. See also Paul Baker, *King and Country Call: New Zealanders, Conscription and the Great War* (Auckland, 1988).
7 C E W Bean, *The Official History of Australia in the War of 1914–18: Vol. VI, The AIF in France during the Allied Offensive, 1918* (hereafter *AOH*) (Sydney, 1942), 896, 937–40; see also Bean's diary for 12 September–12 October 1918, Australian War Memorial (AWM) 606/203, 47–52; P A Pedersen, *Monash as Military Commander* (Melbourne, 1985), 279–80; P S Sadler, *The Paladin: A Life of Major-General Sir John Gellibrand* (Melbourne, 2000), 157, 165, 184–5.
8 *OH, 1918, IV,* 369.
9 *ibid,* 367.
10 *OH, 1918, V,* 67, fn.3; A D Ellis, *The Story of the Fifth Australian Division,* (London, n.d.), 381.
11 To this author's knowledge, only a handful of brigade histories or studies have been published. They include Brigadier-General F C Stanley, *The History of the 89th Brigade, 1914–1918* (Liverpool, 1919), Brigadier-General T Ternan, *The Story of the Tyneside Scottish* (Newcastle, n.d.), 'E R' (ed.), *The 54th Infantry Brigade, 1914–1918: Some Records of Battle and Laughter in France* (Aldershot, 1919) and *A Short History of the 55th Infantry Brigade in the War of 1914–18* (printed for private circulation, London, circa 1919). More recent examples include J Sheen, *Tyneside Irish: A History of the Tyneside Irish Brigade Raised in the North East in World War One* (Barnsley, 1998), G Stewart and J Sheen,

Tyneside Scottish: A History of the Tyneside Scottish Brigade Raised in the North East in World War One (Barnsley, 1999) and D Bilton, *Hull Pals: A History of 92 Infantry Brigade, 31st Division* (Barnsley, 1999).

12 Schreiber, *Shock Army of the British Empire*, 20; Hyatt, *General Sir Arthur Currie*, 101. Both Edmonds and Hyatt point out that Sir Douglas Haig, the Commander-in-Chief of the BEF, initially viewed the 1918 reorganisation as only a temporary expedient and hoped to restore the former twelve-battalion system by adding one American battalion to each British brigade to replace one disbanded British battalion (see *OH, 1918, I*, 63).

13 H R Cumming, *A Brigadier in France, 1917–1918* (London, 1922), 93–4.

14 P Simkins, 'Co-Stars or Supporting Cast? British Divisions in "The Hundred Days", 1918', in P Griffith (ed.), *British Fighting Methods in the Great War* (London, 1996), 56–8.

15 Gellibrand to Bean, 2 May 1929, AWM 8040/1(2).

16 A Farrar-Hockley, *The Somme* (London, 1964), 123; E K G Sixsmith, *British Generalship in the Twentieth Century* (London, 1969), 158; Pedersen, *Monash as Military Commander*, 174; J Keegan, *The Face of Battle* (London, 1976), 259–60; Hyatt, *General Sir Arthur Currie*, 45–6, Sadler, *The Paladin*, 84–5; J M Bourne, British Generals in the First World War', in G D Sheffield (ed.), *Leadership and Command: the Anglo–American Military Experience since 1861* (London, 1997), 101.

17 Hyatt, *General Sir Arthur Currie*, 45.

18 Cumming, *A Brigadier in France*, 97–8.

19 Bourne, 'British Generals in the First World War', 101.

20 Sadler, *The Paladin*, 85, 141.

21 Godley to Pearce, 28 July 1916, AWM 3DRL, Item 2333. Pope later returned to the Western Front to command the 52nd Battalion AIF at Messines in 1917 (see Bean, *AOH, III*, 447 fn.).

22 Roger Lee, 'The Australian Staff: The Forgotten Men of the First AIF', in Dennis and Grey (eds), *1918: Defining Victory*, 118–20. Though mainly an analysis of the staff of the Australian Corps, this paper also provides an excellent outline of staff duties in general during the First World War.

23 Lee, 'The Australian Staff', 121.

24 B Bond and S Robbins (eds), *Staff Officer: The Diaries of Walter Guinness (First Lord Moyne), 1914–1918* (London, 1987), 13.

25 O Lyttelton (Viscount Chandos), *The Memoirs of Lord Chandos* (London, 1962), 74–5.

26 A Eden, *Another World 1897–1917* (London, 1976), 149–50.

27 Bond and Robbins (eds), *Staff Officer*, 150–1, 166.

28 *ibid*, 13; Eden, *Another World*, 149–50.

29 *Preliminary Notes on the Tactical Lessons of the Recent Operations* (SS119), issued by GHQ, July 1916.

30 Brigadier-General H C Rees, 'Notes as to the Battle west of Serre on the morning of 1st July 1916', VIII Corps War Diary, Public Record Office (PRO), WO 95/820.

31 XIII Corps to 3rd, 24th, 35th and 55th Divisions, 'Instructions for continuing the attack on the Falfemont Farm–Guillemont Line', 10 August 1916, PRO, WO 95/896.

32 'Memorandum on attacks', written by General Sir Hubert Gough 'for the guidance of Divisional and Infantry Brigade Commanders' and circulated by Reserve Army Headquarters, 5 October 1918 (SG 43/0/5). A copy can be found in the Reserve (Fifth) Army Headquarters and General Staff War Diary, April–December 1916, PRO, WO 95/518.

33 'Notes on conference held at V Corps Headquarters on 16th November, 1916',
    V Corps Headquarters and General Staff War Diary, August–December 1916,
    PRO, WO 95/747.

34 GHQ to Armies, 13 August 1916 (OB 1762), see First Army Headquarters and
    General Staff War Diary, August–September 1916, PRO, WO 95/166. See also
    B Gudmundsson, *Stormtroop Tactics: Innovation in the German Army 1914–1918*
    (Westport, CT, 1989), particularly 43–90.

35 Currie to Second Army, on 'causes of success and failure in the recent
    operations of the Canadian Corps', 20 November 1917, copy in AWM
    45,47/1.

36 *Notes on Recent Fighting, No. 1* and *Notes on Recent Fighting, No. 4*, 5 and 13
    April 1918.

37 *Preliminary Notes on the Tactical Lessons of the Recent Operations* (SS 119), July
    1916, 7.

38 Major-General W G Walker (GOC 2nd Division) to XIII Corps (copy to X
    Corps), see X Corps Headquarters and General Staff War Diary,
    July–December 1916, PRO, WO 95/851.

39 99th Infantry Brigade Order No. 97, 15 November 1916, V Corps
    Headquarters and General Staff War Diary, August–December 1916, PRO,
    WO 95/747.

40 *Notes on Recent Fighting, No. 1*, 5 April 1918.

41 P Simkins, 'Somme Reprise: Reflections on the Fighting for Albert and
    Bapaume, August 1918', in B Bond et al, *Look to your Front: Studies in the First
    World War by the British Commission for Military History* (Staplehurst, 1999),
    151; R Prior and T Wilson, *Command on the Western Front: The Military Career
    of Sir Henry Rawlinson, 1914–18* (Oxford, 1992), 300, 305, 339, 342. See also
    P Griffith, *Battle Tactics of the Western Front: The British Army's Art of Attack,
    1916–1918* (New Haven CT and London, 1994), 22–3, 27; T Travers, *How the
    War was Won: Command and Technology in the British Army on the Western Front,
    1917–1918* (London, 1992), 109, 145–51, and G D Sheffield, 'The Indispensable
    Factor: The Performance of British Troops in 1918', in Dennis and Grey (eds),
    1918: Defining Victory, 94.

42 See, for instance, C Page, *Command in the Royal Naval Division: A Military
    Biography of Brigadier-General A M Asquith DSO* (Staplehurst, 1999); A Carton
    de Wiart, *Happy Odyssey* (London, 1950); R McMullin, *Pompey Elliott*
    (Melbourne, 2002); J Terraine (ed.), *General Jack's Diary, 1914–1918* (London,
    1964); F P Crozier, *A Brass Hat in No Man's Land* (London, 1930) and C
    Maxwell (ed.), *Frank Maxwell, Brigadier-General, VC, CSI DSO: A Memoir and
    some Letters* (London, 1921).

43 J M Bourne, 'The BEF on the Somme: Some Career Aspects, Part 1, July 1916',
    in *Gun Fire: A Journal of First World War History*, No. 35, 11–14.

44 Mitford was subsequently promoted to command the 42nd (East Lancashire)
    Division in March 1917. He was succeeded, in October 1917, by Arthur Solly-
    Flood.

45 J M Bourne, 'The BEF on the Somme: Some Career Aspects, Part 2, 2 July–19
    November 1916', in *Gun Fire*, No. 39, 18–25.

46 Bourne, 'The BEF on the Somme: Some Career Aspects, Part 1', 12; see also
    John Bourne's address, as Haig Fellow 2002, to the Douglas Haig Fellowship,
    29 January 2002, in *Records*, No. 8, December 2002, 2.

47 J M Bourne, 'The BEF's Generals on 29 September 1918: An Empirical Portrait
    with some British and Australian Comparisons', in Dennis and Grey (eds),
    1918: Defining Victory, 100–5.

48 *ibid*, 110–11.

49 See the entries on Bennett in P Dennis *et al* (eds), *The Oxford Companion to Australian Military History* (Melbourne, 1995), 93, and on Bradford in J M Bourne, *Who's Who in World War One* (London, 2001), 34.

50 I am deeply indebted to Dr John Bourne for the information about George Gater and for his considerable help and advice with other aspects of this chapter.

51 Cumming, *A Brigadier in France*, 95–6.

52 J H Boraston and C Bax, *The Eighth Division in War, 1914–1918* (London, 1926), 150, 235–6, 388.

53 Bean *AOH, V* 298–355, G H F Nichols, *The 18th Division in the Great War* (Edinburgh, 1922), 399; P Simkins, 'The War Experience of a Typical Kitchener Division: The 18th Division, 1914–1918', in H Cecil and P H Liddle (eds), *Facing Armageddon; The First World War Experienced* (London, 1996), 304, 306.

54 D Campbell, 'Introduction' in Cumming, *A Brigadier in France*, 13.

55 F Davies and G Maddocks, *Bloody Red Tabs: General Officer Casualties of the Great War, 1914–1918* (London, 1995), passim.

56 *ibid*, 87–8, quoting from H M Davson, *Memoirs of the Great War* (Aldershot, 1964).

57 A Whitmarsh, 'Tactical and Operational Practice in the British Expeditionary Force: A Divisional Study. The 12th (Eastern) Division, 1915–1918', unpublished MA dissertation, University of Leeds, 1995, 22; P Griffith, *Battle Tactics of the Western Front*, 83, 184–5; S Bidwell and D Graham, *Fire-Power: British Army Weapons and Theories of War, 1904–1945* (London, 1982), 125.

58 Nichols, *The 18th Division in the Great War*, 154–8, *OH, 1917, I*, 105–6.

59 ibid., 232–46; 18th Division, Headquarters and General Staff War Diary, January–December 1917, PRO, WO 95/2016, 53rd Infantry Brigade, Headquarters War Diary, January–December 1917, PRO, WO 95/2135, *OH, 1917, II*, 343–4.

60 Bourne, 'The BEF on the Somme: Some Career Aspects, Part 2', 20–1.

61 E M Andrews, 'Bean and Bullecourt: Weaknesses and Strengths of the Official History of Australia in the First World War', in *Revue Internationale d'Histoire Militaire*, 72 (1990), 32; see also Bean, *AOH, IV*, 433.

62 Bean, *AOH, III*, 601.

63 Andrews, 'Bean and Bullecourt', 26, 35, *OH, 1917, I*, 455–66; Bean, *AOH, IV*, 428, 435; Sadler, *The Paladin*, 128–36; 'Summary of operations for week ended 8 am, Friday 4 May 1917', I Anzac Corps Headquarters and General Staff War Diary, AWM 26, Box 153, Item 1, 2nd Australian Division Headquarters and General Staff War Diary, AWM 4, Item 10, 1/44/21 and 1/44/2, 'Report on Operations from 3rd May to 5th May 1917', 5th Australian Brigade War Diary, 26 April–10 May 1917, AWM 26, Box 166, Item 9, 'Report on the Assault on the Hindenburg Line east of Bullecourt, 3rd May 1917', 6th Australian Brigade War Diary, 26 April–10 May 1917, AWM 26, Box 167, Item 6.

64 See the entry on Bennett in Dennis *et al* (eds), *Oxford Companion to Australian Military History*, 93; Bourne, 'The BEF's Generals on 29 September 1918', in Dennis and Grey (eds), *1918: Defining Victory*, 112–13, see also Bourne, *Who's Who in World War One*, 21, and Bean, *A OH, V*, 571–2.

65 The disputes between Gellibrand and McNicoll are covered in some detail in Sadler, *The Paladin*, 163–6.

66 Bean, *AOH, IV*, 832. Elliott is the subject of a new biography by Ross McMullin, *Pompey Elliott*.

67 Dennis *et al*, *Oxford Companion to Australian Military History*, 224–5; Bourne, 'The BEF's Generals on 29 September 1918', 112.

68 Bean, *AOH, IV,* 791 *et seq*, particularly 832 and fn.140; Elliott's 'Report on Operations of 15th Aust. Inf. Bde. at Polygon Wood on 24th, 25th, 26th and 27th September, 1917' can be found in AWM 51, Item 2. I am extremely grateful to Dr Peter Stanley and my other friends at the Australian War Memorial for providing me with a copy of this document. See also Dennis *et al, Oxford Companion to Australian Military History*, 225.

69 Bean, *AOH, V,* 523–5, 550. Birdwood's letter of 30 April 1918 can be found in the Elliott papers, AWM 2DRL/513, Item 16. There is also a copy in the Monash papers.

70 Brigadier-General J B Jardine to Edmonds, 13 June 1930, PRO CAB 45/135; T Travers, *The Killing Ground: The British Army, The Western Front and the Emergence of Modern Warfare, 1900–1918* (London, 1987), 143.

71 Notes by Brigadier-General H C Rees, July 1916, Robertson papers, Liddell Hart Centre for Military Archives, King's College London (LHCMA/KCL), 1/21/27/2; Rees to Edmonds, 14 November 1929, PRO, CAB 45/137; M Brown, *The Imperial War Museum Book of the Somme* (London, 1996), 37–9; Turner, *Pals: The 11th (Service) Battalion (Accrington), East Lancashire Regiment*, 127.

72 Brigadier-General H C Rees, quoted in Brown, *Imperial War Museum Book of the Somme*, 39.

73 *OH, 1916, I,* 400.

74 *ibid*, 376–7.

75 F I Maxse, *The 18th Division in the Battle of the Ancre*, printed report (known as the 'Red Book'), December 1916, 6; J Baynes, *Far from a Donkey: The Life of General Sir Ivor Maxse* (London, 1995), 156.

76 T R Moreman, 'The Dawn Assault – Friday 14th July 1916', in *Journal of the Society for Army Historical Research*, 71, 287 (1993), 191, 197; T Norman, *The Hell They Called High Wood: The Somme 1916* (London, 1984), 94.

77 Travers, *The Killing Ground*, 13.

78 H W Higginson to Edmonds, 1 January 1934, PRO CAB 45/134.

79 Haig Diary, 8 July 1916, PRO, WO 256/11; Travers, *The Killing Ground*, 169–70, *OH, 1916, II,* 93–4.

80 Carleton died following a heart attack in 1922, aged only 54. The full story of his dismissal and of his successful appeal against it is given in M Brown, *The Imperial War Museum Book of the Western Front* (London, 1993), 125–30. The relevant papers can be found in the Department of Documents, Imperial War Museum, London (IWM).

81 Maxse, *The 18th Division in the Battle of the Ancre*, 17; Baynes, *Far from a Donkey*, 161–2; Simkins, 'The War Experience of a Typical Kitchener Division', 306.

82 P Simkins, 'Somme Footnote: The Battle of the Ancre and the Struggle for Frankfort Trench, November 1916', *Imperial War Museum Review*, 9 (1994), 84–101.

83 Cumming, *A Brigadier in France*, 44, 53, 56–7, 74–84; see also J Walker, *The Blood Tub: General Gough and the Battle of Bullecourt, 1917* (Staplehurst, 1998), 167–70; 7th Division, Headquarters and General Staff War Diary, January–May 1917, PRO, WO 95/1632; 91st Infantry Brigade War Diary, January–November 1917, PRO, WO 95/1667.

84 D Campbell, 'Introduction' in Cumming, *A Brigadier in France*, 13.

85 A Scott and P Middleton Brumwell, *History of the 12th (Eastern) Division in the Great War, 1914–1918* (London, 1923), 99–104; *OH, 1917, I,* 218–220, 248–9.

86 Scott and Brumwell, *History of the 12th (Eastern) Division*, 143–60; *OH, 1917, III,* 185–6.

87 Davies and Maddocks, *Bloody Red Tabs*, 199–200; Becke, *Order of Battle of Divisions, Part 3A*, 1938, 28.

88 C Headlam, *History of the Guards Division in the Great War, 1915–1918*, Vol. II, (London, 1924), 4–6; *OH, 1917, III*, 189–90.

89 S Gillon, *The Story of the 29th Division: A Record of Gallant Deeds* (London, 1925), 161–7; *OH, 1917, III*, 205–210.

90 Sheffield, 'The Indispensable Factor: The Performance of British Troops in 1918', in Dennis and Grey (eds), *1918: Defining Victory*, 93–4.

91 See, in particular, Bean, *AOH, V*, 568–80.

92 *OH, 1918, I*, 509, 514–15; *OH, 1918, II*, 421–3; *OH, 1918, III*, 130.

93 21st Division, Headquarters and General Staff War Diary, January–August 1918, PRO, WO 95/2133; 64th Infantry Brigade War Diary, June 1917–March 1919, PRO, WO 95/2160; *OH, 1918, IV*, 243–7; Davies and Maddocks, *Bloody Red Tabs*, 167–9.

94 Lieutenant-Colonel C A Howard (CO, 1st King's Royal Rifle Corps) to Edmonds, 23 June 1938, PRO, CAB 45/1 85.

95 *OH, 1916, I*, 323, 356, 375, 385; *OH, 1917, I*, 227, 231.

96 See, for example, the memorandum on 'Training of Divisions for Offensive Action', 8 May 1916, given in *OH, 1916, I, Appendices*, Appendix 17.

97 *OH, 1918, IV*, 49–51, 58.

98 *OH, 1918, IV*, 359.

99 *OH, 1918, V*, 220.

100 See *OH, 1917, I*, 205, 228, 248.

101 A Montgomery, *The Story of the Fourth Army in the Battles of the Hundred Days, August 8th to November 11th 1918* (London, 1919), 128–31; Pedersen, *Monash as Military Commander*, 274; J Monash, *The Australian Victories in France in 1918* (London, 1920), 232; *OH, 1918, IV*, 481.

102 Montgomery, *The Story of the Fourth Army in the Hundred Days*, 217–29; 'Operations of XIII Corps between 3 October and 11 November 1918', Fourth Army papers, IWM, Vol. 64; E Wyrall, *The Fiftieth Division, 1914–1919* (London, 1939), 355; *OH, 1918, V*, 308–12, 320–2.

103 See, for example, D Winter, *Haig's Command: A Reassessment* (London, 1991); M Samuels, *Doctrine and Dogma: German and British Infantry Tactics in the First World War* (New York, 1992); and *Command or Control? Command, Training and Tactics in the British and German Armies, 1888–1918* (London, 1995); see also Travers, *The Killing Ground* and *How the War was Won*.

104 *Statistics of the Military Effort of the British Empire during the Great War, 1914–1920* (London, 1922), 269–71; R T Mitchell and G M Smith, *Official History of the War: Medical Services, Casualties and Medical Statistics of the Great War* (London, 1931), 166–75; *OH, 1918, V*, 562; J Nicholls, *Cheerful Sacrifice: The Battle of Arras 1917* (London, 1990), 211.

CHAPTER VIII

Queen of the Battlefield: The Development of Command, Organisation and Tactics in the British Infantry Battalion during the Great War

Chris McCarthy

Before the First World War, infantry was generally regarded as the 'Queen of the Battlefield'. The Western Front, however, was dominated by artillery. But instead of declining into obsolescence, the infantry unit evolved to become a key element in the 'weapons system' that in 1918 carried the BEF to victory. This chapter examines the developments in the British infantry battalion. Much evidence has been drawn from published unit histories; this is a rich source that is still rather underused by historians.

In 1914 a British infantry battalion consisted of four rifle companies. The total strength of each company amounted to 227 officers and men. The company commander was usually a captain or major, who had a subaltern to act as his assistant. The company was divided into four platoons, each commanded by a subaltern, and in turn each of the platoons was divided into four sections, each of twelve men under the control of a Non Commissioned Officer (NCO). In addition, a Headquarters (HQ) company was employed to administer the battalion. This consisted of forty-five men consisting of the Battalion 'Office' and the Signal section made up of a sergeant and eight men under the command of the Signalling Officer of subaltern rank. Similarly, there was a Transport section under the command of the Transport officer, his sergeant and sixteen drivers.

Other individuals essential to the smooth running of the battalion – cooks, shoemakers, drummers, pioneers and provosts sergeants – were all attached to HQ company. This was also the home of the Regimental Sergeant Major, the man whose job it was to implement the orders issued by the battalion commander, known as 'the Colonel' although his rank was actually that of lieutenant colonel. The HQ company also had attached to it the Regimental Medical Officer (RMO), and an Armourer,

173

and eight Army Service Corps drivers. Over and above the four companies, each battalion had a machine-gun section consisting of a lieutenant, sergeant, corporal, two drivers, batman, and twelve privates organised into two six-man gun teams. This, in brief was the organisation of the infantry battalions that went to France with the British Expeditionary Force (BEF) in August 1914. The battalions of the New (or 'Kitchener') Armies were organised on a similar basis as Service battalions of Regular regiments.

In the aftermath of the Boer War, the army had undergone considerable tactical reform. Offensive infantry tactics in 1914 were based on extended order, the theory being that troops would advance in short rushes with covering fire provided by units on their flanks. These rushes could be of battalion, company or platoon strength. The aim was to form a strong firing line and at this stage in the war to reinforce this line with troops in support. When sufficient fire had worn down the defence, the line was to push through the attack.[1] With many changes, this basic policy of 'fire and movement' underpinned British infantry tactics until the end of the war.

The scale of operations on the Western Front, and the length of the casualty lists, meant that the original BEF was soon desperately in need of reinforcement. The first Territorial battalion to be sent to France in 1914 was the 1/14 London Regiment (London Scottish), which arrived on 16 September 1914. By Christmas, twenty-two other territorial battalions had joined them. The role of the Territorial Force (TF) should not be underestimated. During the crisis of autumn 1914, with scattered Regular battalions and the Indian Army still travelling from their far-flung garrisons, the 'Saturday Night Soldiers' were the only trained force Britain had at its immediate disposal. These part-time soldiers, as they were known, gave much needed support to the Regulars, especially during the First Battle of Ypres.

The Territorial Force was a comparatively new organisation, created in March 1908.[2] However, because it was formed from the old Volunteer Force, which performed well in the South African war, there was much continuity in individual battalions. The TF was firmly imbedded into the Regular Army structure, although TF units were intended for home defence. Most battalions were added to the order of battle of existing Regular regiments, the all Territorial London Regiment being an exception. Recruiting for the Volunteers had suffered after the Boer War, with some units such as the London Rifle Brigade falling as low as 241 men in 1908. Paucity of numbers affected the funding from the government, as each battalion had to field thirty per cent of its establishment to qualify for their grant. This was important, as each battalion had to pay for its own accommodation. The eternal problem with any force composed of part-time volunteers is 'turbulence': the constant coming and going of personnel. At any given time only twenty-five per cent of the troops were fully trained, fifty per cent were at various levels of training and the remainder had only recently joined.

The order to mobilise came whilst most Territorial battalions were at annual camp. They were ordered home to prepare for war. On 10 August 1914 the government issued an invitation for complete units to volunteer for Imperial Service, that is to serve overseas. For a Territorial battalion to be sent on active duty eighty per cent of its members had to volunteer for the battalion to recruit to war establishment. At the end of November 1914 Territorial battalions adopted the four-company organisation laid down for the Regular army a year previously. In the London Rifle Brigade (1/5 Londons), A and D companies became No. 1. E and O were No. 2., G and P, No. 3 and H and Q adopted No. 4. The numbers were retained until after the Second Battle of Ypres in 1915, to avoid confusion, after which they reverted to letters.[3] The Liverpool Scottish, however, opted to adopt company titles V, X, Y, Z. More importantly, the move to what contemporaries described as the 'double company' system meant that Territorial units had to adjust their tactical command structure. This could entail some disruption in personnel, as there was now a need for only four company commanders rather than eight, as well as to learn new drill and undertake a modified form of training for 'what came to be known later as "the platoon and company in the attack"'.[4]

When the Territorials arrived in France they still had much to learn. As the historian of the Liverpool Scottish (1/10 King's Liverpool Regiment) noted of November 1914:

> The first sight the Battalion had of a company of Regulars on the march was something of a shock. Many of the men had beards, their clothing was stained and muddy, and quite a number were wearing cap-comforters instead of the regulation flat cap . . . But there was one thing about them that did particularly attract the eye. Every man's rifle was absolutely spotless, not a bad illustration for civilian soldiers of the distinction between the superficial and the essential.[5]

In fact, the coming year was, for combatants of all armies, a year of learning. For the British, 1915 saw the drawing together of the three threads – New Army, TF and Regular – that made up the BEF. All units had to adapt to trench warfare, which did not remain static but rather evolved steadily throughout the year. This learning curve was definitely hampered by the inevitable shortages caused by the British government's failure to foresee or plan for a long attritional war. Between 1914 and 1918 the British Empire developed a war economy capable of sustaining a mass army in a total conflict. In the early days, however, front line troops had to improvise and innovate, and tactics and command structures had to be devised to handle new weapons for trench warfare.

The Hales Grenade, a stick grenade with a tape streamer tail, had been introduced to the British army in 1908, but supplies were very limited. Moreover, they were issued not to the infantry but to the Royal Engineers, who acted as bombers. The Germans first used hand-grenades or bombs in October 1914, and it was quickly appreciated that this was a very useful weapon in trench warfare.[6] This shortage had to be addressed, thus the first bomb seen by most British soldiers was the jam tin bomb. This weapon was just an ordinary small tin, half filled with explosive, and the rest of the space filled with nails or any small scrap metal that would fit in the container. The lid was replaced and a hole punched into it and a piece of safety fuse pushed in. However rough and ready, this weapon seemed to be effective:

> 12 Aug 15; Algeo and his half-dozen bombers did wonders. With cigarettes in their mouths for lighting the fuses of their jam tin bombs, they drove back over thirty Huns armed with Krupp's latest pattern-bomb.[7]

Throughout 1915 the question of the right organisation for specialists such as bombers, carriers and bayonet men was attracting a lot of thought and experimentation. As it turned out this was far from wasted. It was not until after the Battle of Loos that everyone was trained to throw bombs.

In February 1915 infantry brigades created 'grenadier' companies thirty men strong, drawn from each of the battalions within the brigade. These were trained by sappers. Normal practice was to attach twenty bombers to each assault battalion, the remaining men being held in reserve. This was the procedure first used in the battle of Neuve Chapelle in March 1915. It was not until after the fighting in the spring of 1915 that bombers became part of the individual battalions, at the strength of eight men and one NCO per platoon. Later in the year the specialist platoons were disbanded, and all ranks were trained in bombing. In October 1915 the pamphlet CDS74, *Training and Employment of Grenadiers* was published, to be followed in March 1916 by SS398, *The Training and Employment of Bombers.* The change of name was occasioned by the complaints of the Grenadier Guards, who argued that the original nomenclature would cause confusion. SS398 stated that: 'Some battalions have in addition a platoon of battalion bombers, trained and administrated as a separate unit of the battalion organization.' It also stated that 'it was not desirable to lay down any definite organization or establishment for bombers.'[8] However, the same pamphlet, renumbered as SS126 and republished in September 1916, now required each platoon to provide one specially trained bombing squad, of one NCO and eight men. The four platoon squads in a company formed the company bombers 'In addition,' SS126 stipulated, 'if desired and approved by the divisional commander, a separate battalion bombing platoon under the battalion bombing officer, consisting of not more than four bombing squads, may be formed.'[9]

During 1915 there were myriad designs of grenades, including the 'Cricket Ball', 'Bethune' and 'No. 1 Percussion'. However, by the end of the year, the 'Mills Bomb', fitted with a timed fuse, was used very widely and it was to become the British army's standard grenade.

A major limitation of the Mills and other bombs was that its range was restricted to the distance a man could throw. The rifle grenade was an obvious development. The Welsh Guards, formed in early 1915, were trained from the start in the use of rifle grenades. Initially they used the Hales, a percussion grenade with a rod that was placed down the barrel of a rifle and discharged with a blank cartridge. These were very different from the Mills bomb and could be used in no other way. An attempt was made to standardise and have one bomb that could be thrown by hand or fired by rifle. On 7 July 1916 a cup discharger was approved and this enabled the Mills bomb with a different base with a rod screwed in, to be fired or thrown, thus simplifying the supply of bombs. The Welsh Guards received four of these cups for each company on 8 September 1916, and later the number was raised to sixty-four per battalion.[10] Apart from anything else, this last figure is testimony to the significant increase in firepower available to the British infantry battalion between 1914 and 1918.

The machine gun was another weapon central to the conduct of trench warfare. In February 1915 the machine-gun sections were increased to four guns per battalion. These sections were made into machine-gun companies. However, difficulties in production of the Vickers Machine Gun meant the BEF was still 237 machine guns short of its establishment in mid-July 1915. As a substitute, 13th Royal Fusiliers in 37th Division were armed with Lewis guns mounted on Vickers tripods; this was a common expedient in New Army divisions.[11]

In 1915 the Lewis gun, an air-cooled light machine gun, made its first appearance after numerous production teething troubles. Initially one gun per battalion was issued in six selected divisions. This was increased to four per battalion as the guns became available. On 22 October 1915 the Machine Gun Corps was formed, and all Vickers guns came under control of Brigade. This was not a popular move with battalion commanders, as they missed the direct support of their own heavy machine guns. The reorganisation depended on the supply of Lewis guns and was carried out on a brigade basis, by rotation. As soon as every battalion in a brigade received its Lewis guns and trained its gunners, the Vickers and their teams were withdrawn to form the machine-gun company of the brigade.[12] At first the Lewis teams were seen as a direct replacement for the Vickers teams and treated like specialists. But it soon became apparent that with the guns going forward with the attacking troops, more men should be able to operate them, in case of casualties. Increasingly, Lewis Guns were devolved to the front line, and became incorporated into the BEF's emerging assault tactics.

The universal adoption of the four-company battalion had the effect of the platoon replacing the company as the basic tactical unit. The section, commanded by a corporal, thus became the fire unit. This change strengthened the role of the junior NCO; previously, this rank was seen as a stepping-stone to sergeant. These enhanced responsibilities served cruelly to underline the shortage of experienced NCOs in Britain's mass citizen army of 1915. An example appears in the history of the 18th (Eastern) Division:

> There was also the case of the Fusilier officer who was approached by an Oldham man who was doing sentry. 'I've been here six hours,' he said, 'and no one has relieved me.' It was a rainy night, and the trenches were at their slimiest. 'There must be a mistake,' replied the officer, and he sought the man's sergeant, who was sitting dry and snug in a dugout. 'You've a man out there who's been on sentry for six hours. You were to change the sentry every hour.' 'I didn't think it worth while getting more than one man wet,' was the sergeant's explanation.[13]

The Chinese attack was one of the new skills to be mastered by infantrymen in 1915. This was a demonstration or a dummy attack, designed to attract the enemy's attention or fool them into believing that the attack was on a larger scale than it was in reality.

> This illusion was heightened by showing in our trenches scaling leaders and flashing bayonets, by excited blowing of whistles and by rapid covering fire from selected positions; and that the ruse was successful was proved when an examination of our poor dummies showed them to be literally riddled with bullets.[14]

The best battalions considered No Man's Land as their property after dark, sending out patrols to capture prisoners, harass German wiring parties and generally make a nuisance of themselves. Soldiers' feelings about patrols were ambivalent:

> ... patrols, which for the first time or two were nerve racking, came to be quite enjoyable to the young and ardent. In the case of the majority, the novelty did not take many months to wear off, and although there was never any lack of volunteers for a patrol, there was not that sheer enthusiasm to find any excuse for a 'crawl round'.[15]

Patrols soon evolved into raids. SS107, *Notes on Minor Enterprises*, a compilation of experiences of the previous few months, appeared as early as March 1916. It states that raids on enemy trenches took place with parties ranging from thirty to 300 men. Raids were by and large organised by brigade or division, battalions usually mounting large fighting patrols. They were considered very good battle training for the inexperienced troops.

Another art that the BEF had to learn was sniping. At the beginning of 1915 the Germans held the upper hand. The BEF addressed this by starting schools of Scouting, Observation and Sniping. Initially battalion scouts attended the courses so they could go back and teach others. Observation was considered as important as, if not more important than sniping. By 1918, the establishment of scouts was four per company, usually grouped with company HQ. It was considered desirable that every section should maintain a pair of men who had had some training.[16]

By the end of 1915 the BEF was a rather different organisation from that of twelve months earlier, or even the army of Neuve Chapelle. The issue of various pamphlets began to codify the new warfare. These documents, some of which have already been cited, are an invaluable guide to the thinking of the General Staff throughout the war. They do not, however, merely reflect the flow of ideas coming down from on high; they also frequently capture the experience of the front line. It is noticeable that those pamphlets issued in 1915 leaned to the French tactics, in 1916 they swung to publishing captured German documents; but by 1917, after the Somme, until the end of the war the pamphlets were largely homegrown.

By mid-1916 the BEF was beginning to receive war material, from Mills bombs to men, on something like the required scale. From July to November the BEF's main focus was on the Somme. The sheer scale and duration of this battle dwarfed Loos, the BEF's largest previous action. For many battalions, the Somme was their first taste of major battle. Heavy losses were the norm, and the effect on inexperienced units can easily be imagined. Even experienced battalion commanders were shocked by the casualty rate. The experience of 14th Warwickshires was by no means unique:

> The first parade on Pommiers Redoubt was a very sad one; a battalion had practically disappeared, leaving a mere handful to carry on its fine tradition. In two attacks the battalion had lost 22 officers and 618 ORs in eight days. It was possible to take stock of the position and realise how few of the old battalion had survived the ghastly attack. The 1st Birmingham Battalion had practically ceased to exist, for very few of the original officers and men were left.[17]

Another problem was the sheer lack of battle experience among junior officers and NCOs. This was particularly worrying during the semi-open warfare of the Somme, when much tactical responsibility devolved onto platoon and section commanders. All too often it seemed that as soon as officers gained experience they were killed or wounded. Some of the officers who were good in battle lacked skill in training of their battalion, company or platoon when out of the line. These problems were exacerbated by the lack of 'grip' by higher commanders, resulting too often in units being committed to battle piecemeal, with inadequate time for preparation. The example of the 7th Northumberland Fusiliers must stand for many others:

> On the night of April 26th, orders were suddenly received to take over the line from the French, Hardly had this order been carried out than a further order was received to attack on the 27th in conjunction with the French on our right flank. None of us had time to even see the front on which we were to attack. The desperate hurry about everything, and the lack of time for preparations . . . The result of the night's work was nil, and it was impossible to bring up formed parties of men anywhere near the front line by day, it was obvious that the assaulting battalion were not in a position to attack. The operation, consequently, had to be postponed until the following day.[18]

After heavy losses high priority needed to be given to rebuilding battalions, although often there was little time to train and assimilate new drafts:

> The quality of drafts made those of us [in the 2nd Royal Welch Fusiliers] who were used to a different personnel fearful of the immediate future, so every working hour was given to trying to get them into some sort of shape.[19]

Indeed, the Somme showed that many infantrymen, even in nominally Regular battalions, had had only perfunctory initial training in musketry and fire and movement. The bomb became the universal weapon. Battalions spent the rest of the war trying to improve the standard of small arms training. Lieutenant Colonel J L Jack of the 2nd West Yorkshires noted on 24 September 1916:

> Accurate, rapid musketry, a special feature of pre-War British training, has been sadly neglected through undue reliance on the hand-bomb for nearly two years. Although the bomb is the more suitable infantry weapon for trench actions I am certain that first-class rifle marksmanship must prove of high value at times, particularly when troops are in the open during phases of major battles . . . I have

therefore ordered that every man in the front trench is to fire daily, at dawn or dusk, under supervision, two rounds at tins hung on our wire.[20]

One of the most difficult command and control problems lay in ensuring effective co-operation between infantry and artillery. One infantryman noted that:

In the early stages of the Somme artillery programmes were apt to be so rigid and difficulties of communication and control so great that, immediately after a hold-up, a satisfactory re-bombardment followed by a well-organised renewal of the infantry attack was a rarity.

On 7th Division's sector on 1 July, however, 'to the credit of all concerned – including one of the best brigadiers in the Army – this was brought off in ample time'.[21] This was exceptional. Improved co-operation between infantry and gunners was to be one of the key factors in the development of the BEF's art of attack over the next two years.

For all the problems that the Somme revealed, this battle was probably the single most important phase in the BEF's learning curve. Even while the fighting was in progress, the actions were being assessed and lessons disseminated to the wider army through doctrinal pamphlets. To single out one, SS119, entitled *Preliminary notes on the tactical lessons of the recent operations*, is dated July 1916. This pamphlet stresses that attacking infantry should remain as close to the barrage as possible, the duties of 'moppers up' and consolidation of newly captured ground, along with the strictures against the excess use of bombs. However, the full fruits of the tactical lessons of the Somme did not emerge until the issue of three key documents over the winter of 1916–17.

February 1917 saw probably the most important change to the organisation of the battalion throughout the war, with the publication of SS143, *Instructions for the Training of Platoons for Offensive Action* and SS144, *The Normal Formation for the Attack*. These publications in conjunction with SS135, *Instructions for the Training of Divisions for Offensive Action* (December 1916) encapsulated the experience of the war so far. SS143 outlined the change in battalion organisation, making the platoon the key tactical unit. This was the direction in which all armies were heading. The French issued a pamphlet in late 1916 with broadly the same conclusions, and the German stormtroopers utilised the small unit tactics. To some extent the new British doctrine simply codified the practice that had been learned the hard way on the battlefield during the Somme.

The platoon was the smallest unit in the British army that was made up of all the infantry weapons. Its minimum strength was twenty-eight Other

181

Ranks (OR); the maximum, forty-four OR. If its strength fell below the minimum, the platoon ceased to be workable and had to be reinforced. The composition of the platoon was, from February 1917, an HQ section; one section of Bombers (one NCO and eight OR including two bayonet men and two throwers); one section of Lewis Gunners (one NCO and eight OR, including Nos 1 & 2 of the gun); one section of Riflemen (one NCO and eight OR picked shots, scouts, picked bayonet fighters); and one section of Rifle Bombers (one NCO and eight OR including four Bomb Firers). The rifle and bayonet were still considered the primary weapons and every NCO and man was expected to be proficient in their use. The bomb was considered the second weapon of the infantryman. Men were also instructed in the use of the rifle grenade, which was considered the 'howitzer' of the infantry, being used to dislodge the enemy from behind cover or drive him to take cover. Finally the Lewis gun was considered 'a weapon of opportunity', used to kill the enemy above ground and gain superiority of fire. It was thought to be particular suitable for working round the enemy flank or protecting one's own flank.

The normal formation for the attack was known as 'Artillery Formation'. This consisted of the four platoons in a diamond formation, with the riflemen leading and the Bombers and Rifle grenadiers taking the eastern and western positions, with the southern point filled by the Lewis gun section. Platoon HQ was usually located to the front of the Lewis gun section. When attacking trenches, the attacking troops moved into two waves shortly before joining with the enemy. These new tactics continued the process by which command was effectively devolved to junior officers and NCOs. If the platoon was the basic tactical building block, the role of platoon commander – held by a subaltern or even an NCO – was a key tactical command appointment. The BEF's tactical doctrine was shaped by the realisation that it was fighting a platoon and section commander's war.

By April 1917 most battalions to be used in the forthcoming Battle of Arras had practised the new tactical doctrine. In conjunction with a massive and sophisticated artillery bombardment, the new tactics proved their value. The next battle, fought at Messines in June 1917, was the first example of a completely successful battle with limited objectives. It was planned by Plumer's Second Army to the last detail, in part to ease the way of the junior infantry commander. As an officer of 36th Division recalled, battalions rehearsed their attacks 'over ground marked out to represent the German trench system . . . [with] officers from the flanking battalions of divisions' in attendance during exercises to iron out possible snags. A huge model was created of the ridge with a wooden walkway around it, so a whole infantry company 'could examine it at one time'.[22] This was a tangible demonstration of high command's recognition of the necessity and virtues of devolving command to the infantry sub-unit.

Messines was the prelude to the Third Battle of Ypres (July–November

1917). The task of the attacking British troops was complicated by the effective use made by the Germans of 'elastic' tactics designed to provide defence in depth. The defenders dispensed with regular lines of trenches, as these made a good aiming point for artillery and were consequently quickly obliterated. The Germans now based their defences around 'pill boxes' placed in mutual support, shell holes, and immediate counter-attacks to regain lost ground. To counter these tactics the British in turn evolved various methods. As during the Somme, these revised British tactics were founded on the experience of recent fighting.[23]

One method was to use an artillery barrage in great depth to negate German counter-attacks, while infantry battalions adopted a variation of SS143 tactics: an elastic formation in the form of a thin line of skirmishers followed by 'worms', lines of sections in single file. Particular attention was paid to 'mopping up' to deal with isolate pill boxes. The greater flexibility given to the platoon by the February 1917 reorganisation proved invaluable in dealing with pill boxes, to such an extent that increasingly German defenders recognised that they were death traps in the event of a determined infantry attack. Once ground had been captured, companies formed strong points in good tactical positions. These were to stop any determined counter-attacks. Other units were stationed as counter-counter-attack troops, ready to move forward and meet the expected enemy repost. This account of an action by 1/4 Londons on 25 November 1917 gives a flavour of tactics used:

> The Lewis gun sections took up a position near our blocks so as to fire along the trench and prevent any movement in the open. For about 50 yards very little opposition was met with but the leading bombing section was then held up by stick bombs and suffered eight casualties, which included the leading bombers. To overcome this fire, fire was opened for several minutes with No. 23 and 24 Rifle Grenades, and the trench was searched forward for about 100 yards.
> The shooting was very accurate and the enemy were driven back . . . The advance was continued by bounds of from twenty to forty yards under cover of salvoes of rifle grenades.[24]

In contrast to the experience all too common in 1916, battalions were often used in a sensible fashion during Plumer's (if not Gough's) operations in Third Ypres. Once used in an attack, they were withdrawn as soon as feasible, and then taken out of the line for rest. The constant stream of minor attacks that were a feature of the Somme battles was largely avoided. Largely, but not entirely. On 3 December 1917 the New Zealand Division attacked at Polderhoek Château. 'There was no use attempting to disguise the fact that the attack failed', wrote an officer of the Division, although on the whole the opposition encountered, though stiff, was no greater than the opposition which NZ troops had successfully overcome on many previous occasions. The attack had been held up neither by mud or wire.

Reasons. The men, though several days were spent in practising the attack, were not intensively trained to the necessary standard. A large portion of the officers and men were reinforcement drafts, unfamiliar with hostile shelling or our own barrage. The troops on the right left the assembly trenches too soon, by their returning to them, and starting forward again by their pressing into our own barrage. Strength of enemy defences. Isolated nature of the attack drew intense artillery and MG fire. The period allowed for training for the attack was far too short, and gave neither officers, NCOs nor men a chance to know and feel confidence in each other; and it had also been interrupted by wet weather.[25]

This frank piece of analysis is, among other things, an illustration of the centrality of low-level leadership to tactical success in 1917. Even an undeniably elite formation like the New Zealand Division could be rendered ineffective if, for whatever reasons, junior commanders did not prove up to the task. Inexperienced soldiers are always at a disadvantage in battle. One battalion historian commented that:

> Whether it is that the seasoned warrior has an instinctive sense of self preservation, or that he notices and knows the signs which indicate danger, one cannot say, but it was a remarkable feat that casualties among new drafts were always appreciably higher than among those who had served some time in the line.

However, a hard core of experienced officers and NCOs could pull the rest through.[26]

In 1918 the infantry of the BEF faced some of the greatest challenges of the war. The Allies were thrown on to the strategic defensive, and thus the British infantry had first to concentrate on static defensive warfare. For many soldiers, this was their first taste of this type of soldiering. After the German breakthrough of 21 March infantrymen had to learn how to conduct mobile defensive operations, something that had not been on the agenda since 1914. The problems were compounded by restructuring of units and formations. From August 1918 onwards, the BEF was faced with another set of challenges: learning to conduct mobile offensive operations.

The British were not well prepared to fight a defensive battle in the spring of 1918. While huge strides had been made in the art of the attack, the defence had been neglected. GHQ had issued a manual that drew upon the German experience of 'elastic' defence in depth. Gone was the old idea of defending rigid lines of trenches. Now, the notion was to wear down the attackers by forcing them to push through a layered defence, weakly held at the extremities, before they came up against the main line of resistance. At the appropriate moment, the defenders would counter-attack. Unfortunately, it is far from certain that the concept was properly understood by the staff and commanders or the troops who had to carry it out.

> Orders were given to cover this and that contingency, only to be modified or cancelled later. The posts which had originally been intended as outposts only and not as strong points, from which a stout defence could be put up, were now ordered to be held to the last, a costly proceeding, as experience showed.[27]

The difficulties were compounded by the need to convert trenches to the new defensive system, which entailed infantry doing much manual labour, and that ate into the time available for training. 'Since 1916 our troops had been accustomed to an offensive role,' wrote the historian of the Royal Scots, 'and consequently they had not devoted the same attention to the construction of defensive systems as had the Germans. The leeway could not be made up in the course of a few weeks . . .'[28]

These problems were exacerbated by the decision, forced upon a reluctant BEF, to take over trenches formerly held by the French, and in February 1918 by the reorganisation of formation compelled by the manpower shortage. Divisions were reduced from twelve fighting battalions (plus one pioneer unit) to nine, and brigades from four battalions to three. A total of 141 battalions were disbanded, and their personnel – in many cases disgruntled – were posted to other units to keep them up to strength. In Haig's words, this meant that:

> the fighting efficiency of units was lowered at a critical moment. An unfamiliar grouping of units was introduced thereby, necessitating new methods of tactical handling of the troops and the discarding of old methods to which subordinate commanders had been accustomed.[29]

The whole sorry process was summarised by the historian of the Coldstream Guards as follows:

> our troops who were expected to repel . . . [a] concentrated onslaught were very considerably weaker than they were before they were menaced by so grave a danger, they were made responsible for a longer line than they had ever held in the past, their defences were not as perfect as they would have been had there been time to make

them secure, and they were ordered at the last moment to adopt new formations which made it more difficult for them to resist attack, and interfered with their training which was still defective and unsuited to defensive warfare.[30]

These factors, among others, help to explain the German breakthrough on Fifth Army's front near St Quentin on 21 March 1918. However, just seven days later, British defenders performed well in defeating a further German offensive on the Scarpe:

> Our defences in that sector were comparatively speaking strong ... [and] on this occasion the enemy was not befriended by fog, for the day was bright and clear ... The weight of his columns and the bravery of his troops carried them through our line of outposts; but on reaching the battle zone he was met by the accurate fire of all arms in front, as well as in flank and rear by the garrisons of our outposts. There he was stopped and thrown back with very heavy loss ... [L]ater in the evening we counter-attacked with success and pushed out a new outpost line.[31]

Thus, under favourable conditions British infantry could make highly effective use of defence-in-depth tactics.

The defensive mobile operations initiated on 21 March 1918 forced the British infantry to master some skills very different from those needed in position warfare. The 'on-the-job training' was bloody as troops conducted a fighting retreat against a skilful and aggressive enemy. Even more than in the trench warfare period, junior commanders – officers, NCOs and even senior privates – shouldered a huge burden of responsibility as units became more dispersed and communications from the centre were fractured:

> [. . .] 26 March, 1918, was one of the most trying days experienced by the Cambridgeshires during the whole campaign ... Parties under those stubborn fighters, [Lieutenants] Lacey and Wright, became detached, and had perforce to fight for three days alongside other units until they were able to rejoin.
>
> It was a Lewis-gunner's day; 'artists' like Lance-corporal Muffett and Private Bonnett took up positions with a store of drums and waited for the oncoming hordes. They never had to wait long; their stay was limited by the number of drums their overheated guns could fire. Both these performers staggered back after dark carrying their guns, but many nameless Lewis-gun crews were heard firing long after the enemy waves had surged past them ...
>
> Yet throughout the day [Major] Saint and [Captain] Wood,

working together, kept the Battalion together as a fighting unit. Towards evening, more dead than alive, they marshalled the attenuated Companies and platoons into the selected position. By this time the Black Watch and the Cambridgeshire platoons were intermingled and a joint H.Q. was formed . . .

There was no rest for the officers . . . at a conference that night officers fell asleep standing, whilst making their reports.[32]

Evidence such as this – and much else could be cited – suggests that officers had a much higher level of competence than many, including the Official Historian, J E Edmonds, have suggested. Moreover, the level of initiative displayed by British NCOs and Other Ranks, often regarded as negligible, should be reassessed. British infantry during the March Retreat coped with an ever greater devolution of command, as the leaders of small groups fighting a dispersed battle became the key to holding the BEF together. These men tended to be young in years, although they were often battle-experienced. One such was Lieutenant-Colonel J A Taylor, appointed to command 13th Royal Scots in April 1918 at the age of 26. He was killed in action only four months later.[33]

The sheer endurance and stubbornness of the infantry helped to compensate for what they might have lacked in tactical skill. The 7th Royal West Kents (18th Division) were involved on 21 March at the beginning of the German Somme offensive, and also at the end, in the fighting for Villers Bretonneux in the third week of April:

To have lost forty officers and over a thousand men within three weeks and yet be required to return to the fighting line after less than a fortnight's rest shows what the demands were to which the British infantry of 1918 proved themselves equal. That battalions so constantly shattered, so constantly reconstituted and almost re-created, could possess a full measure of cohesion, training and skill was not to be expected, but it was extraordinary how quickly the new drafts assimilated the old traditions and how they emulated standards of courage, devotion and endurance which their predecessors had established. It is hard to do justice to the men of the 7th Battalion who went through the long strain of these days, in which they were constantly fighting rear-guard actions against heavy odds under trying and disadvantageous conditions.[34]

It is fair to say that not every battalion was as resilient as this one, but while the BEF's battle-line bent under the strain, it never shattered; and thus the Germans were unable to convert their tactical successes into decisive victory.

The BEF that took the offensive in August 1918 differed in many ways from the force that had fought on the defensive in the spring. The reorganisation of February was repeated in the late spring. Entire divisions were reconstituted, 30th Division for example, with battalions being disbanded or moved and fresh units arriving. 6th Black Watch (51st Division) spent a fortnight in early August in rest and reorganisation:

> For the third time in five months the Battalion was rebuilt and large drafts of men arrived; a well contested football match between teams of the newcomers showed old members of the 6th that the new drafts were as good as had been their predecessors.[35]

Some differences between British and Dominion units widened in 1918. By this stage Australia alone relied purely on volunteers, and had retained the four battalion brigades, although this meant casualties were increasingly difficult to replace and units were often numerically weak. The Canadians and New Zealanders, by contrast, had adopted conscription and by various methods succeeded in keeping their divisions (still organised in four battalion brigades) up to strength. These formations were significantly larger than their British or Australian equivalents. Plans for American battalions to be permanently assigned to British brigades came to nothing, although many units, including the 17th Royal Fusiliers, received an American Medical Officer. In 1918 the BEF was very much a conscript army, with a leavening of the remaining volunteers and even a few pre-war Regulars and Territorials. Britain was finding it increasingly difficult to find men for the army, and in 1918 battalions were perhaps 500 rather than 900 strong.

To some extent, additional firepower compensated for the manpower shortage. Numbers of Lewis guns had increased steadily over the previous three years. In November 1915 1st Welsh Guards

> received one Lewis Gun. They received a second gun in December 1915, six more in March 1916, and a further eight . . . in August 1916 . . . The number of guns was again increased in 1918 by eight in January and eight in April – in fact, there were so many they could not be manned, although by that time every man in the battalion knew all about the gun [i.e., how to operate it].[36]

By 1918 each battalion had thirty-six Lewis guns, including two per platoon. Additional fire support came from eight trench mortars, sixteen or so rifle-bombers, and, on occasion, attached tanks and guns – in addition, of course, to the support customarily given by the artillery. In February 1918 sub-units underwent further evolution to capitalise on available firepower. The platoon was usually split into two half-platoons of fifteen or twenty men, each commanded by a sergeant. The half-platoon consisted of a section of Lewis gunners and a mixed section of riflemen and rifle-bombers, the section commanders being corporals or lance-corporals. The bombing section had now disappeared, the bomb being the quintessential weapon of trench warfare, while the reorganisation of February 1918 correctly anticipated the imminent re-appearance of modern warfare.[37] As a modern historian has commented, all this denoted a remarkable change in attitude from 1916, when it was considered that a platoon had to contain twenty-eight men to be of any use on the battlefield.[38] According to an official pamphlet issued during the Hundred Days, a section of three men was still viable as a fighting unit.[39]

During 1918 doctrinal pamphlets continued to be issued, codifying tactical best practice, often underlining the importance of the small unit.[40] This point was emphasised by the commander of 4th (Guards) Brigade, a combined-arms formation of infantry, artillery and machine-gun units attached to the Cavalry Corps. Lecturing the newly arrived 1st Honourable Artillery Company, he stressed that in the mobile fighting ahead:

> We shall be split up and therefore you N.C.Os, and very likely some of the old soldiers, will be very much on your own. You won't have your platoon commander very close to you; platoons very likely will not have their company commanders, and the C.O. will not be able to exercise the same amount of supervision as he would do if the battalion were more concentrated. You will all have to act very much on your own, and not wait to be told everything.[41]

From early August until the end of the war the BEF was continually on the offensive, and in this phase, British infantry proved that they were flexible enough to cope with a variety of complex tasks in yet another context: that of mobile offensive warfare. On 21 August, in the Battle of Albert, 2nd Royal Scots advanced through a mist, across open ground 'without any conspicuous landmarks' by compass bearings.[42] 6th Black Watch, rebuilt in early August, made a series of successful attacks in the latter part of the month. By early September, fighting had entered a new phase and the Battalion spent a week 'in training and practising advanced guard formations', for 'the pursuit of the German army had now indeed begun'. This was a form of warfare very different from the mobile defensive work of the spring, or the semi-open and trench-to-trench attacks of earlier years, and once again the BEF had to learn more-or-less on the job. The Germans conducted a fighting retreat, eventually turning to fight on a good defensive position. On 24 October 6th Black Watch made an assault crossing of the River Escallion, carrying 'temporary bridges' with them in the face of intense machine-gun fire that caused heavy casualties:

In spite of this fire, however, and of the difficulties of the river crossing, the 6th resolutely pushed forward and, largely due to Second Lieutenant J M Walker's successful leadership, achieved the crossing. Realizing that the bridges were useless, Walker dashed forward with the survivors of his platoon and by joining hands these men struggled across the river. After cleaning his Lewis gun under cover of the opposite bank, Walker disposed of a machine-gun post in a house nearby. He then pushed forward round the village on the right, taking seventy-eight prisoners. With the coming of daylight, enemy resistance grew less, and the Battalion gained its objective.[43]

There are many other examples of effective leadership, which, added to other improvements (in weapons, and tactics, as well as in command and staff work at all levels up to and including GHQ) helped to make the British infantry a formidable opponent in the Hundred Days of 1918. The experience of 1st Gordon Highlanders (3rd Division) was discussed by Cyril Falls, a highly perceptive commentator. This battalion, nominally a Regular unit, was in September 1918 'an eager but young battalion, with inexperienced platoon commanders'. Many of the Other Ranks were 18 or 19 years old. Attacking the Hindenburg Line and beyond, however, it was successful, not least because the performance of its commanders offered proof 'of the saying that it is junior officers who win battles'. The war diary pointed out that for the attack of 27 September 1st Gordons had less than its full complement of NCOs, and suffered casualties among those that it had; 'section commanders were lance-corporals or privates'. During a subsequent attack on 1 October,

> junior officers, quickly learning their work, had shown skill as well as bold leadership. A couple of days of this open fighting and manoeuvre taught them more than a series of trench-to-trench attacks – and left more survivors to profit by the lessons.[44]

Finally, the process of learning can be illustrated by examining two actions fought by 1st Welsh Guards. On 11 October 1918 the battalion attacked near St Vaast, supported by one section of machine guns and two trench mortars, with a battery of RFA in support. Although largely successful, the regimental history was critical of the operation. Co-operation of the machine guns and trench mortars was defective, and

> it is possible that the formation adopted by the Battalion in this instance was not flexible enough, a relic, no doubt, of the set piece attacks to which it had become accustomed, and there is no question that its will to manoeuvre was hampered by the orders which laid such emphasis on liaison with flank units – another relic of trench

warfare. . . . [Also] the Brigade Commander's conference and the reconnaissance of the ground during daylight in anticipation of orders that were not received until long after darkness had set in.[45]

Three weeks later, on 5 November, the CO of 1st Welsh Guards was given verbal orders by the brigade commander to take a position around Buvignies village. The Battalion commander then carried out a reconnaissance of the ground, and consulted with the CO of the battalion on his right, and also with the artillery commander. Then in order to 'save time . . . orders were dictated to Company commanders and discussed with them'. This Orders group ended at 8.00pm. At midnight, formal orders arrived from brigade. Orders were then issued to the battalion, and reached the companies 'early in the morning'; they were only slightly different from those issued earlier. The attack, in fact the last one to be conducted by the Welsh Guards during the war, commenced at 6.00am on 6 November and was successful.[46]

This small operation reveals a number of interesting aspects. The 'flash to bang' time of the planning was very short. On the Somme in 1916, an operation ordered and then executed that quickly would have been likely to fail, given the inexperience of staff, commanders and troops. That the brigade commander felt able to issue verbal orders, to be confirmed in writing later, is a sign of the trust that had been built up between commanders at different levels, as is the CO's consultation with his company commanders. On receiving verbal instructions, the CO made use of available daylight to conduct a personal reconnaissance, set planning into motion and anticipated (largely correctly) the final orders. This was the mark of a command structure that had adapted well to fluid, open warfare. An infantry officer of 21st Division explicitly compared the clumsy methods of 1916 with those of the Hundred Days: 'It is very important to remember that the artillery had improved their technique just as had the staffs and the infantry.'[47]

The British infantry battalion of November 1918 had undergone considerable evolution from its ancestor of August 1914. It was smaller, but with far greater firepower, and it was less a general purpose unit than an integrated collection of specialist sub-units. It had emerged as an essential element in the BEF's 'weapons system' that brought together various arms into a synergistic whole. Bill Rawling has written of the Canadian Corps that in the Hundred Days of 1918:

Each soldier was a specialist with a specific role to play in battle . . . but he was [also] a jack of all trades, ready to use bomb, rifle-grenade, Lewis gun, or rifle if need be . . . [it was] an army of technicians, which even in the infantry battalions, specialized in particular aspects of fighting battles.[48]

Much the same could be said of infantry battalions raised in other parts of the Empire, including Britain. Moreover, alongside tactical and technological innovations evolved flexible and effective methods of command and control. Whether or not it truly remained 'queen of the battlefield', the command, organisation and tactics of the infantry of the BEF had kept pace with the extraordinary changes in warfare between 1914 and 1918.

NOTES

1   The preceding paragraphs are based on *Field Service Manual 1913. Infantry Battalion (Expeditionary Force)* 40 WO 1658, *War Establishments of New Armies 1915, 40* WO 2425; *Field Service Pocket Book 1914,* 40, WO 2923, all in Public Record Office (PRO).

2   For the TF see I F W Beckett, 'The Territorial Force' in I F W Becken and K Simpson (eds), *A Nation at Arms* (Manchester, 1985), 128–47.

3   Anon, *History of the London Rifle Brigade 1859–1919* (London, 1921), 72.

4   Anon, *The 23rd London Regiment 1798–1919* (London, 1936), 13.

5   A M McGilchrist, *The Liverpool Scottish 1900–1919* (London, 1930), 21.

6   J E Edmonds, *Military Operation, France and Belgium 1915,* Vol. I (London, 1927), 95.

7   F C Hitchcock, *Stand To* (London, 1937), 70.

8   SS398, *The Training and Employment of Bombers.*

9   SS126, *The Training and Employment of Bombers* (Sept. 1916).

10 C H Dudley Ward, *History of the Welsh Guards* (London, new edition, 1988), 150.

11 Edmonds, *Military Operations, France and Belgium, 1915,* Vol. II (London, 1928), 86; G Chapman, *A Passionate Prodigality* (London, 1933), 32.

12 Edmonds, *Military Operations, France and Belgium, 1916,* Vol. I (London, 1932), 64.

13 G H F Nichols, *The 18th Division in the Great War* (London, 1922), 22.

14 Anon, *A War Record of the 21st London Regiment (First Surrey Rifles),* (privately published, nd), 42.

15 R O Russell, *The History of the 11th (Lewisham) Battalion, The Queen's Own Royal West Kent Regiment* (London, 1934), 48.

16 SS195 *Scouting and Patrolling. Issued by the General Staff December 1917,* 6.

17 J E B Fairclough, *The First Birmingham Battalion in the Great War* (Birmingham, 1933), 63.

18 F Buckley *War History of the Seventh Northumberland Fusiliers* (Newcastle upon Tyne, nd), 13.

19 J C Dunn, *The War the Infantry Knew 1914–19* (London, new edition, 1987), 245.

20 J Terraine (ed.), *General Jack's Diary* (London, new edition, 2000), 169–70.

21 C Falls, *The Life of A Regiment,* Vol. IV, *The Gordon Highlanders in the First World War 1914–1919* (Aberdeen, 1958), 83.

22 C Falls, *History of the 36th (Ulster) Division* (Belfast, 1922), 83.

23 V H B Majendie, *A History of the 1st Battalion Somerset Light Infantry* (Taunton, 1921), 61.

24 F O Grimwade, *The War History of the 4th Battalion The London Regiment (Royal Fusiliers) 1914–19* (London, 1922), 339.

25 D Ferguson, *The History of the Canterbury Regiment, NZEF 1914–1919* (Auckland, 1929), 217.

26   Russell, *Lewisham Battalion*, 139.
27   O F Bailey and H M Hollier, *'The Kensingtons' 13th London Regiment* (London, nd), 150.
28   J Ewing, *The Royal Scots 1914–1919*, II (Edinburgh, 1925), 556–7.
29   Quoted in Sir J Ross-of-Bladensburg, *The Coldstream Guards 1914–18*, Vol. II (London, 1928), 171.
30   *ibid*, 172.
31   *ibid*, 216–17.
32   E Riddell and M C Clayton, *The Cambridgeshires 1914 to 1919* (Cambridge, 1934), 159–60.
33   Ewing, *Royal Scots* Vol. II, 639, 651.
34   C T Atkinson, *The Queen's Own Royal West Kent Regiment 1914–1919* (London, 1924), 385
35   A G Wauchope (ed.), *A History of the Black Watch (Royal Highlanders) in the Great War, 1914–1918*, Vol. II (London, 1926), 198.
36   Dudley Ward, *History of Welsh Guards*, 150.
37   SS143, Feb. 1918.
38   B Rawling, *Surviving Trench Warfare: Technology and the Canadian Corps, 1915–1918* (Toronto, 1992), 175.
39   C Dudley Ward, *The Welsh Regiment of Foot Guards 1915–1918* (London, 1936), 133 fn.1.
40   For example, GHQ letter NO.O.B./1919, 28 September 1918.
41   G Gould Walker, *The Honourable Artillery Company in the Great War 1914–1919* (London, 1930), 105.
42   Ewing, *Royal Scots*, 661.
43   Wauchope. *Black Watch*, 199–200.
44   Falls, *The Life of a Regiment* Vol. IV, 245–8.
45   Dudley Ward, *Welsh Regiment of Foot Guards*, 125–6.
46   *Ibid* 134–7. For the operations orders, see Dudley Ward, *History of Welsh Guards*, 365–7.
47   D V Kelly, *39 Months with the 'Tigers', 1915–1918* (London, 1930), 138.
48   Rawling, *Surviving Trench Warfare*, 217.

CHAPTER IX

Command of Artillery:
the case of Herbert Uniacke

Sanders Marble

Although the First World War is remembered for the quantities of artillery used, artillery commanders have not received the attention paid to infantrymen and cavalrymen. While few artillerymen left collections of papers, there is a more important reason: gunners subordinated themselves, and the artillery, to the infantry and cavalry, which were seen as the primary combat arms. This chapter will examine the role of artillery commanders through the example of Herbert Uniacke, who commanded artillery from brigade to Army level. His career enables us to see the role of different echelons of command, and also the evolution of combat methods. As Uniacke left a body of papers, and did not always hide his opinions, it is often possible to see where he made a difference.

Herbert Crofton Campbell Uniacke was born in 1866 and went to the Royal Military Academy in 1883. After two years at Woolwich he was commissioned and posted to the Royal Field Artillery in 1885 and saw mainly garrison duty until 1914. His rise through the commissioned ranks was unexceptional, and only two points about his pre-war service are particularly worthy of mention. First, Uniacke's battery was stationed in India throughout the Boer War, and so his baptism of fire was delayed until 1914. He was thus rare among his peers in lacking any campaign medals prior to the First World War. Still, Uniacke studied the Boer War, and advocated more modern gunnery methods than had been demonstrated in South Africa. Second, he had developed an interest and aptitude for training. For almost a year before war broke out Uniacke was effectively head of the School of Horse and Field Artillery in Britain, the main training establishment. At the time there was neither a central school nor a doctrine; Uniacke wanted to change this, and during the First World War he would repeatedly butt his head against obstacles to achieving his aim.

Little of Uniacke's pre-war thoughts on artillery have survived. Tim Travers notes one incident at the 1913 manoeuvres when Uniacke lined up two batteries of Royal Horse Artillery (RHA) on Salisbury Plain to see which detachment could fire first.[1] Without being unkind to the RHA, this type of display was its stock in trade and Uniacke may have been producing what onlookers expected to see, rather than what he believed would be the wartime role of horse artillery.

Because he was not commanding a combat unit in August 1914, Uniacke did not go to France until November, when 5th Brigade RHA was improvised from schools and from batteries kept below strength as a peacetime economy measure. Uniacke's time had presumably been occupied with organising training programmes for Kitchener divisions, for he has been credited with creating a 'New Army artillery school'.[2] This seems generous, unless the establishment closed shortly thereafter, for no record of it remains.

Uniacke commanded 5th Brigade RHA from November 1914 until February 1915.[3] It formed part of the artillery of 8th Division, itself assembled from units gathered from around the Empire. His period of command was uneventful, as the Division held a quiet sector at a relatively quiet time of the war, and the combatants all lacked enough shells to revive the fighting.

As Uniacke had no opportunity to distinguish himself in action, his selection to command a new and important heavy artillery unit in February 1915 should be attributed to his pre-war reputation. The unit was at first called Second Group, General Headquarters Artillery, but a month later became Reserve Heavy Artillery Group No. 2 and soon thereafter Second Heavy Artillery Reserve Group (HARG). The name is less important than the function: specialisation of command. In 1914 the BEF mobilised very few units of heavy guns and all the artillery was directly subordinated to the infantry. Indeed, while there were Commanders, Royal Artillery (CRA) in each division they had little to do because the artillery was divided and attached to the infantry brigades, which operated almost as brigade groups. When heavy artillery trickled out to France the same pattern was followed – it was parcelled out to divisions rather than being centrally organised. Thus flexibility of fire was sacrificed, for, unless the divisions could reach private arrangements, artillery attached to one division would not fire in support of its neighbours.

The formation of GHQ Artillery was the first hesitant step away from this system. Uniacke and George Franks (commander of First Group) were put in command of the heavy artillery that had previously been allotted to divisions. But Uniacke and Franks themselves reported to the commanders of those same divisions. Thus the effect was to create a new subordinate command, yet at the same time to improve the technical handling of artillery as the divisional CRAs would be freed of some of the extra units with which they had been burdened. While a small step, it was about the most that was technically possible. At the time the BEF lacked such communications necessities as telephone cable and switchboards, and communication is the first requirement for centralised fire control. Throughout 1915 several headquarters (and even observation posts) had to be co-located in order to share the available telephones. Similarly, the artillery had not developed the routines and expertise that later allowed rapid and accurate shifting of fire.

Uniacke's group soon took part in the BEF's first attack of 1915, the Battle of Neuve Chapelle. He was allowed no role in planning the battle. Rawlinson and Haig dominated the former, and Rawlinson made the decisions about artillery after consulting the gunners.[4] Uniacke's war diary[5] goes into battery ammunition expenditures and targets, details rather than policy. He put his energies into the one area where he had responsibility: counter-battery (CB) work. Because he commanded the guns that would be most effective at CB fire, and he had close liaison with the Royal Flying Corps, and because higher headquarters would be too busy to manage artillery operations minute-by-minute, Uniacke was left to his own devices. He developed an elaborate chart that showed at a glance which batteries could hit targets in each grid square. With this, German batteries could be engaged rapidly and as effectively as possible given the material shortages and technical limitations of early 1915.

During the rest of 1915 the position of the HARG changed as the combatants grappled with trench warfare, something that itself changed rapidly during 1915. Broadly, in quiet times a HARG commanded heavy artillery within a corps area, responsible to the Corps Commander. However, they also had fluctuating responsibility for CB work and dealt with the Major General, Royal Artillery (MGRA) at each Army HQ. Without any precedents, a great deal depended on individuals. 1st HARG pondered CB policy; 4th HARG developed a more effective paper organisation.[6] Uniacke developed new techniques of working with the RFC, apparently being the first to put an aeroplane in the sky with a battery 'on call', waiting for a target.[7] He also seems to have developed the 'zone call' system rapidly whereby any aircraft that spotted activity would report the location and type with a simple code; response times were cut through pre-planning.[8] Uniacke also insisted on more uniformity within his Group. Negatively, this could be viewed as interference from above. More positively, in a BEF composed of some Regulars, many inexperienced Territorials, and also completely green Kitchener volunteers, with a personalised command system, trying to develop a doctrine while still fighting, Uniacke brought some order to his subordinate units. This seems to have been a conscious policy, which he repeated later.

Besides CB the other main task of heavy artillery was to carry out bombardments. Neither Uniacke, nor any other artilleryman, had much influence here because the BEF rated strategy more important than tactics and furthermore centred tactics on the infantry. Artillery commanders were generally consulted during planning; when time permitted the discussions could be extensive. However, because the artillery only supported the attack, the final decisions were made by *formation* commanders at division, corps or army level, after weighing the representations of the infantry, engineers and RFC. Thus the input of artillerymen was masked by the command structure; all orders came from the formation commander because he had legal command authority. Artillerymen would, from the framework laid down and consultations with others, develop their orders down to battery level. Different levels would work on different parts of the plan: divisions handled wire-cutting and some harassing fire; CB and more harassing fire was planned by corps (HARGs in 1915); bombardment was shared between divisions and higher levels.

It is worth briefly examining how a bombardment actually worked in 1915. Unfortunately, no detailed notes or recollections survive about how Uniacke handled matters around Hooge, in September, but contemporary operations at Loos were carefully studied.[9] Army and corps commanders prioritised target categories for bombardment; this was then combined with the amount of ammunition available to set the amounts for each category per sector. The front-line infantry brigades then worked with the artillery covering that same sector to pick out the targets of special local importance. Targets for the next day would be selected on the basis of the success of each day's fire; the infantry would have their say and would have the advantage not only of direct observation from the front line but daily aerial photographs. Wire-cutting worked similarly, with the guns covering a given sector responsible to the infantry for cutting that wire. The infantry could also ask that special attention be given to certain areas or demand that fire continue until they were satisfied with the results. Overlaid upon this destruction of German forward trenches was fire farther to the rear. This was out of sight of the infantry and was left to artillerymen, the HARGs. Targets included German HQs, observation posts, reserves and billets; train, trench and road junctions; telephone exchanges and guns. Harassing fire was also centrally controlled. With a finite number of guns to do the work, two different HQs had to reconcile their orders. One HQ worked out the shelling of forward trenches, while the other planned deeper targets. Orders were finally issued over the signature of the General Staff because the artillery chain of command was still muddled.

This system had some advantages. It used the detailed local knowledge of the infantry directly to guide the bombardment, thus improving the infantry's confidence in the artillery. Generally, given adequate supplies of ammunition, the German trenches were battered beyond use and wire was adequately cut. This was especially important, as the infantry were very concerned with (and insistent about) wire-cutting. Some elements of this practice survived well into 1917. But there were serious drawbacks too. It worked well at the beginning of an offensive, but once infantry brigades were replaced because of losses, local knowledge evaporated, liaison in general suffered, and a system that relied upon close liaison suffered in proportion.

Overall, the system was complicated and proved inefficient. Personnel difficulties only exacerbated the problems in September 1915, the only large-scale test. At Loos, First Army attacked with two corps, each operating a different system of artillery command. Rawlinson, commanding IV Corps, distrusted his titular Artillery Adviser and worked around him. Gough of I Corps worked better with his, but there was still overlap with First Army's MGRA. Subsidiary and diversionary attacks were mounted along the British front; Uniacke's part was supporting V Corps around Hooge. Uniacke reported to two masters, Second Army and V Corps, for some of the same activities. At the same time the Army Commander (Herbert Plumer) inserted his MGRA to take command of all artillery supporting V Corps. Legally, Uniacke could command his guns and the CRAs could command theirs, but neither could command the other, leading to difficult positions for the HARG commander, the Artillery Adviser and divisional CRAs. The Artillery Adviser had no command authority, and the MGRA had power only (as in this case) when specially appointed. It is a tribute to the professionalism and tact of all concerned that the system worked at all.

In the winter of 1915–16 significant changes took place at GHQ and subsequently in artillery command. The first was the arrival of John Headlam as the new MGRA at GHQ. Headlam had been MGRA at Second Army and was the man inserted to command the artillery of V Corps in September. The second was that a few weeks later, in December 1915, Sir Douglas Haig rose from First Army to command the whole BEF. Haig had the experience of Loos fresh in his mind. Within weeks Haig and Headlam had combined to reorganise artillery command throughout the BEF.

CRAs now only commanded the field artillery supporting their division. This might be more than the theoretical establishment if the division had been reinforced, but, however many pieces were allotted, they commanded only field artillery. At corps level the Artillery Adviser had a new title and – for the first time – power. He was now Brigadier General, Royal Artillery (BGRA) and explicitly placed above the CRAs. He would co-ordinate between them (for the infantry still had great influence) and act as the artillery spokesman to the corps commander. The last element was the Commander, Corps Heavy Artillery (CHA). After an initial hiccup when the CHA appeared to be the equal of the BGRA, he became firmly established as the subordinate. This structure had a few flaws (mostly concerning field artillery) that would be ironed out in 1917, but it greatly simplified the commands and responsibilities of CRAs and CHAs. It meant they could learn their duties and that only the BGRA had to understand how to mix artillery. Practically speaking, there was little turnover. All but one Artillery Adviser was made into a BGRA. HARGs, which had proliferated throughout 1915, became CHA staffs.

Uniacke had, in mid-November 1915, been made Artillery Adviser at V Corps (apparently ratifying his position; the incumbent had done and would continue to do little), still occupying a section of the Ypres Salient. In April he was exchanged with the BGRA of III Corps in the Somme region. This was a deliberate step, for Uniacke had been identified as an excellent officer and several such were selected to take part in the planning of the Somme offensive.[10] Shortly thereafter Haig moved Headlam out of GHQ and brought in Noel Birch, who was both very competent and well liked by Haig. However, the CIGS, Sir William Robertson, recommended Uniacke for the GHQ post, indicating the extent of his reputation by this stage.[11]

Uniacke remained at III Corps only until the end of July 1916. Notes from an early conference show organisation and also subtlety – for instance German reserve troops were not to be shelled too early, for they would have time to recover.[12] Similarly, as the British lacked enough artillery to destroy many German guns, it was important not to fire lightly and early; better to force them to move late and at least reduce their efficiency just before the attack. By June plans had firmed up considerably and III Corps, like the rest of the Army, practised its creeping barrage under cover of the general bombardment.[13] Yet in an operation as large as the Somme attack, even a corps was a cog in the machine and matters were settled higher up. Rawlinson at one point decided some artillery matters with his own Chief of Staff and MGRA, then left the details to the subordinate artillerymen and the general staff officers.[14] Furthermore, the corps was not yet a strong enough echelon of command to insist that the component divisions obey its wishes. For instance, while the principle of the creeping barrage was outlined at Army level, the actual orders were laid down by the divisions and corps could only do their best to co-ordinate. On this matter, Uniacke was firmer than some BGRAs, and both divisions of III Corps set the same pace, a sign of something he was shortly to emphasise. Unfortunately, the pace was intentionally set faster than the infantry could advance, so the barrage and the infantry soon became separated and the barrage was ineffective.[15] III Corps did not do well when the offensive began, although the Corps Commander had loyally expressed himself 'quite satisfied' when Haig enquired about the progress of the bombardment.[16]

III Corps' failure did not, however, halt Uniacke's rise. By the end of July he had been made MGRA of Hubert Gough's Reserve Army, a job he would hold for almost two years through some of the heaviest fighting of the war. The position of MGRA was technically one of influence rather than power. However Uniacke might sign himself, he was *not* a commanding officer. The first MGRAs had been appointed in early 1915 with two roles. Ordinarily they would oversee the artillery in the armies but they could be detailed to temporary command of artillery groupings. The latter happened extraordinarily rarely, apparently once in 1915 and once in 1917. Otherwise they co-ordinated the artillery of the corps within their army. One of the MGRA's few clear powers was to delineate CB areas for each corps. He also worked on allotting guns between corps, ammunition supply (mainly a question of priorities), and what was termed 'supervision'.[17] Not being a formal commander, the MGRA could not issue orders or instructions of his own; instead they had to go through the General Staff, being signed by or for the Senior General Staff Officer. Only gradually was this procedure loosened so that Uniacke (and other MGRAs) could handle some matters directly. Certainly, for several months, Hubert Gough (and Neill Malcolm, his chief of staff) gave Uniacke little rope, maintaining a close personal interest in artillery matters and ensuring that the GS cleared any orders.[18]

Despite few formal powers, there was plenty of work for an active MGRA, and lazy men did not rise to this level. Uniacke studied the tactical and technical evolution of the artillery, the rest of the BEF and, of course, the Germans. He spread effective methods throughout Reserve Army; he also warned against ideas that failed. Seeing artillery as part of a combined arms team, Uniacke talked to Army, corps and divisional commanders, not just artillerymen.[19] Training was a particular concern, especially for a man with a long interest in technical standards of gunnery. Uniacke looked to increase the professionalism not just of the gun detachments, but also subordinate artillery commanders. He did this by requiring four daily reports: deliberate shoots (CB), neutralising fire (CB and trench retaliation), hostile activity and British bombardments.[20] While doubtless cursing the paperwork, the corps had to pay attention to all these aspects, although the Australians, with their fine disregard for paperwork, seem to have ignored Uniacke. That Uniacke was not simply obsessed with paperwork is shown by his later behaviour; he cracked the whip early, but by August 1916 required fewer reports, and in 1917 Uniacke stopped requiring the reports because he had achieved what he sought.

For several months during the Somme campaign, the Reserve Army worked mainly in support of Fourth Army's operations, largely by CB work against German artillery that flanked Rawlinson's advance. Uniacke was intimately involved in this, because the counter-battery struggle was the closest thing the Royal Artillery had to a private war. He did what he could, including creating a temporary and unofficial CB office as part of his HQ, but there were severe limitations. There was still a shortage of artillery, and Fourth Army had a higher priority for guns. Various helpful technologies would not pay off until 1917. Maps still had unacceptable margins of error. Aerial spotting was imperfectly organised; whenever boundaries were changed the gunners and RFC had to learn the new sector.[21] Gunners had not become accustomed to doing complex mathematics before every shoot, causing larger margins of error.

In later stages of the Somme, Fourth and Reserve Armies shared attacks, and Uniacke worked on bombardments and infantry support as well as CB. Bombardments would still be co-ordinated with the infantry formations and their commanders, but Uniacke laid down guidelines. For instance when the Canadians entered the line in September 1916 they were told how many rounds were needed to destroy a yard of German trench.[22] Uniacke stayed in close touch with front-line conditions, and changed his advice when necessary – for instance three weeks later reducing the weight of shelling because now the German positions were not so formidable.[23] However, Uniacke was acting as a technician, not making policy decisions; if Gough wanted a trench line obliterated then Uniacke planned that, but if the goal was a quick attack then Uniacke did what he could in the time available. If corps and army commanders decided that time was no object then orders would follow: 'The above sections of trench will be destroyed by deliberate shooting . . . No limit to number of rounds fired on each spot, except that each section of trench must be completely obliterated.'[24]

Gough, while learning to trust Uniacke, still maintained the formal organisation for artillery orders. This meant Uniacke would settle matters amongst the artillerymen, but then a General Staff officer would sign the orders. Uniacke spent a tremendous amount of time devising new ways to make creeping barrages more effective, but his signature is absent from the documents. The creeping barrage had been identified early as a vital aid to the infantry. Indeed, so important did it become that junior infantry officers might think riflemen a 'very slight support' to the artillery.[25] But with communications as imperfect as they were throughout the First World War, the question was always what should be done where the infantry met strong resistance or the creeping barrage advanced faster than the infantry. There was no one answer but Uniacke tried what he could. Specifically, he tried to give infantry battalion and brigade commanders a particular battery of guns to deal with local targets. This had serious drawbacks, being vulnerable to any failure of communications, and it also risked drawing the guns away from firing on a more important target. In 1917 part of this problem would be solved because more guns were available. Uniacke did not believe that the generals farther to the rear had more information or were in a better position to decide; he did not think the artillery should conquer and the infantry occupy. Instead he was doing everything he could to perfect the artillery as support for the men in direct combat – the infantry.

As the weather worsened into the harshest spell for years, fighting declined over the winter of 1916–17. In late November the BEF stopped its offensive, only mounting occasional local attacks in keeping with a policy to keep pressure on the Germans. With fewer infantry involved, the artillery played a large part in these operations. The artillery was to be especially active in destruction and harassment; each corps used its local knowledge to devise plans. Once these were ready, Uniacke knitted the separate corps schemes into an Army-wide plan, mixing in CB, and his own nasty tricks for harassing fire. Army HQ then melded the local infantry attacks with the artillery plans. All this was ready within ten days, and the results were once again issued over Neill Malcolm's signature.[26] Once the outlines had been settled by Uniacke, the detailed week-by-week work was left to the corps whose bombardment plans were again signed by the GS. With three corps in the line over the winter, Fifth Army's active artillery policy meant firing over 2,000,000 shells.[27]

Another part of the winter programme was training. Complaints about the level of training of Territorial and New Army divisions had begun as soon as they arrived in France; now there was little to choose between them and Regular divisions. There were few regulars left while the new units had plenty of on-the-job experience. Schools mushroomed behind the lines training both individuals and whole units. GHQ tried to standardise instruction, but most things were left to army or corps schools. The most important artillery school was actually back in England, on the site that would later become the Royal School of Artillery. With his interest in training Uniacke would undoubtedly have been active, perhaps more active than some of his subordinates appreciated, but little information survives about the time units spent training.

As winter waned, the Germans made a strategic withdrawal to the Hindenburg Line, shortening their frontage, increasing their reserves, and dislocating Allied logistics for the forthcoming spring offensive. Fifth Army (as Reserve Army had been renamed) took part in the advance, doing their best to cut off German rear-guards but being able to do little more than maintain contact. For units that had experienced nothing but trench warfare this brief taste of movement was confusing rather than exhilarating, and senior artillerymen had to teach techniques that were useless in trench warfare. Fourth Army wrote an elaborate report afterwards that guided the next winter's training programme but Gough's troops were busy preparing to attack. The dislocation of supply lines meant that Fifth Army could only make a subsidiary attack to help the Third Army's offensive around Arras, but they did what they could. Uniacke took less of a role in Fifth Army's advance and attack for a very good reason: he had been detached to Third Army.

Once the decision to attack at Arras had been taken, planners turned to the details of the attack. The Army Commander, Allenby, wanted to do something new: an attack using surprise.[28] He wanted a short but correspondingly intense bombardment and was counting on the Germans to react slowly, as the BEF had in the past used long bombardments. Haig was more conservative and eventually won the argument by removing Allenby's MGRA in what was clearly a warning shot. The man appointed to Third Army was ill, and in a unique move Uniacke was loaned to Third Army to sort out the artillery plan in the short time available.[29] Uniacke produced a very effective artillery plan on more traditional lines, partly because he was told to but also because he felt little more was possible at the time.[30]

Before his attachment to Third Army, Uniacke had been on another mission. Haig had long wanted to attack from the Ypres Salient and needed plans to convince the Cabinet and the French. Several people were put to work on the question, from junior colonels in GHQ's operations branch to Henry Rawlinson, by now the most experienced Army commander. Rawlinson's plan was not terribly sensible, and may have been an indication that he thought the Salient the wrong place for an offensive. Uniacke was the one telling Rawlinson about the problems Ypres posed for the artillery, and had been specially selected over Rawlinson's own artillery adviser.[31] In any event, Haig temporarily dropped Ypres as the location for an offensive.

Fifth Army's part in the spring offensive was the undistinguished fighting around Bullecourt. The results could largely have been predicted before so many lives were lost. Hasty attacks failed with heavy losses. Once adequate time was allowed for preparations (not just by the artillery) the village was finally wrested from the Germans. Until then it was a matter of pitting troops whose only advantage was courage against defenders who held all the other cards. It was not the BEF's finest hour, and Uniacke passed over it in his annual review, for the lessons were plain for all to see and larger events had intervened.

After the fighting around Arras had died down, Fifth Army was transferred to Ypres to prepare an offensive there. Intended to break the German lines and at least sweep them from the Belgian coast, it was more ambitious in scope and resources than Arras. Gough had been chosen because he was a thruster; if anyone would pursue after the breakthrough, it was him. And he, along with Uniacke, was confident of a breakthrough. The baseline for planning their attack was issued just days after the storming of Messines Ridge:

> . . . It has been conclusively proved that with the artillery at our disposal, a carefully organised and thoroughly prepared attack can break through any defences which the enemy can devise. The great initial successes of the 1st July, 1916, 13th November 1916, and 9th

April [1917] are sufficient proof that this claim is not too great a claim. The Second Army attack on the 7th June furnished further proof . . .[32]

Uniacke was ambivalent about the situation at Ypres, recognising the simple geographical fact that the British would be advancing farther into a salient that, regardless of the efforts of the RFC at downing German aircraft, was overlooked on all sides.[33] At the same time the Germans were desperately bolstering their defences, especially building pill boxes. It can only have been absolute confidence in the Royal Artillery (and, to a degree, Uniacke's handling of it) that meant the bombardment was left off the agenda of the first conference about the forthcoming attack.[34] A fortnight later the next conference did not even have an artillery officer present, even though the participants knew 'the question of artillery support was the principal difficulty' in how far the infantry could advance the first day.[35] Uniacke attended the next conference and began trying to turn Gough's ideas into reality. Gough had drawn the easy distinction between attacking an organised enemy and an unorganised one, but the planners had to deal with a more complicated world. Uniacke played the key role in settling artillery matters: gun and ammunition requirements, bombardment priorities, CB work, battery positions, air support, details down to the types of shells and fuses for the barrage. Much of this had to be done while the preliminary bombardment was underway, because the extensive German defences required a long bombardment.

Gough was relying heavily on artillery preparation before the attack and support during the attack to allow the infantry to make a big advance without getting disorganised and vulnerable to a counter-attack. Other commanders were just as confident, including some with better historical reputations than Gough. As the bombardment and CB work pressed on, Uniacke's confidence rose too. At first the Germans had fought back and the British gunners, packed into the Salient under German observation, had taken heavy losses. But gradually the Royal Artillery gained superiority and losses dropped, and the Germans shifted to area shelling for disruption rather than trying to destroy particular targets. The Germans also pulled their guns back to places the British could not reach. This was hailed as a CB success but when the British infantry advanced the German guns would be back in range. Finally, the Germans had adopted new tactics of recoiling before the first British attack then counter-attacking, which meant Gough's decision to rush as far as possible on the first day was being used against him. All in all, Fifth Army got caught up in the details before 31 July and lost sight of the big picture.

The first day of the Third Battle of Ypres was only a very partial success. The BEF gained ground but everywhere the Germans still held the key points. Yet the offensive had a momentum of its own and Fifth Army kept battering away at the Germans. Tactics took priority over operations and strategy. It availed the BEF little that people like Uniacke were fast developing better tactics, always reacting rapidly to German changes and sometimes anticipating them, because better tactics could not compensate for the geographical situation.[36]

Eventually Fifth Army's progress became so unsatisfactory that the emphasis was shifted to Second Army. Uniacke was still busy, for Second Army needed flanking artillery support. It was not glamorous work but he did it thoroughly. He also threw himself into the winter training programme the BEF began after the fighting came to an exhausted close. Because the BEF shifted to the defensive, rather than only pausing in its attacks as over the previous winter, more troops could be pulled out of the line for training; they were also more experienced, so training could focus on different areas. This made a great difference in the training pro-gramme. Expertise in gunnery had been acquired by experience, so mobility was the missing element. Mid-ranking officers were a key group that was taught more about operating on their own in mobile operations. Some of the reports after the opening battles in the spring of 1918 pay eloquent testimony to the usefulness of training in mobile operations. This was something that senior commanders had noted in March and April 1917 and filed away until they had a chance to do something about it.[37]

During 1917 Uniacke (indeed artillerymen generally) had more operational freedom than in 1916. This came about not because the British army had again changed its command structure, but because artillerymen had shown themselves trustworthy within the new system. Gunners did not try to fight a separate war; they recognised their role was to support the infantry and they did their best to do so. After Passchendaele, Uniacke drew up a thorough 103-page report about artillery, what it had done through 1917, what it should do in 1918 and the changes needed. He dwelt on the need for changing artillery tactics to 'allow our Infantry to assault with a reasonable prospect of success, and gain their objective with the minimum of loss – *always bearing in mind that the final decisive factor is the bayonet of the Infantry soldier.*'[38] Neither Uniacke nor other artillery com-manders were calling for the war to be centred on the guns, but neither did they think the war should be fought in the same old way. They would be searching for the best way to integrate manpower and firepower until the last shot was fired, and some looked to reform the army after the war.

After Cambrai (November–December 1917) the BEF halted operations for the winter. Fifth Army, still in the morass around Ypres, gratefully ceased the harassing fire, bombardments, raids and patrols that charac-terised 'quiet' times for British troops.[39] Early in 1918 Fifth Army was shifted from the Ypres Salient to the opposite flank of the BEF and took over ground from the French. This meant an immense amount of work for units that were below strength and worn out from long campaigning. As the army adopted a new divisional organisation and new defensive ideas (defence in depth was now the watch-word, however ill-defined), there were a series of conferences; Uniacke attended on an equal basis with infantry commanders.[40] After British plans were settled and until the Germans launched their attack, there was relatively little for senior British commanders to do except see to details. Uniacke spent about one day a week in his office on paperwork (typically when the weather was bad), the rest of his time seeing things and being seen. Among other things, he studied defence against tanks, with interesting results: he concluded that tanks were not the main danger, 'but the facilities [they] give for the enemy's *Infantry* to break into our defences'. Thus only designated anti-tank guns should shoot at tanks and other artillery should 'destroy the enemy's infantry'.[41] He did study the new German infiltration tactics (then called 'Riga' tactics), although in this case forewarned was still not forearmed.

It is again important to see what powers a high-ranking artillery commander had, what he could do to affect a battle. There were frequent alarms about impending German attacks, but Uniacke had limited options. He could shift the reserve brigades (which were simultaneously training) to new locations; he could order more ammunition forward from the dumps (if there was labour available); he could devise bombardment plans to test German reactions. This last was perhaps the most useful, because watching what the Germans did after the BEF shelled bridges and junctions gave valuable clues. If repairs were slow, or the Germans gave up after repeated damage, an attack was unlikely. If they made repairs regardless of effort and cost, the omens were very different. Intelligence about German artillery became more important. If the Germans moved guns in it was an obvious sign, but more subtly the numbers of empty positions, amount of ammunition dumped, quantity of registering fire, and deployment of the active batteries all provided clues. Unfortunately, however accurately Fifth Army diagnosed an attack on their front, German feints and deceptions caused other armies to report activity.

With less fighting, the staff was given the opportunity for more paperwork. The main change for senior artillerymen was a return to the 1916 system whereby the General Staff had to sign artillery papers. Uniacke was livid. He saw the 'petrifying influence of the Gen[l] Staff Manual ... This is a retrograde step of the worst description' because artillery had performed very well in 1917 with looser, more practical, arrangements.[42] Uniacke decided to fight the change, even if opposition cost him his position. He finished his self-described 'screed' a week before the German offensive was unleashed. Given that there was a real battle to fight, the paper war came to an end.[43]

The Germans opened their offensive on 21 March following their new tactics. They nearly broke through the British lines and only a fighting retreat prevented a collapse. Command and control broke down into a soldiers' battle. Gough could only try to reinforce where the need was greatest and Uniacke could do little more than arrange ammunition supplies and prise replacement guns from the Ordnance Department.[44]

Fifth Army rode out the storm as reinforcements arrived and the Germans faltered through exhaustion. Perhaps unfairly, given the ratio of forces, Fifth Army HQ was replaced by Fourth Army although the troops in the line stayed the same. Gough was made a scapegoat for the army's weakness and his staff went with him. Uniacke had confidence in Gough and intended 'to stick to Goughie'. Once Gough was relieved of even token duties Uniacke's ire bubbled forth again.[45] At first Fifth Army HQ was put to reconnoitring reserve lines; once that was done there was little to fill the days beyond overseeing training. A brigade commander wrote at the time: 'General Uniacke spent much of his time at the school, and under his guidance you may be sure that the instruction was thorough and up-to-date.'[46] Uniacke plotted against Charles Budworth, MGRA of Fourth Army, who wanted to take over the Fifth Army's Artillery School. As long as he was in France, Uniacke maintained ownership, but Budworth pounced when Uniacke went home to watch a demonstration and all he could do was pour his vitriol into his diary: 'd-d impertinence' and 'perfectly iniquitous'.[47]

In mid-July Uniacke was appointed Deputy Inspector General for Training with particular responsibility for artillery training. He had long been active in training and during the lull of the 1917–18 winter renewed calls for a central artillery school.[48] Now given an opportunity, he tried to restructure training with greater central control of the syllabi.

> By doing away with Army Schools, uniformity of instruction would at last be secured and that is greatly needed. Only too often instructors will not stick to THE BOOK, but teach fancy Systems of their own – very fancy they often are, and confusing to young officers going from one school to another.[49]

Uniacke's work involved visits, inspections and conferences, so again he managed to escape the office. The British army lacked a central organ for developing doctrine (it was another of the tasks of the General Staff) and the new Inspector General of Training (IGT), Sir Ivor Maxse, stepped into the breach. He interpreted his mission as not just overseeing training, but deciding what that training should be, and thus the tactics and operations of the future army. Uniacke took this up for the artillery, at the same time overseeing the publication of leaflets concerning the latest German tactics and discussing what artillery the BEF should have for the 1919 campaign.[50] Training involved integrating the components of the BEF into a combined-arms team and Uniacke's responsibility for artillery meant he was involved in everything: close support of infantry, work with infantry and tanks, use of smoke, and a hundred other details.[51] Maxse and Uniacke were not conducting an isolated seminar, as they examined reports from the front line. The IGT drew its information from divisional reports, filed as soon as the troops left the front line, German documents translated for clues on what the Germans would do next, and private correspondence filling any gaps.

Tim Travers notes that IGT did not make changes as fast as Armies, but IGT was farther from the front and also watching to see which British innovations worked before spreading them all across the BEF.[52] Regardless of how fast IGT were thinking, they had more time for it than operational HQs, and as soon as the fighting slackened GHQ's Birch asked Uniacke what should be done next. Uniacke seized the opportunity to campaign for his pet project, a central artillery school.[53] There was now too much technical gunnery being taught, he said, and it was time for tactics to be emphasised. Open warfare was coming, either if the war was resumed in 1919 or in future wars; the key personnel to train were battery commanders. His arguments, presented in a whirlwind visit to the War Office and backed by Birch, were accepted and the School of Artillery opened in 1920.

The First World War was an episode in the career of Herbert Uniacke. It did not shape him, and he did what he could to shape it. He trod on most rungs of the ladder of artillery command and all along he searched for ways to make the artillery efficient, so that it could successfully play its supporting role. He experienced the frustrations of a system that was overly bureaucratic and did not allow for goodwill by the parties involved (perhaps a legacy of nineteenth-century campaigns with wrangles over seniority) and that hampered use of artillery. Whatever the limitations, Uniacke did his best and often his personal qualities were recognised by bending the rules. As he gained influence he worked to have the rules changed, but that only happened after the war. Uniacke also worked hard to improve artillery within the system's limitations, first pressing for technical proficiency then tactical application. His calls in 1918 for better horsemastership may sound archaic, but were serious, because that was what was needed. Uniacke realised the details of one war would soon be left behind, but training would never go amiss. He worked hard during the First World War to establish a workable chain of command for artillery, and to make the artillery effective so that it could do what was needed.

NOTES

1   T Travers, *The Killing Ground: The British Army, the Western Front and the Emergence of Modern Warfare, 1900–1918* (London, 1987), 42.

2   S Bidwell and D Graham, *Firepower: British Army Weapons and Theories of Warfare, 1904–1945* (London, 1982), 301. n. 101.

3   War diary, Public Record Office, Kew (PRO), WO 95 11693.

4   Rawlinson's diaries, Churchill Archives Centre, Churchill College, Cambridge (hereafter CAC), RWLN, 24 Feb 1915 to 3 Mar 1915; IV Corps War Diary, PRO, WO95/707.

5   War diary, PRO, WO95/87.

6   War diaries, PRO, WO95/86 and WO95/89.

7   War diary, PRO, WO95/87, 8 May 1915.

8   War diary, PRO, WO95/87, 14 Jun 1915 and 5 Aug 1915. The lack of explanation of the 'ZZ' call in June suggests it was not new, although its paternity cannot be precisely established.

9   War diary, No. 1 HARG, PRO, WO95/86, Sep 1915.

10 Memo by J H Davidson, 4 March 1916, PRO, WO158/19; Rawlinson Diary, CAC, RWLN, 24 January 1916.

11 Haig Diary (PRO, WO256), letter from Robertson, 10 May 1916.

12 PRO, WO95/690, April–June 1916.

13 Measures like this would ensure that Uniacke's name was entered into what became almost a sweepstakes for the title of 'inventor of the creeping barrage'. See H W L Waller's letter of 18 April 1930, PRO, Cab 45/138 and on the question of the creeping barrage's origins, this author's dissertation, '"The Infantry cannot do with a gun less": The place of the artillery in the BEF, 1914–1918', University of London, 1998, Chapter 5.

14 Rawlinson Diary, CAC, RWLN, 1 June 1916.

15 See A F Becke, 'The Coming of the Creeping Barrage', *Journal of the Royal Artillery,* 58, 1, 19–42.

16 Haig Diary, PRO, WO256, 29 June 1916. Sir William Pulteney would receive few offices of special trust after 1 July.

17 This list comes from a memo by Birch (MGRA at GHQ) showing an MORA's limits, arguing more authority to gunners would yield a more effective artillery to formation commanders. Birch to Secretary Royal Artillery Institution (hereafter RAI), 9 Aug 1916, Uniacke Papers, RAI, III/13.

18 PRO, WO95/340, 10 Oct 1916, includes Artillery Instructions detailing the rate of advance for a creeping barrage and technical matters, over Malcolm's signature. PRO, WO95/518 shows the involvement of Gough and Malcolm in the second half of July 1916. Many procedures had been settled before Uniacke's arrival.

19 In August Gough asked a Corps Commander, rather than the artillerymen, how many guns and shells various attack would need. The Corps Commander in question (the Earl of Cavan) would have taken advice from the gunners, but Gough was working through the proper channels. PRO, WO158/336, 3 Aug 1916.

20 See II Corps BGRA diary, 25–26 July 1916, PRO, WO95/65.

21 A year later Uniacke was still receiving memos urging better methods. 'Statement on the Desirability of Standardisation of Method of Ranging for use in Co-operation of Aircraft with Artillery', Lieutenant Colonel Ludlow Hewitt (OC III Wing RFC) to Uniacke, 16 Aug 1917, Uniacke Papers, RAI, VIII/5.

22 The numbers varied with the calibre of the guns firing: 4.5" howitzers

required four shells per yard: 6" howitzers only 2.5 shells/yard and heavier howitzers 1.5 shells/yard. PRO, WO95/1059, Canadian Corps Artillery Instruction No. 25, 12 Sep 1916.

23 PRO, WO95/1059, Artillery Instruction No. 28, 4 Oct 1916.

24 PRO, WO95/1059, Artillery instruction No. 42, 10 Oct 1916.

25 PRO, WO158/344, Fifth Army Somme Experiences. 'Memorandum on trench to trench attack by a battalion commander in the Fifth Army', GA43/0/8, 31 Oct 1916.

26 PRO WO158/341 and 341, 21, 27 Nov and 1 Dec 1916.

27 Uniacke Papers, RAI, VII/1.

28 Allenby Papers, Liddell Hart Centre for Military Archives, King's College London (hereafter LHCMA), Allenby 6/VII/7.

29 LHCMA, Allenby 6/VII/7: R H Johnson 19 July c1937, PRO, CAB45/116. R StC Lecky, the permanent replacement, was thought a more malleable character and not as innovative as Uniacke. PRO, CAB45/137, PRO, C E Vickery, 14 Feb 1938, CAB45/116; R Read (?), 6 Jan 1930.

30 Uniacke was later willing to use very short bombardments.

31 Haig Diary, PRO, 25 Jan 1917; Rawlinson Diary, CAC, RWLN 27 Jan 1917, Bidwell and Graham, *Firepower*, 90.

32 PRO, WO158/249, Fifth Army SG671/1, 7 June 1917.

33 Bidwell and Graham, *Firepower*, 100.

34 Maxse Papers, Department of Documents, Imperial War Museum, London (hereafter IWM), folder 35/1. 'Notes for Conference at Fifth Army', 23 May 1917. This issue was raised from the floor, so some officers were dealing in brass tacks.

35 PRO, WO95/519, Conference at Lovie Château, 6 June 1917.

36 Uniacke's 'Attack Barrages, as modified by the enemy's latest tactics' is both thorough and thoughtful, Maxse Papers, IWM, folder 35/2. GOCRA Fifth Army RA225, 25 Aug 1917. See also his 'Artillery Notes', undated but from early in Third Ypres, in the same folder.

37 PRO, WO158/343 has after action reports, which as many units as possible (down to batteries) were to file. Uniacke skimmed the highlights of these for an article in the *Journal of the Royal Artillery*, 'Actions Performed by the Artillery of the Fifth Army', 45, 8 (1919) and W H F Weber wrote a five-part article about his brigade, 'Being a Tactical Study of the Field Artillery Group in Retreat', 46, 8–12 (1920).

38 Uniacke Papers, RAI, VII/2, original emphasis.

39 Uniacke Papers, RAI, VII/3, Artillery Instructions No. 5, 27 Dec 1917.

40 Uniacke's private diary for 1918 survives in his papers at the RAI; it will be referred to as Diary. Diary, 3 and 4 Feb. Fifth Army first devised its own defence plans; a second conference at GHQ discussed plans across the BEF.

41 Artillery Instructions No. 5, 7 Jan 1918.

42 Diary, 11 and 12 March.

43 Diary, 15 March.

44 Gough's only mention of Uniacke in his memoirs, *Soldiering On,* is for 'commandeering' guns.

45 Diary, 28 March and 5 April. Interestingly. Uniacke had always written of Gough as 'the Army Commander' and his first mention of him by name or nickname came when Fifth Army was relieved.

46 N Fraser-Tytler, *Field Guns in France* (Brighton, 1995), 242.

47 Diary, 21 April et seq. Uniacke was upset with Budworth, who he thought had delayed taking over as MGRA until the situation improved: 28 and 29 March.

48   Diary, 24 February 1918.
49   Fraser-Tytler, 243. Fraser-Tytler was an instructor at the Fifth Army school, and so would have been aware of Uniacke's opinions.
50   Uniacke Papers, RAI, I, II, III and IX. See also Diary from July onwards.
51   Uniacke Papers, RAI, IV.
52   T Travers, *How the War Was Won: Command and Technology in the British Army on the Western Front, 1917–1918* (London, 1992), 150.
53   Diary, October–December 1918, Maxse Papers, IWM, folder 53/2 'Artillery Notes', 2 October 1918.

Index